Grace Bradley
March 9 1988
Recommended in
Mystery of Bible Class
by Carol Parrish

The
Steppingstones

The Steppingstones

◇

James A.
Scarborough

MERIGOLD SPIRITUAL CENTER
Merigold, Mississippi 38759

For Shelley, Douglas, and Laurel,
children whom God has shared

ISBN 0-9618823-0-1

CONTENTS

Acknowledgment vi
Preface vii
Abbreviations ix

PART ONE
The Source of Truth
I

PART TWO
God's Creation
73

PART THREE
Reconciliation
129

ACKNOWLEDGMENTS

The author wishes to express his deep gratitude to those who have helped in the writing of this book.

Foremost among those dear souls is John Howie, whose unfailing love, support, insight, interest, and wit have brightened many moments. He has shown a rare willingness to back up his convictions with his own expenditure of time, energy, and personal resources. Much of the impetus to complete this book owes its origin to John Howie.

Carol Howie has diligently checked hundreds of Scripture references for accuracy and context. She has contributed valuable suggestions for improving the clarity of the text, in addition to her kind gift of typing the final manuscript.

Brenda Payne has been a bright ray of light with her enthusiasm, interest, sense of humor, and sensitive insights into the ways of God. Her love and her sharing of spiritual discoveries were responsible for setting the author on the path toward understanding.

Keith Alford has contributed many warm hours of stimulating conversations on an unlimited range of subjects. His sharing of friendship and of ideas has been valuable.

Several people, some of whom hold beliefs differing from those expressed in these pages, have, nevertheless, given of themselves in different ways. The author wishes to thank the following: Rev. Dale Hensarling for his concern, compassion, and personal guidance; Dr. Henry Outlaw, for his tolerance, acceptance, and personal support; Brenda Heflin and Shara Howie, for their interest and kindness in reading parts of the manuscript; Dr. Bill Sullivan for his interest and voluntary proofreading of the manuscript; Johannes Greber, for marking the trail, and, most of all, thanks to the Spirit Who guided him.

To all of these friends, and to dozens of others who remain unnamed, the author extends his heartfelt thanks and love.

PREFACE

This book was written by a Christian for other Christians. As such, the existence of God, and the identity of Jesus of Nazareth as the Messiah, are taken as starting points. Beyond that, not even the churches agree. It is the intent of this book to present a logically consistent understanding of some aspects of our existence. The conclusions reached serve that purpose, but they often differ with the usual teachings.

This book is not directed to the theologian locked into a doctrinal position, nor to the clergyman bound by the beliefs of his creed. It is directed to the sincere and inquiring seeker who senses there are discrepancies in what he has been taught, who senses that things are not right with what he believes, but who cannot fight his way through the dogma to arrive at the truth. Especially is this book sent to those honest souls who decline to disconnect their brains upon entering the church doors, who search for order in the chaos of Christianity, and, finding none, give up in despair. How, indeed, could they resolve the conflict between common sense and the allegedly unanswerable questions?

Why did God create Earth? And Satan? And give him domain over the world? Why did God place us, His children, on Earth under Satan? Why not in Heaven to start with?

Why does God, with His infinite power, allow Satan to deceive and trap humans? Why does He allow illness and death? Could God not stop these things?

We are taught that Christ defeated Satan, but where is the victory if the largest part of mankind is destined for the tortures of Hell for not having known Christ? Would a loving Father create such a place of terror and then doom most of His children to it?

Where is God's love in allowing children to be born deformed, or retarded, or crippled? Does the existence of a child begin at conception, at birth, or at some other time? Why is a harmless child said to be already a hardened sinner in the sight of God? How could a righteous God pass guilt by inheritance from Adam onward? Where is His justice in punishing children for the sins of the fathers?

Why is acceptance of Christ as Lord necessary for salvation? Why is it not sufficient to simply believe in God, since most creeds teach that Christ was, in fact, God? If Christ was God, then to Whom did He pray? And where was the need to pray at all?

The list of such questions confronting the believer continues at length. Unfortunately, modern Christianity is virtually impotent to supply convincing answers. It is, therefore, not surprising that many thinking people reject the entire concept of God, while others must temporarily forsake the rational part of their minds in order to believe what they hear of Him. However, the answers are available, and available in a form easily understood by any person of even modest ability. Some of these answers are given explicitly in this book. Others are found between the lines. In spite of that, *The Steppingstones* is not so much a book of answers as it is a collection of truths which are steps in the direction toward the Source of truth.

The contents of this book are verifiable to any reader having the skill to read and the willingness to think. The reasoning used in the arguments presented can easily be followed by anyone whose mind has not been anaesthetized by previously held doctrines. All historical facts mentioned are so readily available and well known as not to require documentation. The reader need not be a scholar.

Long lists of references could have been used to give the illusion of credibility to this book. Instead, references have been minimized and, in addition, intentionally restricted to those which require no special training on the part of the reader. The concepts expressed in this book must stand or fall according to their own merit.

James A. Scarborough
August, 1986

ABBREVIATIONS

Several translations of the Bible have been used in search of the clearest and most accurate renderings of various passages. Since the Authorized King James Version holds a position of unique esteem in the hearts of so many Christians, it has been used as the standard reference wherever possible. As such, a Biblical quotation comes from that version unless otherwise indicated. On a few occasions, passages are from translations made by Goodspeed, Moffatt, or Wuest, and are so indicated. From time to time, the translations employed in *Communication with the Spirit World of God,* by Johannes Greber, are used, and are designated simply by the name "Greber," followed by a page number.

The various translations used are indicated by the following abbreviations:

Authorized King James Version. . . . . AKJ
New International Version. . . . . NIV
New American Standard. . . . . NAS
New English Bible . . . . NEB
The New Testament, Greber translation . . . . GNT

From time to time, certain points have been emphasized in Scriptural passages by printing one or more words completely in capital letters, or by inserting a clarifying word in brackets. Whenever the present author has added emphasis in this way, it is signified by the abbreviation: *em add.*

PART ONE

The Source of Truth

———————◇———————

CHAPTER I

The Heavens Declare

"The heavens declare the glory of God; and the firma-
ment sheweth his handywork" (Psa 19:1)

IN dawning awareness early man gazed upward at the sparkling
lights in the night sky and wondered. He dreamed and imag-
ined. He created names and personalities for the stars and
searched for meaning among the constellations. Astrology and
numerous myths remain with us as remnants of man's futile mus-
ings.

Mankind still gazes at the stars but now uses complex instruments to enhance his perception. The stars tell their stories clearer
now. They speak not by myths and horoscopes, but by their
actions under the influence of universal forces. The nuclear, grav-
itational, and electrical forces leave their signatures on the light
rays, bringing "messages" from the stars. These light rays intrinsically carry the messages that we read. Light which left stars
millions of years ago and trillions of miles away arrives at Earth
with information about the conditions in the universe. The messages are code-like, to be sure, and a degree of scientific skill is
needed to decode them, but the information is there to be found.

In studying this information about the universe, we find clues to
the nature of the Creator. For example, analyses of starlight reveal
that the same laws of nature that apply here are in force in the rest
of the universe. The laws of nature are the laws established by the
Creator of all nature. That is to say, laws of nature are laws of God
Who established them. As such, some of the Craftsman is revealed

in His handiwork, "for since the creation of the world His invisible attributes, His eternal power and divine nature, have been clearly seen, being understood through what has been made" (Rom 1:20 NAS).

Applying this concept to the results of starlight analyses, we discover that, since the laws of nature are the same trillions of miles distant as they are here, God behaves the same way at all places. Since the light left the stars millions of years ago, it further reveals to us that the laws of nature, and of God, were the same then as now.

God is the Same at All Times and at All Places

His universality and immutability were also imparted to His first-born Son, of Whom it is said, He is "the same yesterday, and today, and forever" (Heb 13:8).

As we study the behavior of nature in other areas, we immediately find that the laws governing the behavior of the forces in nature are so precise that they cannot even be expressed in words. Language is inadequate to express the behavior of electrical forces. Gravity cannot be well described by words. In order to deal with the forces of nature, one must use the precise language of mathematics. Only the language of mathematics is sufficiently precise to describe the governing forces of the universe. There is nothing whimsical or indefinite about the character of God. He is precise to many decimal places. Thus we find that:

God is Mathematically Precise

We may choose to disregard the laws of nature if we wish. We may choose to ignore the danger of a high voltage, but be electrocuted nonetheless. We may disregard gravity, but still die in a fall. We may not believe in powered flight, but an airplane flies unaware of our disbelief. In general,

God's Laws Apply Irrespective of Man's Awareness of Them, Understanding of Them, or Belief in Them

In the same vein, we notice that the laws of chemistry must be obeyed whether they are applied by a criminal making poison, or by a technician producing medicine. Neither person has any advantage over the laws of chemistry. The same laws of electricity apply in precisely the same way to power a telephone, whether the telephone is used by a loving friend, or an angry enemy. The message makes no difference. The same rules governing electricity apply for either party.

God's Laws are Impartial

The laws governing the behavior of matter and forces behave the same regardless of who, when, or where we are, irrespective of our thoughts, for God is no respecter of persons (see Acts 10:34). The laws have no anger and no love. They have no feeling. They simply are.

In order to use the forces in nature for our purposes, we have to cooperate with them by adapting to them. We must change: the laws will not. In order to make an airplane fly, it must be designed in careful obedience to the laws of aerodynamics, force, and gravity. The aircraft does not remain in the air by violating the law of gravity, but by using other forces in the proper ways to overcome gravity. Many other examples could be produced which show that we have to work with natural laws in consideration and obedience to their nature. They will not conform to us. We must adapt. In short,

God's Laws Cannot be Violated

The eternal, immutable laws established eons ago by the Creator are still in effect with mathematical precision. All of them are obeyed and none are violated in the workings of His creation. Observe, for instance, the creation of a stately oak tree. The process proceeds step by tiny step, atom by atom, in accordance with all the known laws of genetics and chemistry. Each cell is formed purposefully, each branch and leaf planned in advance, based on the genetic code carried by the acorn. It requires considerable time for the Master Architect to build this tree by using the laws He long ago laid down with infinite wisdom. All of His creations take time.

The creation of a dog proceeds in a similar fashion, using chemically coded instructions in the genetic material, and proceeding from single cell to embryo, to puppy, to dog. All without violating any natural laws. The creation of a human follows the same pattern. It is step by step, atom by atom, causal, purposeful, and planned in advance in every detail. And it is not instanteous.

God Obeys His Own Laws. He Never Violates Any of Them.

This realization has immediate applicability to the creation story as related in the book of Genesis. There is no evidence of an instantaneous creation of any thing in all of nature, and much evidence to the contrary. Whereas nature reflects the workings of God, the idea that He instantaneously called humans into existence reflects human misunderstanding of the Biblical story.

A closely related idea is that creation took place in six literal days. Although the literal word for day is used in Genesis, it is contrary to all scientific evidence that it be intended as literally true. The use of the word day must, therefore, be symbolic. This conclusion is forced on Biblical grounds by the summarizing statement, "in the day that the Lord God made the earth and the heavens," (Gen 2:4), wherein the word for a literal day here is applied to the previously mentioned six-day creation period. One literal day cannot equal six literal days. Six is not equal to one. So, whether we proceed from scientific evidence, or whether we start from the Bible, we arrive at the same conclusion about creation: it did not occur in six twenty-four hour time periods.

Men sometimes take "day" to have its literal meaning despite no real evidence for that interpretation and much against it. If we choose to interpret literally, despite the contradiction such an interpretation causes with Genesis 2:4 mentioned above, should we not apply the same standards of interpretation to the rest of the Bible? If we do so, then we have to believe that Jesus is literally a grapevine and we are truly branches (see John 15:5). We also are required to believe that we are literally sheep (see John 10) at the same time. Neither is literally possible.

It might be well to summarize at this point the characteristics of the laws of nature. They may be synthesized into this one law:

There is No Magic

This one concept, alone, opens the way to an understanding of the so-called supernatural and miraculous happenings in the Bible and in the modern world. We know that in His dealings with the physical universe, God works through His inviolable laws in a causal, orderly, and purposeful way. Consistent with His character, He works in like manner in the phenomena we have heretofore classified as supernatural or miraculous. This short book is a steppingstone on the path to understanding these phenomena and the plan God has for the salvation of man. At this point in history, however, mankind knows virtually nothing about the laws of God governing such phenomena. Enough research has been done to verify the reality of the supernatural and miraculous, but not enough to result in a clear mathematical understanding. However, this much is certain:

Man Does Not Know all of the Laws of Nature (of God)

The events which seem to be supernatural have behind them the conscious application of God's laws controlling His creation. The understanding of these events has been effectively blocked, however. The way to understanding is blocked for those people who do not accept the reality of such happenings. The road is blocked by fear of the supernatural. The path is barricaded by church teachings against the very kind of phenomena which their Bibles describe. And the words themselves are stumbling blocks.

The word "supernatural" conveys the idea of going beyond the laws of nature. But those laws are the laws of God. Nothing whatever can occur beyond the scope of His laws. Thus, nothing is truly supernatural, merely beyond our present human understanding of the natural.

The same applies to the word "miraculous." If taken to mean an occurrence beyond the laws applying to nature, then "miraculous" conveys the same impossible idea which gives the skeptics good grounds for rejecting the miracles of Christ. As St. Augustine put it, "Miracles are not contrary to nature, but only contrary to what we know about nature." The misuse of words thereby becomes yet another stumbling block on the path to understanding.

Surely the technological devices of today would appear as magic to the people of Christ's time. Imagine Mary Magdalene's delight and surprise at discovering an electric hair dryer. Visualize Phillip riding a helicopter to Azotus, lepers being cured by injections of antibiotics, Paul speaking to the men of Athens through a public address system. Any of these events would appear miraculous to the people of that day. And so they would be, because they would be events completely beyond the understanding of the witnesses. But that in no way renders the events incredible. They are simply incomprehensible. The phenomena themselves are real enough. It is the explanations and interpretations of them which are wrong.

Matter can be depended upon to react the same way every time, under the same experimental circumstances. The Creator of matter exhibits these same characteristics of reliability and dependability, and in some ways, predictability. That is, He has said what He would do in certain situations and we may be fully confident that He will respond as He promised. His Word will be kept.

So far we have considered only God's workings in inanimate matter. We now arrive at a subject of supreme importance: God's dealings with man. In this case, though, there is little laboratory evidence. Few experiments have recorded the voice of an angel or subjected one to physical examination. We generally must rely on earlier records of angelic appearances and on the messages they delivered to understand what purpose God has in mind regarding man. We usually turn to the written testimony of earlier witnesses. We turn to the Bible.

———————◇———————

CHAPTER 2

The Bibles

C HRISTIANS have relied on the Bible for nearly two thousand years as the source of learning God's truths. Insight into God's dealings with humanity and guidance for right living are found within the pages of this great Book. It is taken as the basis for all Christian beliefs, giving rise to the widely held sentiment that, "the Bible is the inerrant Word of God." That is to say, the Bible is God's complete revelation to man and it is without error. Since this sentiment, or some version of it, comprises a driving force directing us to the Bible, it warrants close scrutiny. If the Bible does indeed meet this description, then we need look no further for the truth. If, on the other hand, the Bible fails to support this description, then our search but begins with that noble Book. When a person asserts that the Bible is the inerrant Word of God, it is fair to ask which Bible the speaker means.

There are several "Bibles," all different and all claiming divine inspiration, not to mention numerous other books for which that claim is made. Shall we study the King James version, or the Douay version containing the Apocrypha? Or the *Torah,* or the *Book of Mormon?* The *Bhagavad-Ghita* and the *Tibetan Book of the Dead* lay claim to knowledge from beyond the Earth. The *Aquarian Gospel of Jesus* from around the turn of the century allegedly is inspired. The lengthy *O.A.H.S.P.E. Bible* from the middle of the last century lays claim to divine inspiration. For purposes of the present discussion, in our search for the inerrant Word of God, we will confine ourselves to the modern Christian Bibles.

Scholars disagree on which books should be included in the Bible. The *Book of Mormon* is different from the Catholic Bible, and both differ from the protestant Bibles. To make matters worse, the protestant Bibles do not all contain the same verses in their books. There is no proof as to which books were inspired. We have only a long tradition of accepted books. Tradition is quite a different matter from proof.

The early Christians did not hold all the same books sacred that we do today. Nor did they always agree on which manuscripts were inspired. The books of Hebrews and James were not always considered inspired. Many early churches did not consider II John and III John to be valid. Furthermore, II Peter was not considered Scripture by many of the early church fathers, being so different in form and expression from I Peter. The Revelation to John was considered spurious by a great many early church leaders. Many books were omitted from our Bible for such reasons.

Among the omitted books we find the book of Enoch. An Ethiopian version of the book of Enoch was discovered in Abyssinia in 1773. Fragments of different Enoch manuscripts written in Aramaic, some containing sections not found in the Ethiopian manuscript, were discovered in a Qumran cave near Jerusalem in 1952. Many quotations from it, and parallels to it, have been identified in the letters (epistles) of Paul and in the sayings of Christ. The book of Enoch is mentioned and quoted in Jude (Jude 1:14–15) as being Scriptural. If we cite Jude as Holy Scripture, then should we not accord the same status for Enoch? We do not attempt to resolve this problem here, only to point out that it exists.

Other books considered Scriptural by the early church were the epistles of Clement, a compatriot of Paul. The Gospel According to Thomas is quite similar to the accepted Gospels, and it possibly predates all of them. The Shepherd of Hermas was so highly regarded in post-apostolic days as to be classed among the Scriptures. Numerous other manuscripts not found in the Scriptures were claimed by early Christians to be inspired.

The Old Testament is no more definite in this regard than is the

New Testament. It mentions several Holy books which it does not itself contain. The Book of the Wars of the Lord is mentioned and quoted (see Num 21:14–15). The Book of Jasher is mentioned and quoted, both in Joshua (Josh 10:12–13), and in II Samuel (II Sam 1:17–27). There are other books mentioned by the writer of Chronicles, such as those written by Samuel the Seer, Nathan the Prophet, Shemaiah the Prophet, and others, plus The Book of the Kings of Judah and Israel and The Book of Acts of Uzziah (see I Chron 29:29; II Chron 9:29, 12:15, 13:22, 20:34, 26:22, 32:32).

We note at this point that the collection of ancient writings which we call the Bible is a very special selection of ancient Holy writings. The selection was made by people unknown to us, and whose criteria for judging the writings are unspecified. Yet, once the traditional books became established as Scriptures, the human force of reverent habit established that collection as "the" Bible. Men, therefore, determined in the chaotic early days of Christianity what we would read and revere as Holy today.

It is of little help to read that "All scripture is inspired by God" (II Tim 3:16 NAS), unless we know which writings are Scripture and which are not, and unless we also have original manuscripts of them. This verse is usually taken to apply to our Bibles but, as we have shown, we do not know with certainty to which Scriptures the verse refers. We do know that the reference is not applicable to the New Testament, for the simple reason that it did not yet exist when the verse was written. Nevertheless, this verse is often used as validation for the modern Bibles and was translated in its usual form to serve that purpose. It fails in that purpose when written as "every inspired scripture" (NEB) or, more accurately, "Every Scripture THAT is inspired by a spirit of God" (GNT) *(em. add.)*. In this rendering, it is simply a statement of the self-evident truth that "if God said it, it is true." The problem still remains as to which of the words are from God, and which are due to men.

Disagreements in the translations of the modern Bibles are not insignificant, especially when they differ on critical points. The opening verse of the book of John, a powerful verse used in proofs of the Divinity of Christ, is such an example. "In the beginning was the Word, and the Word was with God, and the Word was God" (John 1:1 NAS). In this form, the passage supports the

Deity of Christ, a doctrine crucial to most Christian churches. The same verse in the following translation gives little support to that doctrine: "In the beginning was the Word, and the Word was with God, and the Word was divine" (John 1:1, Moffatt translation). This translation leaves open the possibility that Christ was not God, Himself, but one of the beings in Heaven whose nature was like the Divine nature of God. The doctrine is not supported at all in another translation: "In the beginning was the Word, and the Word was with God; and the Word was a god" (John 1:1 GNT). In this translation one reads that Christ was a heavenly being, one of many, and was "a god" in the same sense that ancient people thought of angels as gods.

It is evident that translations can be honestly done and yet still be skewed to support conflicting doctrines. We must conclude, at this point, that there are different Bibles which differ in places in critical ways. This is evident despite the fact that they are all based on conscientious and honest translations by skilled men using the best available manuscripts. But they disagree in places, nevertheless.

We have, so far, addressed the selection of the contents of the Bibles made by men in earlier times and have pointed out certain disagreements in translation. Let us now examine the important issue of inerrancy and, in so doing, limit ourselves to the Bibles containing the same books as the classic Authorized King James Version (hereafter, Bible references are AKJ, unless otherwise noted).

To be inerrant is to be without error. Thus, an inerrant book contains no contradictions, as two opposing statements cannot both be true. According to logic they may both be false or, at most, one might be true. However, if two statements are in opposition, they cannot both be true. The demonstration of a contradiction in a Bible therefore proves that it is not totally without error. If it contains any error, then it is not totally from God. There are quite a few contradictions from which to draw examples. We will present only a few.

Were the Apostles told to take no shoes (sandals) nor staves (see Matt 10:10), or were they told to take nothing except a staff and to wear their sandals (see Mark 6:8–9)?

Did the chief priests buy the "field of blood" (Matt 27:3–7), or was it purchased by Judas himself (see Acts 1:18–19)?

Are we justified by faith alone by the grace of God (see Rom 3:23–27; Eph 2:8–9), or is it that "a man is justified by works, and not by faith alone" (Jas 2:24 NAS)? This is by no means a trivial issue.

Were two of every kind taken aboard the ark (see Gen 6:19), or were seven pairs of some kinds taken (see Gen 7:2–5)?

Is it true that "No man hath seen God at any time" (John 1:18), or is it true that "and the Lord spake unto Moses face to face, as a man speaketh unto his friend" (Ex 33:11)?

Did the Lord inspire David to take a census of his people (see II Sam 24:1) and then severely punish him for doing so, or did the inspiration come from Satan (see I Chron 21:1)?

Will whoever who "shall call on the name of the Lord . . . be saved" (Acts 2:21), or is it that not all who call upon the name of the Lord will be saved (see Matt 7:21)?

How did King Saul die? Was it suicide, by falling on his own sword (see I Sam 31:4–6)? Was he slain by the Lord (see I Chron 10:14)? Or was he slain by an Amalekite (see II Sam 1:8–19)? Or by the Philistines at Gilboa (see II Sam 21:12)?

How should we respond to foolish claims? Here are two ways. "Do not answer a fool according to his folly, or you will be like him yourself" (Prov 26:4 NIV). "Answer a fool according to his folly, or he will be wise in his own eyes" (Prov 26:5 NIV).

When the Lord spoke to Saul of Tarsus on the road to Damascus, were Saul's companions standing speechless (see Acts 9:7), or had they fallen to the ground (see Acts 26:14)? Did his companions see the light but not hear the voice (see Acts 22:9), or did they hear the voice and not see the light (see Acts 9:7)?

These contradictions are but a few of many to be found in our Bibles. They suffice to show that the Biblical books do, in fact, contain some errors. Therefore, the Bibles are not inerrant.

By the same token, it is equally impossible that all the words in the Bibles are from God, since they cannot all be correct. Therefore, the statement that the Bible is the inerrant word of God fails utterly, and is a statement containing within it the falsehood that there is one Bible. An accurate rewording might read, "Some

Bibles contain some of the words which probably came from God, but I'm not sure which." The original claim is a shadow which disappears when exposed to light.

Instead of current translations, most scholars and theologians assert that they rely on the original manuscripts as their ultimate source of God's uncontaminated truth. This assertion, which enables many people to sustain a belief in inerrancy, is based on the implication that original manuscripts exist. This is a false implication; there are no original manuscripts. There are no copies of originals, not even copies of copies. At the present time, there are several thousand so-called manuscripts and fragments, differing substantially from one another on some points. When the Bible was first translated into Latin (the *Vulgate*) by Saint Jerome around 400 A.D., he stated that there were over three thousand so-called manuscripts then, and that no two agreed on all points. After being instructed to make the translation, he protested that he would have to use his own judgment, fill in verses here and there, and generally edit and correct. Saint Jerome said, "Even those who condemn me as an impious forger must admit that we can no longer speak of such a thing as 'truth' when there are variations in that which is said to be true." Yet, at the insistence of Pope Damasus, Jerome was required to make the translation. His *Vulgate* was later decreed to be "the inspired word of God" by the Council of Trent.

Jerome explained that his researches and interviews revealed that the copyists sometimes dozed while at work, that sometimes verses were changed or added in order to clarify the manuscripts, and that some changes were confessed to have been deliberately made in order to substantiate prior church doctrine. Indeed, some of the oldest manuscripts now available show words rubbed out and written over repeatedly as church dogma developed through the early centuries. Little is to be seen in the way of Divine inspiration in the melange of adulterated documents. In spite of these difficulties, Jerome made his translation into Latin.

Divine inspiration in the New Testament is, in fact, claimed only in the book of Revelation. The authors of the other New Testament books say nothing about supernatural help in their writing, in contrast to the Old Testament, whose writers felt duty bound to state clearly when a statement came from God. On the contrary, Luke expressly states that he compiled his accounts (Luke and Acts) in quite a human way by collecting accounts of eyewitnesses and by studying the written accounts of other writers (see Luke 1:1–3). John states that he personally witnessed the events he relates, and says that his story is authentic on that account. This same personal source of information is also claimed for the books of Matthew and Mark. The various Epistles of Paul contain basic information such as would be addressed by a pastor to a distant congregation. Paul claims to be relaying information from the Lord in only a few passages.

Thus, the Apostles do not say their writings were done with supernatural aid. Let us emphasize, however, that truth can remain truth, whether given directly by God or reported by an honest man. No detailed proof is needed to show that the Apostles were honest men who truly believed they were telling the truth. One need only look at the prices they paid for proclaiming the Gospel to see that they believed what they wrote. They gained no earthly riches and no glory in their lifetimes. They endured difficult times, persecution, and violent deaths but, independently of each other, stood by their stories. It goes against all we know of human nature to suppose those men were not truthful witnesses for their Lord. Yet He did not write their books and letters for them. They did it themselves. Consequently, for example, the Gospel according to John is just what it claims to be: the good news as remembered and as understood by John—nothing more, and certainly nothing less. The New Testament writings can, therefore, be essentially true without invoking an unsupportable claim of Divine inspiration. We will proceed on that basis, bearing in mind that human authors, copyists, and translators are not infallible.

In the foregoing, we have pointed out that the oldest manuscripts have been the victims of many word changes. That fact, alone, lays to rest the idea that God protects the Scriptures from the erring hands of man. To illustrate how easy it was for earlier scribes copying the manuscripts to change words, whether by accident or on purpose, a few accidents from modern times are recalled.

In proofreading a Bible being prepared for publication, a man in

1805 questioned whether a certain comma should be removed. In answer to his question, the editor wrote "to remain" in the margin. These two words were later included in the text, altering Galatians 4:29 to read, "But as then he that was born after the flesh persecuted him that was born after the spirit *to remain,* even so it is now" *(em. add.).*

An edition in 1717 headed the twentieth chapter of Luke "The parable of the "vinegar" instead of "vineyard.""

An 1806 edition of the Bible has the "r" left out of "fishers" in Ezekiel 47:10, causing the verse to read, "and it shall come to pass that the *fishes* will stand upon it" *(em. add.).*

Still another Bible from 1810 makes an odd mistake in Luke 14:26: "If any man come to me and hate not his father, and mother, and wife, and children, and brethren, and sisters, yea, and his own *wife* also, he cannot be my disciple" *(em. add.).* The word, "wife," should have been "life."

There are a number of similar examples. It seems to be quite easy for errors to creep into the Scriptures. It was even easier in the early centuries when copies were made by hand and few people could read them. By presenting even one example of alterations made in the Scriptures, we prove that they can be altered in spite of the stern warnings against it (see Deut 4:2; Prov 30:6; Rev 22:18–19). The fact that Scriptures can be, and had been, altered by man is the very reason for these warnings.

The ultimate source of truth is God. God, either in Person, or through Christ, or through the Holy Spirit, constitutes the primary source of the truth. If He gives a message to a man and the man relays it, then the man is a secondary source of the truth. Such a truth can, therefore, contain human error. If the man relays the truth by writing, and the letter is then recopied several times and also translated into a new language, the resulting letter is at best a tertiary source. As such, it would not be admissable as evidence in a modern court of law. We have that very situation with the Bibles.

To find the truth in its original purity one must ask of the original Source. "Call to Me, and I will answer you, and I will tell you great and mighty things, which you do not know" (Jer 33:3 NAS).

Even though our present Bibles are imperfect, they have, in

their most ancient versions, endorsement from high spiritual authority. The Apostles, as secondary sources, testify to the inspiration of the Scriptures. "For the prophecy came not in old time by the will of man: but holy men of God spake as they were moved by the Holy Ghost" (II Pet 1:21). However, the Apostles and Christ do not always quote the Old Testament Scriptures in the way they have come down to us today. As one example, Psalms 68:18 (NIV) reads, "When you ascended on high, you led captives in your train; you received gifts from men, even from the rebellious—that you, O Lord God, might dwell there." When this passage is quoted in Ephesians, however, the end part is omitted (or had it been added in Psalms?). The second person "you" is changed to the third person "he," and the verb accompanying "gifts" (received) is replaced by its opposite (gave). The verse in Ephesians reads, "This is why it says: 'When he ascended on high, he led captives in his train and GAVE GIFTS TO MEN' " (Eph 4:8 NIV (em. add.). The Scriptures referenced by the Apostles and by Christ were not identical to our Old Testament. John writes, "as the scripture hath said, out of his belly shall flow rivers of living water" (John 7:38), but this statement is nowhere in our Old Testament.

Neither do the New Testament writers each quote Christ in exactly the same way. There are several examples of this. The Lord's prayer reported by Luke (Luke 11:2–4) is shorter than reported by Matthew (Matt 6:9–13). Either the one version has been shortened, or the other has been amended. We, unfortunately, do not have certain knowledge of exactly what Christ said.

In spite of the many flaws in the Writings, their strongest endorsement comes from Christ, Who must be taken as a primary source if He is correctly quoted. He freqently quoted passages from the Law and the Prophets, on more occasions than need be referenced here. His quotes do not, however, always agree in detail with our present copies of the Old Testament. However, He had the position and the authority to correct, and to interpret or extend, the words given through the prophets. The strength of His testimony is so powerful that we will take the Scriptures very seriously indeed, but not with blind faith. In the final analysis, the faith of a Christian must rest in the Person of God, not in the Noble Book. Faith is confident trust in God, not blind reverence for the Bibles, nor intellectual acceptance of a set of doctrines.

We find ourselves today in the situation of having Bibles flawed by occasional contradictions and inconsistent manuscripts. Nothing short of Divine guidance suffices to sort out the golden nuggets of truth from the ore. One wonders what precautions Christ could have taken to preserve the truth for us, and whether He took those precautions. As we shall see, He did, in fact, take appropriate measures to assure that the truth would always be available to His followers. It was not by writing books.

During Christ's mission on Earth, He omitted doing one thing which shouts out at us by its absence. He wrote no books.

He could surely read and write, as evidenced by His outwitting the scholars of the Scriptures at age twelve. Since he spoke to audiences who spoke Aramaic, Greek, and Latin, and since there is no evidence He ever used a translator, it is probable that He was not only literate, but multilingual. Yet, in spite of this, He did not write His own Gospel. We find in our Bibles the Gospel according to John, according to Luke, and so on, but we do not find a book called the Gospel According to Jesus. Even if we suppose that Jesus could not write, He could certainly have dictated His plan of salvation in His own words to one of the professional scribes of that day. There were scribes who could take down His sermons in shorthand, if necessary. Could it be that our Lord knew full well that "written matter is the sport of fate" (anon)?

It is also conspicuous that Christ did not instruct the Apostles to write books. He sent them out with instructions to teach, to heal the sick, to cast out demons in His name, and to preach the gospel, but not to write books (see Matt 28:19–20; Mark 6:7, 16:15–18; Luke 9:1–2, 24:47; Acts 1:8).

What a blessing it would have been if Christ or His Apostles had unambiguously written down the plan of salvation to stand for all time. What a curse it would be if the Master had done so, and sinful man had altered His truth into a mixture of truth and error. Our difficult quest for the truth would be almost impossible in that event, for we would be locked into a faulty document believed to be uncontaminated truth from the Lord Himself. We are almost in that condition now with the popular views held of the Bibles. Yet our fate could have been even more difficult than it is.

Our Lord knew a way around all these sources of error. He did not write anything down where man could tamper with it and distort it. He had a better way. He intended to reveal the rest of His truth later on by means of His spirits.

Christ revealed very little in His ministry that was new information. He testified of God and of His own identity. He urged people to come through Him to the Father. He exhorted people to live a life of love. Otherwise, He explained little that was not already in the Old Testament. People were not ready for it. Even to His own Apostles He said, "There is still much that I could say to you, but the burden would be too great for you now. However, when he comes who is the Spirit of truth, he will guide you into all the truth" (John 16:13 NEB). Christ promised to send the Holy Spirit to teach mankind all we need to know, to "lead us into all truth." Although it is generally believed that the revelation of the truth ended with the New Testament, that cannot be so without contradicting this promise from Christ. Christ specifically said among His last recorded words that much more was yet to be revealed, "all truth," and that it would be brought later by a Spirit.

These truths which He promised to send are not contained in the Gospels for the obvious reason that those books cover only the time up to Christ's ascension, at which point the Holy Spirit had not yet been sent. We search the Epistles in vain for these great and mighty truths, but find they contain essentially the same information as the Gospels. We search the book of Revelation and find that no two men seem to agree on what this highly symbolic book really means in its entirety. It cannot be maintained, therefore, that these additional truths Christ promised to reveal are revealed in the New Testament. In spite of this, Christians believe that Christ promised truthfully and that He keeps His promises. Unfortunately, we are usually entrapped by the dogma that the New Testament ended all messages from God. Let us escape from this snare and search for evidence that Christ kept His promise. It is easy to find that He did.

From the first century after His resurrection down to the present, people have reported visits by the Spirit or by angels, and, on occasion, claim to have been instructed in the true understanding of the Scriptures. Those people were often branded as heretics and burned at the stake, or tortured into submission, until the churches lost the power to do so. Other recipients of Christ's promise have endured other persecutions as well. Who are the persecutors? Other Christians.

Paul met with ridicule in his encounter with Festus (see Acts 26:24), who declared Paul to be crazy when Paul told him more than he was ready to grasp. This was the same fate met by Jesus, when even His own family, at one time, thought that He was out of His mind (see Mark 3:21 NEB) and others thought He was possessed by a devil (see John 7:20). Even His brothers did not believe in Him (see John 7:5). It is not surprising, then, that His later followers, to whom He had truly sent the Spirit, were treated badly. Surely the servant is not greater than the Master (see John 13:16).

The greatest weapon the Christian has in his struggle to escape Satan's rule is the Truth. "And ye shall know the truth, and the truth shall make you free" (John 8:32). Consider the councils of Hell plotting how to thwart the truth. First convince both sheep and shepherds that all the truth available has already been given. Then persuade the shepherds to declare the Scriptures closed and the revelations ended. Having thus blocked the people from receiving the rest of the truth, contaminate with errors the spiritual food which they do have. Serve God's children a set of doctrines contrived by faulty human thinking. Threaten them with eternal punishment if they do not swallow all these beliefs. As a result, those who eat of this food will likely find their faith weak and their growth in knowledge stunted. Others will choose to remain hungry rather than eat of it.

There is more truth to be had than is revealed in the Bibles. We know that the source of truth must be God Himself. It is of Him that we inquire. It is He Who will answer in His own ways by means of His Holy Spirit. Never has He instructed us to ask a rabbi, priest, professor, or theologian. Always He says, "Inquire of me and I will answer you."

In what way will He answer? To find out, let us see how He has answered in the past, bearing in mind that He is the same today as He was then.

◇

CHAPTER 3

God Speaks

Gᴏᴅ had promised to send answers to questions put to Him. "Call unto me, and I will answer thee, and show thee great and mighty things, which thou knowest not" (Jer 33:3). Later on, Christ promised that if we seek we shall find, that if we ask it will be answered (see Matt 7:7). This was to happen when the seeker is ready for it, as Christ withheld a great deal even from His Apostles because they were not yet able to grasp it (see John 16:12).

The prayerful seeker is often drawn to churches, ministers, and Bibles for these important answers. The Bibles contain a portion of the truth revealed millennia ago, admixed with unknown amounts of human alterations. The ministers have learned and followed the creeds of their respective churches and cannot be expected to go much beyond that. The churches, themselves, come in hundreds of varieties, each one basing its beliefs on Bibles which disagree on both trivial and significant points, each one teaching doctrines reasoned by fallible humans from imperfect documents. Sometimes an article of devout faith to one church is the heresy of another. Once we attempt to understand beyond the basics of God, Christ, and Love, we find Christianity in a shambles and able to exhibit few, if any, clear answers. Surely, God is not the Author of confusion (see I Cor 14:33).

Accordingly, if God has indeed drawn the seeker to churches, ministers, and Bibles, these can only be regarded as way stations along the road to more of the truth. The remainder of the truth must come from God. If, in answer to our prayers for understanding, we are brought to a way station, we can choose to remain there indefinitely, but only at the cost of traveling no further on the road to the Truth God promised.

God did not intend that erring human agencies should be the sole dispensers of His Truth. On the contrary, Christ expressly declared that His spirits would bring the remainder of such truth as is comprehensible to man (see John 16:13). His promise confirms the Old Testament pledges that God would answer and supply the truth by His spirits (see, for example, Jer 33:3; Joel 2:28). It appears that these pledges will not be honored merely for the asking. More than that is required of us.

There were times when the people could not expect an answer from God: "And word from the Lord was rare in those days, visions were infrequent," (I Sam 3:1 NAS). The cause of God's silence was explained by the usual reasons: "these men have set up their idols in their heart, and put the stumbling block of their iniquity before their face: should I be inquired of at all by them?" (Ezek 14:3).

Take the case of King Saul. When the King strayed from a life in the Lord, then God did not answer him (see I Sam 14:36–37), "neither by dreams, nor by Urim, nor by prophets" (I Sam 28:6). God's conditions for His sending an answer are stated by Isaiah (Isa 58: 2–9) and others, wherein He requires honest efforts toward living good lives in exchange for His communication. Thus God decides to whom His responses will be sent, and He decides by His own criteria. His judgment may be very different from ours, as evidenced by the conversion of Paul. This great Apostle had participated in the misguided persecution of the early Christians, yet the intent of his heart was clear to the Lord, who summoned Paul to be His servant. Paul later received truths promised by God and reaffirmed by Christ. Paul's letters say little about how he received his instructions from the Lord, other than that God's spirits were involved. It is clear that Paul's instructions into the secrets of the faith came from above (see I Cor 2:13), for Paul was never sent to one of the other Apostles for training, although the distance was not great. On the contrary, Paul represented himself to them as an equal, already one of them. Paul acquired his knowledge by inquiring of God, with God somehow answering. With this in view, we ask, "How does God answer?"

Although God promises to answer us, He does not generally answer in Person, but sends His responses via His agents. These agents are His spirits. In the Old Testament, a spirit agent of God is often called "the angel of the Lord," or simply, "the angel." In the New Testament the agent is usually called "the holy Spirit," as distinguished from "the evil spirit." A careful reading of both Old and New Testaments reveals that almost all communication from God is through His agents, even though the Scriptures might say, "Thus saith Jehovah." Although we are assured that the words were sent from God, He did not personally bring them except in rare cases.

As an example of this, consider the famous burning bush episode in Exodus. We read there that it was an angel of the Lord appearing as flame in the bush (Ex. 3:2), but the angel speaks for God in His name (Ex 3:6). In our own experience, we have had someone relate a message to us from someone else. Though the message is brought by a messenger, not the principal sender, if it is delivered accurately we are truthful in saying that, in a sense, we heard from our friend and are justified in quoting him.

An example of a physical artifact being used by a messenger is found in the Biblical account of David's inquiry of God through Abiathar, the priest. Abiathar operated the breastplate attached to a garment called the ephod. As the breastplate was used to spell out the answer from God, the Scripture relates that "the Lord said" (see I Sam 23:9–12), when in fact the Lord made no sound at all. Again, it is somewhat the same as communication between people. If we receive a letter from a friend, we say we heard from that friend and we might quote him as such. Actually, we heard nothing with our ears; we received a letter brought by the postman. The postman is the carrier of the message. Here he compares with the angel who carried God's message, 'delivered by whatever means.

In these and other ways, God uses intermediaries, angels, in virtually all of His communications with man. It is of great importance, then, for us to learn how God's spirit agents manifest themselves and carry out their assignments. The Bibles make frequent reference to the word of God coming to the prophets of old. However, the Bibles are usually silent as to how God's messages came, stating simply that they did come. How did the prophets receive their answers? There were many ways (see Heb 1:1).

According to television and movies, God speaks by using a resonant voice coming from the air. The Scriptures, however, do not support Hollywood's theology. On the contrary, communication by means of a voice from God was rarely employed. God almost never communicated in Person, but as a matter of course sent His messages by means of His spirit messengers called angels, or Holy spirits. Thus we can expect answers to our prayers to be brought not by God himself, but by His spirits, the inhabitants of His great spirit-world which we call Heaven. "Are not all angels simply ministering spirits sent out to help those who are to regain the salvation that is theirs by inheritance?" (Heb 1:14 GNT). We are not addressing the question of why God deals with man almost exclusively through His spirit agents, we are simply observing that He does.

Sometimes God does communicate by an audible voice. John reported a voice from Heaven that some hearers thought was thunder (see John 12:28–29), and a voice from Heaven spoke to Nebuchadnezzar (see Dan 4:31). The voice comes not from the empty air, however, but from a cloudlet, or small fogginess. In this regard, recall Moses and Aaron in the book of Exodus, especially regarding the cloud between the wings of the cherubim in the Tent of Meeting from whence the Voice spoke. The Voice speaking to Christ at the transfiguration likewise came from a cloudlet (see Matt 17:5).

The writers of the Old Testament do not carefully distinguish as to who spoke from the cloudlets, whether it was God, Christ, or an angel of the Lord. Sometimes the writers confuse the matter by saying it was God, then a few verses later say it was an angel (see Ex 13:21, 14:19). On another occasion, we first read that an angel is speaking, only to have subsequent verses begin stating it is God (see Ex 3). Sometimes we are not told who the speaker is, just that an unidentified voice spoke (see Num 7:89). In any event, if the message was delivered by an authorized spirit agent of God, the witnesses were truthful enough in reporting that "God said," especially in view of the witnesses' ignorance of whose voice they had, in fact, heard.

Another awesome way in which God sends His word is via angels materialized in solid form. This may involve only a part of the body of the spirit, such as the materialized finger which wrote a message on the wall for King Belshazzar. "Suddenly the fingers of a man's hand emerged and began writing opposite the lampstand on the plaster of the wall of the king's palace" (Dan 5:5 NAS). This was not the hand of God, but that of one of His angelic spirits, for we read later on that "the hand was SENT from Him" (Dan 5:24 NAS) *(em. add.)*.

Materializations of the complete bodies of certain high beings did occur on special occasions. Gabriel materialized before Daniel and was referred to as "the man Gabriel" (Dan 8:15–17, 9:21). Moses and Elijah talked with Christ in the presence of Peter, John, and James (see Matt 17:3). An angel of the Lord sat down with Gideon and spoke with him (see Judges 6:11–18). The most frequent materializations of a high Spirit are those of Christ, Who appeared several times after His resurrection (e.g., Luke 24:15–31; John 20:14, 20:19, 20:26, 21:4). There were also angelic visitations to Abraham, Lot, and others.

How did the prophets receive their answers as they followed the instructions, "ask me of things to come concerning my sons, and concerning the work of my hands command ye me" (Isa 45:11)? The methods God uses to communicate are much more diverse than the familiar examples given so far. God communicates with man in many and varying ways (see Heb 1:1). He might instill some inner urging or awaken our conscience. Occasionally, the answer to a problem simply occurs full-grown in our minds. However, it is difficult to know for certain where these vague feelings or fully developed ideas originate in every case, much less can we put exact words to them and claim that God spoke to us. There are ways God communicates in which He is much more explicit.

One method He uses is inspirational writing, wherein a person is caused to hear, or see in a vision, the words he is to write. The person then writes of his own volition, being fully aware of what he is writing. It can also occur that he knows only that he is writing, but not what he is writing. It may also be that he is not conscious at all, but is in a trance state. Upon awakening he learns the contents of what he has written.

King David used another method when he inquired of the Lord. This writer of many of the Psalms used the ephod with the breastplate of judgment attached to it: "But David strengthened himself in the Lord his God. Then David said to Abiathar . . . 'Please bring me the ephod [breastplate of judgment].' And David inquired of the Lord" *(em. add.),* and the Lord answered him (see I Sam 30:6–8 NAS). This breastplate was a golden planchette inlaid with jewels, each jewel representing both a letter of the Hebrew alphabet and one of the tribes of Israel. By these engraved stones, words were spelled out using the Urim and the Thummim in a way resembling a modern Ouija board. The breastplate, or breast-piece, is also referred to in Scripture as a graven image.

This method of inquiring of God was in common use for centuries. It first began when God gave Moses detailed instructions for making the ephod and its attached breastplate (see Ex. 28:6–30). Moses consecrated Aaron and his sons as priests (see Ex 28:41) with the special ability to operate the breastplate as the means of making decisions for the Israelites. Moses personally placed the breastplate on Aaron and put the Urim and Thummim in the breastplate (see Lev 8:8). Long after Moses, Micah "made an ephod and a breastplate of divination, and consecrated one of his sons, who became his priest" (Judges 17:5, Greber) (also see Judges 8:27 regarding Gideon).

Saul also had been answered on previous occasions by the breastplate with the Urim and Thummim. After straying from God, Saul inquired of Him unsuccessfully, for "the Lord answered him not, neither by dreams, nor by Urim, nor by prophets" (I Sam 28:6).

Inquiring of God today by using a breastplate would be condemned universally as Satanic. Is there a church anywhere whose board of elders would prayerfully consult a breastplate of judgment for any decision whatever? Yet, David did. Part of the reluctance of modern man to recognize God's ancient ways of communicating is due to our confusion regarding the activities of God's angels as compared with the way Satan's angels work.

There are many resemblances between the ways God's angels bring His answers and the ways demonstrated by Satan's angels. Let us recall the great display of good and evil power in the duel between Moses and the Pharaoh's magicians. The works done by both the good and evil forces were virtually identical. This is understandable if we but bear in mind that God made laws of nature which govern both the Earth and the spirit realm, and that these eternal, immutable laws cannot be broken by the inhabitants of either domain. The same methods are used by both sides.

It is like this: God made the laws of electricity. If someone wishes to broadcast the truth on television, he must comply with these laws. If, on the other hand, someone wishes to broadcast lies, he finds that the same laws of electricity apply, nevertheless.

Both the higher and lower forces were active in divination. Careful reading of the story of Joseph reveals that he "divined" by means of a silver cup, and that it was common knowledge that God sometimes communicated in this way (see Gen 44:5 et seq.). We are not told in this story exactly how the cup was being used, but we know that cups have been used for a long time for casting dice, casting lots, reading tea leaves, or the like. On another occasion, Joshua located the thief, Achan, by lot, implying that the method was reliable to the point of deciding capital punishment. Jonah was chosen as the cause of the storm (see Jonah 1:7–12), and Matthias was selected to replace Judas as the twelfth Apostle (see Acts 1:26), both by the casting of lots. None of the parties casting lots was involved in Satanism. Each was a servant of God. By way of contrast, when the soldiers cast lots of dividing the garments of Christ, they were not using them to receive guidance from God. As always then, we see that we cannot decide whether a spirit phenomenon is from the good or the evil side by investigating the occurrence itself. The discernment can be quite difficult.

Thus, dreams and visions can be induced by Christ's forces, and also by Satan's forces. Such communications from the forces of God were common in Biblical times. Their contents were often quoted in our Bibles as words from God, saying "thus saith Jehovah." The book of Revelation is almost entirely the result of such a vision, as is much of the book of Daniel. Dreams and visions are of little use unless the Lord somehow reveals their meanings. Dreams, visions, and their interpretations were usually received by a man or woman especially gifted for that purpose. Such persons were referred to as seers, prophets, soothsayers, priests, conjurers, diviners, or other titles, depending mostly on the Biblical translation. These individuals might have had the gift of seeing events occurring at a distance, a gift exhibited by Elisha, Elijah, and Jesus. Elisha told the Israelites the secret plans of the warring King of Syria, who thought that he must have an Israelite spy in his household (see II Kings 6:8–12). Elijah knew that his servant had overtaken Naaman and received a reward for Elijah's curing of Naaman's leprosy (see II Kings 5:25–26). Jesus saw Nathanael by this gift of distant sight while Nathanael was yet lying beneath the fig tree (see John 1:48). A person with this gift of clairvoyance was often called a seer.

A common way of inquiring of God in Old Testament days was by consulting a prophet. A prophet was a person who had the ability to relinquish control of his body to a spirit other than himself, whereby the spirit could then converse with the people present by use of the person's human organs of speech. A person whose body is being so used is in what is called a trance. We read of Peter, Paul, and other men of God going into trances and prophesying (see Acts 10:10 *et seq.;* Acts 22:17; Num 24:4). This illustrates how widely known that phenomenon was in their day. If the spirit using the body was a spirit sent from God, our Bibles call the man a prophet of God, or simply a prophet. If the spirit in control was one of Satan's spirits, the Bibles call that person a false prophet (e.g., I Kings 18:22; I Kings 22:23–24; Micah 3:5, 3:11; I Cor 14:32). A spirit, good or evil, may use the human body to produce a spoken message. If the message, so spoken, is in the native language of the listeners, the Bibles call it prophecy. This is the "ecstatic utterance" which we are exhorted to permit (I Cor 14:39; I Thess 5:20). This is the influence of the spirit of prophecy we are instructed not to quench (see I Thess 5:19). The message, so given, will be in the prophet's own voice, although the accent may be different. As such, a hearer may suspect fraud or deception. As proof that the message does not come from the mind of the prophet, the spirit in control may speak in another language, or "tongue" (I Cor 14:21), not a language known by the prophet. This is, then, a sign to the unbeliever that the message is genuine, that is, from the spirit (see I Cor 14:22). Speaking in this way, in "tongues of men and of angels" (I Cor 13:1), was a common occurrence among the Apostolic congregations, most especially those encouraged by Paul.

We note here that a special spiritual gift is evidenced by those persons speaking by the spirit in their own, or in other, languages. The degree of development of this gift is often minimal, however, resulting in an aimless babbling of syllables. Such *glossallalia* is the most common, present-day representation of the Pauline gift of tongues. It serves but poorly to illustrate the value of the gift. In this weak degree of spirit control, there may be no detectable message, no reliable way of separating spirit influence from humanly induced words and, above all, no way to test (try) the spirit (see I John 4:1–2). Both the hearer and speaker are unable to verify the source of utterance, whether from the Holy spirit or from the evil spirit.

There are still other methods of communication not listed here which are used by the spirits in God's service. The variety of ways seem virtually endless. More often than not, we are not told how God communicated. For example, Rebekah, the wife of Isaac, had the following experience: "Twins were struggling in her womb and she said, 'Why has this befallen me?'. So she went to consult Jehovah" (Gen 25:22, Greber). We are not told anything about the special place where she went, but clearly she knew exactly where to go and what to do to consult Jehovah. This verse matter-of-factly says she went to consult Jehovah, as though it were an everyday matter which did not need further clarification. Where did Rebekah go?

Did she go to some special place to have her conscience moved by a vague feeling? Or perhaps to talk to a voice from a small puff of fog? Did she go to a man whose hand was moved by a spirit from God to write an answer for her? Could she have gone, as King David did, to consult a prophet who used a breastplate to spell out her answer? Could she have gone to find her own silver cup of divination, to read tea leaves or cast lots for an answer?

Perhaps she went somewhere to be alone, where in the solitude she could pass into a trance state and see her answer in a vision. Or perhaps there was some place she could go where an angel would materialize and talk things over with her. Perhaps she consulted Jehovah by speaking to one of His angels using the borrowed body of a prophet of God.

These ways of receiving God's answers, in evidence in the Scriptures, are unacceptable to almost all Christians of today. Such manifestations are generally viewed as Satanic exhibitions or, at the very least, delusions. The ways in which the words of God in the Scriptures came to the prophets of old are unacceptable to the very people who believe those Scriptures.

What did other Israelites do to inquire of God? "Formerly in Israel, when a man went to inquire of God, he used to say, 'Come, let us go to the seer'; for he who is called a prophet now was formerly called a seer" (I Sam 9:9 NAS). Over and over we read of the widespread dependence the Israelites placed on their prophets for inquiring of God. "Is there not here a prophet of the Lord, that we may inquire of the Lord by him?" (II Kings 3:11).

Priests who were also prophets, or seers, were not rare in those days. Samuel was a seer (see I Sam 9:19; I Chron 9:22) who, at times, wore the ephod (see I Sam 2:18), as did David's priest and friend, Abiathar (see I Sam 30:7–8). Zadok, the priest, was a seer (see II Sam 15:27), along with Nathan and Gad (see I Chron 29:29). The Lord used a number of others by whom He spoke to Judah and Israel (see II Kings 17:13). An Edomite slew eighty-five such men in the town of Nob, alone (see I Sam 22:18). Only Abiathar escaped and fled with his ephod to take refuge with David (see I Sam 22:20–23). Women such as Huldah (see II Kings 22:14), Deborah (see Judges 4:4), and Miriam (see Ex 15:20), were seers or prophets (prophetesses). These men and women were able to receive communications from God as brought by His spirits using the aforementioned methods, and others. Their special talent, or gift, required more than just their being from the lineage of Aaron and Levi. Those with this latent talent needed development and training. Schools for the prophets existed for that purpose.

The prophetess, Huldah, ran a school for prophets in Jerusalem (see II Kings 22:14). Samuel was head of a school for prophets in

Ramah. Schools for prophets were also located in Bethel (see II Kings 2:3) and Jericho (see II Kings 2:5, 2:15). Ezekiel headed a school for prophets, which attracted more students than he could accommodate. The student prophets approached him saying, "Look, the place where we meet with you is too small for us. Let us go to the Jordan, where each of us can get a pole; and let us build a place there for us to live" (II Kings 6:1–2 NIV).

At such schools, the prophet in training could learn divination by use of the breastplate and the Urim and Thummim. He learned meditation and the skill of passing into a trance condition, in which a spirit from God could take control of his body and speak through it. Alternatively, in such a trance, the prophet might hear words from the Lord or see visions (see Num 24:4, 24:15–16). These ways in which God communicated to man through His prophets in Bible times are held in low esteem when they occur today. It is as though modern Christians pray for guidance, but insist that it be invisible and intangible. Our misunderstanding of the injunctions in Leviticus has contributed greatly to this ignorance.

Truly, the Scriptures forbid inquiring of the dead (see Lev 19:26, 19:31, 20:6; Isa 8:19), the dead being Satan, the Prince of Death, and all those fallen spirits who serve him. On the other hand, the Scriptures openly direct us to inquire of the Living God through Christ, the Prince of Life, Who will answer by His spirit agents, the living. Did Christ sin by "consulting the dead" when He spoke with the deceased Moses and Elijah? Of course not. Although departed from the physical body, Moses and Elijah are in the service of the living God and are numbered among His living.

Leviticus prohibits divination for contacting the dead, the evil spirits, yet divination was used by Samuel, Joseph, and other prophets of God (see Micah 3:7). Lots were cast by servants asking of God and, by the same token, were used by those opposed to God in the story of Haman in the book of Esther. In short, lots were used to communicate either with God or with the evil one. It is not the method used for inquiry which constitutes idolatry or consulting with the dead. Instead, it is the source of the response which determines whether the response is of good or evil. This was the case when the Israelites asked Gideon to rule over them (see Judges 8:22–27 NAS). He declined, saying "the Lord shall rule over you" (verse 23). In order that the people could inquire of the Lord, Gideon made an ephod with its golden breastplate and placed it in his city. Unfortunately, "all Israel played the harlot with it there" (verse 27) by consulting the lower spirits. As another example, the righteous Daniel could not be forced into idolatry even at the risk of his life. It is inconceivable, then, that Daniel would break the Levitical injunction against inquiring of the dead. Yet Daniel was chief of the diviners, soothsayers, conjurers, and magicians, himself being especially gifted in those areas (see Dan 2:48, 4:9, 5:11. Translations vary).

God is the same now as then, and He can answer in the same ways. For the most part, it is true, He relies on ways imperceptible to our senses, but the more spectacular ways are becoming ever more common, as foretold for the last days by Joel, "I will pour out My Spirit on all mankind; and your sons and daughters will prophesy, your old men will dream dreams, your young men will see visions . . . I will pour out My Spirit in those days" (Joel 2:28–29 NAS).

The Scriptures reveal little about the details of the training that took place in a school for prophets, just as they are frequently silent about other day-to-day matters already familiar to the people of that time. Hence, we are told little of what transpired in the schools of Huldah and Elijah, in the same way that we are told no details of what took place in an early church service held by Peter and Paul. At the same time, we are told that spiritual gifts, such as the gift of prophecy, are widely distributed among believers. Like other gifts, they need development by the bearer of the gift. A concert pianist and an Olympic gymnast have in common their persistent practice and self-discipline in bringing to full flower the latent gifts that God bestowed on them. In like manner, God requires effort on our part if we wish to develop whatever spiritual gifts we carry. What do the Scriptures recommend we do?

Foremost among our actions is yielding to Him. Trust and faith in God are fundamental (see Matt 13:58, 21:22; Mark 11:24). A state of tense self-will prohibits yielding to the Spirit. Spiritual gifts seldom appear in a person or in a group where tension, inhibition, or fear are present, or where rigid and stilted forms of worship prevail. Attitude is most important.

Attitudes of love and forgiveness of others are vital (see Psa 66:18; Matt 6:14–15; Mark 11:25–26). We are told not to even enter a worship service if we have anything against another person (see Matt 5:23–24). Clean hearts and clean minds are conducive to receiving God's guidance (see I Pet 3:12).

The time of worship shall include song and music (see I Sam 2:1–10; II Chron 23:18; Matt 26:30; Acts 16:25; I Cor 14:15; Rev 5:9–10). Paul and Silas sang hymns of praise in jail. David played his music. Christ sang hymns. Music helps to quiet the mind and soothe the emotions.

If other people are present, it is fitting to join hands in prayer and song as a token of unity and love for one another and for God. Prayer and praise are our contribution to the conversation with God. Even Jesus prayed (see Luke 18:1–8; Phil 4–6; I Tim 2:1–3).

After our active part in the conversation is finished, we are to be quiet and receptive. Otherwise, we have a one-way conversation, which is not a conversation at all. Since a meditative state of consciousness may be attained, a quiet place away from worldly distractions is preferable. Jesus often prayed alone in a quiet place at a quiet time. The upper room of the Apostles was also such a place (see Matt 6:6; Acts 1:13).

Lastly, practice is required. Just as the pianist and gymnast develop their natural gifts by practice, so too does spiritual ability to receive God's response grow by steadfast application of ourselves to that end. This includes attempting to be always in a state of inner attunement with the Almighty, this attunement being meant by the admonition to "pray continuously" (Luke 21:36; Rom 12:12; Eph 6:18; I Thess 5:17).

By putting together these aspects of communication with God we arrive at a sort of prescription for worship. Such a worship service requires attitudes of love, forgiveness, trust, attunement, and faith. Our active contributions are song, praise, and prayer. Our passive contribution is a meditative and receptive inner calm while we await His reply. Except for this last component, the description applies to most church services.

In the churches we receive a sermon in the place of a direct response from God. Yet Christ promised a more direct reply by means of His spirits. This reply may be received in the meditative, passive state as a clear thought, a word, an idea, or perhaps a feeling. As the receptive gift improves with practice, the worshipper may receive visions, read words written in the darkness of his closed eyelids, or perhaps hear a faint voice not heard by other people present. If the supplicant has an even greater developing gift in this regard, he may pass into a trance and an agent of the Lord may use his body to deliver a message in his native tongue, or in another language. In special rare cases, the entire range of Biblical phenomena are possible, according to the will of God in the matter. It is this great gift of first-hand knowledge that has been rejected by modern Christianity through misunderstanding and fear. Despite the warnings against quenching the spirit (see I Thess 5:19), the spirit has been quenched.

Most churches preach against present day revelation of God's will by His Spirit in the ways described here. In doing so, such churches place themselves in an untenable position, for they unwittingly argue that Christ will not fulfill His promise to answer directly. In that stance these churches tragically stand in the front ranks of the forces fighting to quench the Spirit of God. If personal revelation cannot occur, then the Bible itself is unacceptable, having come in just that way to its respective writers. It appears that God is not silent; we have chosen to be deaf.

If today's Christian were to see any of the events mentioned here, would he not be likely to reject them as being Satanic, as being the dreaded witchcraft and contact with the dead so strongly forbidden in Leviticus? How could he distinguish whether the communication comes from above or from below? Discernment is the critical gift here.

Discernment in the Biblical sense is more than simply good judgment. It is the gift of being able to distinguish between evil spirit influence and Holy spirit influence, "the ability to distinguish between spirits" (I Cor 12:10 NIV). Discernment can be difficult, indeed. If an angel appears praising God, it is easy enough to discern that this angel is one of God's spirits. It is quite another matter to feel inwardly drawn toward a certain course of action and to definitely know from whence the impetus comes—whether from a spirit of Christ, or from a spirit of Satan, or from one's own mind.

We cannot distinguish between guidance by God's spirits and

Satan's spirits simply on the basis of the phenomena they cause when contacting us. The phenomena have the same appearance in both cases because both sides, necessarily, can operate only within the universal laws God established governing His creation. Both warring factions can induce visions, dreams, thoughts, desires, emotions, and attitudes. Both factions can spell out words using a breastplate. Both can speak through a person in trance. Both can casue audible voices or materializations at times. Paul mentions the ability to distinguish between spirits as one of the gifts that a Christian may receive from above. If the believer lacks that special gift of discernment, then he may rely on other means.

The spirit can be questioned directly if it is speaking aloud by controlling a human body. The same is true if it is speaking from a cloudlet. "Beloved, do not believe EVERY spirit, but test the SPIRITS to see whether THEY are from God; because many false prophets have gone out into the world. By this you know THE Spirit of God; EVERY spirit that confesses that Jesus Christ has come in the flesh is from God" (I John 4:1–2 NAS) *(em add)*. The next verse states that a spirit who will not admit Jesus was the Christ is a spirit from Satan. This is expressed more clearly as, "This is how you can find out whether a spirit comes from God; every spirit who confesses that Jesus Christ appeared on Earth as a man, comes from God, while every spirit who seeks to destroy belief in Jesus as our lord incarnated does not come from God, but is sent by the adversary of Christ" (I John 4:2–3 GNT). In this way shall the spirit testify of Christ, for "he shall testify of me" (John 15:26).

If the spirit is merely influencing the human prophet, but not in total and sole control of his body, then the test of I John is not conclusive. In this case, the message can be, and usually is, influenced by the human instrument so that the words are not infallible. This is generally the case in those churches who practice speaking in tongues.

In the usual event that the spirit influence cannot be directly tested, we cannot reliably determine the source of the inspiration. In this case, a good deal of human judgment is required. We are told, "Do not stifle inspiration, and do not despise prophetic utterances, but bring them all to the test and then keep what is

good in them and avoid the bad of whatever kind" (I Thess 5:19–
22 NEB). We can further determine the nature of the spirits by
carefully noticing the results of the inspiration, for "by their fruits
shall ye know them" (Matt 7:20).

Let us suppose that a spirit agent of God testifies of Christ (see
John 15:26) and also passes the tests of I John (see 4:1–3). Suppose,
further, that the fruits of the spirit are "love, joy, peace, patience,
kindness, goodness, faithfulness, gentleness, self-control" (Gal
5:22–23 NAS), and that the spirit opens the Scriptures to understanding (as in Luke 24:27). If all these conditions are satisfied,
then the spirit qualifies without doubt as a Holy one sent according to the promise of God. The truth given by this spirit would
constitute a pearl of great price. Such contact has been made at
various times since Christ.

The most outstanding such contact took place in the first half of
this century, when an angelic being spoke at length with the priest,
Johannes Greber. Pastor Greber was instructed to write the information given him into a book. The book would then clarify God's
ways of communication so that modern man could understand
them and recognize them in the pages of the Scriptures. The book
would also explain the great fundamental questions of Christianity
by simply quoting the explanations brought by the spirit from
God. This book stands virtually alone as a unique source of
knowledge about the beyond, and of Christ. As such, it cannot be
recommended too highly as the key which unlocks the Scriptures.
Pastor Greber's book, *Communication with the Spirit World of God:
Its Laws and Purpose,* is available at a modest cost from the Johannes
Greber Memorial Foundation, 139 Hillside Avenue, Teaneck,
New Jersey 07666.

The Greber book unravels the knot of manmade doctrines
which entangle the modern Christian. In so doing, the book
confirms the truth of the prediction Paul wrote to Timothy: that
men have turned to fables and doctrines inspired by demons (see I
Tim 4:1).

We find ourselves today having no shortage of learned professors and theologians, but having a severe shortage of rational
answers about the causes and course of our existence. It is as
though we are "always wanting to be taught, but are incapable of

reaching a knowledge of the truth" (II Tim 3:7 NEB). We often find that we are described by Paul's words regarding such people who "do not have the slightest understanding of the terms that they use or the things of which they speak with so much assurance" (I Tim 1:7 GNT). Understanding the terms used in the Scriptures is prerequisite to understanding spiritual matters. With this in mind, we turn to a brief study of certain Biblical words.

◇

The Words of God

THE religious beliefs of countless Christians are based primarily upon English translations of the Scriptures. It is a matter of importance, then, to see if this foundation is an accurate reflection of the earliest documents. To this end we will look briefly at some of the difficulties involved in the translation process. We will look at pitfalls involved with the brevity of translations, idioms, word-for-word equivalents, and intentional ambiguity. It will not be necessary to deal with differences in grammar, tense, syntax, and so on.

A student of the Scriptures is necessarily a student of words. It is not possible for the seeker to find the full richness conveyed by the Scriptural accounts unless he first discovers the meanings of the words used. We are not referring to the English words, but to the words used in the original languages.

In the Greek manuscripts of the New Testament, for example, one frequently finds a Greek word which requires an English sentence, or even a paragraph, to bring out its meaning. Since Biblical translations are held to a minimum of words, much meaning can be lost. At times, then, a translation may be brief to the point of obscuring the full meaning. A verse illustrating this states that it is God's intention "to sum up" all things in Christ (Eph 1:10 NAS). One finds that the words briefly translated as "to sum up" mean "to bring back to, and to gather around, the main point." A Greek preposition used therein points back to a previous condition where no separation existed (Vincent, *Vol. III*). This verse carries the implication that at some point in prehistory we were not separated from Christ, but that a separation occurred and a re-unification with Christ is Divinely willed. The richness of meaning of this verse is sacrificed by the brevity of the translation. Translations with brevity in mind inevitably leave out some of the meaning and alter some of the rest.

Let us turn now to the challenge of making a word-for-word translation. Upon comparing one language with another one finds that the meanings of words and the mental images they evoke seldom correspond exactly. Accordingly, it is often not a simple task for a translator to render a New Testament phrase in Koine Greek[1] into an English phrase having exactly the same meaning. The task is made even more difficult if the Greek word is thought to have a special meaning in the New Testament different from its meaning everywhere else in the Greek language. This remarkable supposition invites previously held doctrinal beliefs to enter into the translation of the documents from which those very beliefs are alleged to have come, a kind of circular illogic which renders the beliefs unreliable.

Be that as it may, let us briefly illustrate the difficulty posed by the word-for-word process with an exercise in translating a fictitious foreign language. Suppose we find the phrase "ha rennt" and that we consult a bilingual dictionary for the meanings of these words. We find that "ha" means either "it" or "he" in English, and that "rennt" may mean any of the following: "run, jog, sprint, lope, trot." Depending upon the pronoun chosen ("it" or "he") and the verb chosen, we arrive at ten possible translations of "ha rennt," such as "it runs," "he sprints," and so on. The point is simply this: there is no one-to-one correspondence between words of one language and another. Accordingly, no word-for-word translation of a Bible can exist. It is not even a theoretical possibility.

It is difficult to understand how a person with a knowledge of two languages can claim a word-for-word translation of the Bible

---

1. An amalgam of Greek dialects, during the time of the Roman Empire, that replaced classical Greek.

exists when, on the one hand, there is no single, unique Bible and, on the other hand, no word-for-word translation is possible. A word-for-word translation is an impossibility. It cannot exist.

A translation is, at best, meaning-for-meaning, not the fictitious word-for-word. In order to accomplish such a translation, however, the translator must know the meaning of the writings. This is particularly difficult when the meanings of the words are not clearly known. The exact meaning of a great many Greek and Hebrew words is conjectural. Meanings are deduced based on the theological beliefs of the translators, or on the context in which the words are found, or upon related words from similar roots. It sometimes happens that there is no single English word which represents an adequate translation. Let us look at a passage from the writings of Paul to illustrate this point.

> For we know that if the earthly tent which is our house is torn down, we have a building from God, a house not made with hands, eternal in the heavens. For indeed in this house we groan, longing to be clothed with our dwelling from heaven; inasmuch as we, having put it on, shall not be found naked (II Cor 5:1–3 NAS).

What is the meaning of this passage? What is the meaning of this strange reference Paul makes to nakedness? The passage becomes clear upon learning that the word translated as "naked" means "without a physical body." The word was used by Greek writers referring to disembodied spirits (Vincent, *Vol. III*). Paul is simply stating that, after our struggles in the physical body (tent, house) are finished, we shall have a spirit body (building, house, dwelling) eternal in the heavens.

In addition to the language problems mentioned so far, another problem is that languages have great numbers of phrases which do not mean what they literally say. Such phrases are called idioms. Idioms require, for their accurate translation, a virtual day-to-day speaking knowledge of the languages and an intimate knowledge of the culture. As such, they represent special difficulties for the translator. As a modern example, we find the phrase *vor drei Jahre* in German would be literally translated as "before, or, in front of, three years." The corresponding idiom in French is *il y a trois ans,* literally translated as "it there has three years." Neither the French nor the German idioms translate literally into meaningful English, but both translate into the English idiomatic equivalent "three years ago." This sort of problem gave rise to the incorrect translation of Paul's ascent into Heaven as being "above fourteen years ago" (II Cor 12:2), as the Greek idiom was not understood at the time of the King James translation (Vincent, *Vol. III*).

It is quite clear at this point in the discussion that language is a tricky business. (Is it a business? Does it have the intention to trick?) But let us not go overboard. (Do we have permission to climb over the side of the ship into the water?) A great deal of human judgment and experience enters into making a translation. It is not a mathematically precise endeavor. The translator must make many choices and, by virtue of these choices, the translator is, to a greater or lesser extent, also an interpreter. All Bible translations are, therefore, interpretations of the manuscripts from which they were derived.

Translation includes interpretation. Such is the nature of languages.

Quite naturally, the honest and conscientious scholars who have labored on Biblical translations have exhausted every avenue to ensure that their translations are as accurate as possible under the circumstances. It is, nevertheless, not suprising that different versions of the Bible can differ markedly in the doctrines they will support. Owing to the human judgment involved in the translation process and in the selection of suitable early documents as reference points, it is not difficult to find places where different versions of the Bible support opposing views of doctrine with the same verse. Such a situation occurs in the book of Luke, in which it is related that a woman exclaimed to Jesus, "Blessed is the womb that bore You, and the breasts at which You nursed" (Luke 11:27 NAS). Jesus is reported to have replied, "Yea" (Luke 11:28 AKJ), "On the contrary" (NAS), "Rather" (NIV), "No" (NEB, GNT).

This remarkable selection of responses allows each reader to find justification for his view of Mary, the mother of Jesus, by choosing the translation that agrees with his bias. Christ's true meaning is obscured here.

We have taken a glimpse at some of the problems faced by translators due to idioms, the quest for brevity, and the lack of word-for-word correspondences between languages. Each of these aspects introduces errors or, at the very least, inaccuracies into the translation. We have seen that word-for-word translations

do not exist and that translation includes a degree of interpretation. It is remarkable that the various translations are sometimes as
similar as they are.

Nevertheless, there are considerable portions of the Bibles
which remain obscure despite the skill of the translators. Certain
of these passages were not intended to be understood, at least not
until the end of the age. In particular, parts of the Old Testament
relating to the end times and to the eventual fates of Israel and
Judah were often given in symbolic or otherwise confusing language. The express purpose for this was so the prophecies would
not be understood until after they had been fulfilled, and "then
shall you know that I am the Lord" (Isa 49:23 and others). Many of
the Old Testament books, especially those of Ezekiel, Elijah,
Isaiah, and Daniel, contain intentionally obscure passages, while
in the New Testament, the book of Revelation is the outstanding
example of obscurity. Quite apart from any problems due to faulty
translations or flawed manuscripts, we have no hope of understanding passages which God intended to keep veiled until the
end, unless we are, in fact, in those final days. Then, He said, we
shall understand them (Jer 23:20, 30:24; Dan 12:9).

Christ further hid the meaning of many of His teachings from
the masses. He did this by speaking in parables. When asked why
He spoke to the crowds in parables, Christ explained that God had
not yet granted them the privilege of understanding the secrets of
the kingdom of Heaven (see Matt 13:10–16). They were to hear,
but not understand, and to see, but not perceive, as prophesied
through Isaiah (see Isa 6:9–10). At the same time, Christ took His
true followers aside and explained the parables to them, His disciples having been granted the blessing of that knowledge by the
Father (see Matt 13:36–52, 15:15–20; Mark 4:10–12, 4:34). We see
here that truth is a precious gift from God, the benefit of which He
does not allow His enemies. Indeed, no one is even drawn to
Christ as the source of truth unless it is first granted to him by the
Father (see John 6:65).

Whatever the various Divine reasons may be for this, at least one
of them is clear: the truth carries with it the power to escape from
Satan's deceptions. The most effective weapon at the adversary's
disposal is the mixture of truth and error, whereby humans are
denied knowledge of their true identity and of the purpose of their

existence. We then vacillate between one set of doctrines inspired by demons (see I Tim 4:6), and another. Thus deluded by Satan's deceits, we erring pilgrims often fail to find a strong faith in God. We frequently give up the search for God altogether and live as though He did not exist. The freedom and power to escape from our spiritual ignorance into the light, and to escape from Earth itself into Heaven, are the inheritance of each child of God if he will but open his mind to receive. Then shall he realize the fulfillment of Christ's promise to those who are truly His disciples, "you shall know the truth, and the truth shall make you free" (John 8:32 NAS). Let us now turn our attention to the meaning of a small selection of key words upon which Christian beliefs are based.

Love and Fear

Throughout the Old Testament we find repeated admonitions to fear God. These warnings have worked their way into our language in the form of the complimentary description, "a God-fearing man." How can we reconcile instructions to fear God with the many other Biblical instructions to love God? We cannot both love and fear a person at the same time, since these sentiments are mutually antagonistic. The one prohibits the other. This is pointed out in the New Testament where it says, "There is no fear in love; but perfect love casteth out fear, because fear involves punishment, and the one who fears is not perfected in love" (I John 4:18 NAS).

Fear of God centers around fear of punishment. As such it is a deadly weapon for weakening the faith of God's children by contaminating their love for Him with fear. Should a small child fear his earthly father? It would be a sick and neurotic family in which a child would be afraid of impending torture from his father if he did something wrong. Yet we are led to believe this of our heavenly Father, although He has said, "Can a woman forget her nursing child, and have no compassion on the son of her womb? Even these may forget, but I' will not forget you." (Isa 49:15 NAS).

Fear of God makes no sense at all. This reaction is based on faulty translations. It owes its origination to the infiltration of false teachings in the earliest days of the church. At that time, false prophets and false teachers were at large, even before the Apostles had died. The Scriptures abound with warnings against these false teachings. Nevertheless, controversies raged. Doctrinal beliefs were sometimes established according to which warring faction had the greater force. It was in this historical setting that our basic doctrines crystallized. Scripture verses were translated, sometimes falsified, occasionally manufactured, and, above all, interpreted in such a way as to substantiate the doctrines held by the organized church in power at the time. Essentially these same beliefs are held by almost all denominations of today. The great majority of movements that emerged from the Reformation some five hundred years ago—Baptist, Pentecostal, Methodist, Episcopal, Presbyterian, Quaker—retained the beliefs of the second century church. One of the insidious translations perpetuated from those days is the word "fear" in the Old and New Testaments. This was further used in the King James version and persists today.

Let us look at a sampling of verses containing the Hebrew word translated as "fear."

"Blessed is every one that feareth the Lord; that walketh in His ways" (Psa 128:1).

"And in thy fear will I worship toward thy holy temple" (Psa 5:7).

"Fear God, and keep His commandments: for this is the whole duty of man" (Eccl 12:13).

"The fear of the Lord is the beginning of wisdom" (Psa 111:10 NAS; Prov 9:10).

"The fear of the Lord is the beginning of knowledge" (Prov 1:7 NAS).

In these cases the word translated "fear" should have been translated as "reverent love." Some Bibles do in fact mention in the margins this other meaning of the Hebrew word, giving alternate meanings of it as, variously, "reverence," "deep love," "awe," or "honor." Notice the vast difference in the previous verses when the corrected translations are used:

"Blessed is he that honors the Lord and walketh in His ways" (Psa 128:1).

"And in reverent awe and love will I worship toward thy holy temple" (Psa 5:7).

"Love God and keep His commandments, for this is the whole duty of man" (Eccl 12:13).

"Reverence for the Lord is the beginning of wisdom" (Psa 111:10; Prov 9:10).

"The love of the Lord is the beginning of knowledge" (Prov 1:7).

There are certain places where the word "fear" really means fear, but not when applied to our relationship to God. In the following two passages, the translation "fear" appears to be the correct rendering:

"A wise man feareth, and departeth from evil: but the fool rageth, and is confident" (Prov 14:16)
"But whoso hearkeneth unto Me shall dwell safely, and shall be quiet from fear of evil" (Prov 1:33).

The instructions are quite clear. The Old and New Testaments agree on our recommended attitude toward God. It is to love Him without fear (see Deut 6:5; Matt 22:37–40; John 15:12; Heb 4:16; I John 4:7–8). This attitude of utter confidence in the love of our Father for us is necessary if we wish to learn. It is not truly a compliment at all to be called a "God-fearing man."

Can we learn new things about the workings of God if we are paralyzed by the fear that we might inadvertently make some error in doctrine? Should we be in fear of Divine vengeance if we err? To answer that question again, let us look at what the Lord actually did to people who believed and acted wrongly.

One thief on the cross cursed and ridiculed Jesus, the other changed his mind at the last moment. Jesus accepted his change of heart immediately and responded to him, "Today shalt thou be with me in paradise" (Luke 23:43).

Christ did not condemn the woman caught in adultery who was brought before Him for condemnation. Neither did He scold her. He simply forgave her and sent her on her way with the admonition to sin no more.

Paul had zealously persecuted early Christians. When Jesus appeared to Paul, He did not even scold him, but simply asked, "Paul, why do you persecute Me?" (Acts 9:4). Paul later explained that he was used by Christ as an apostle despite his previous sins, because he had acted out of ignorance (I Tim 1:12–13).

As a final example, consider Christ's attitude toward His tormentors while He was being crucified. It was not vengeance, not hate. It was love. He said, "Father forgive them," and added a reason, "for they do not know what they are doing" (Luke 23:24 NAS).

In conclusion, we see that there is absolutely no reason for an honest seeker of the truth to be afraid of anything. This fear is simply a lack of trust in God's love. This conclusion is important, because we cannot grow in knowledge if we are bound by fear to previously held beliefs which might be incorrect.

"For God hath not given us the spirit of fear; but of power, and of love, and of a sound mind" (II Tim 1:7). Therefore, if we feel fear, we may be sure that its source is not God, but the evil one. We shall proceed in this spirit.

Spirit and Soul

"For God has not given us a spirit of timidity, but of power and love and discipline" (II Tim 1:7 NAS). This translation refers to "a spirit" in contrast to "the spirit" quoted earlier. It is not made clear whether there is only one such spirit or many. The following translation suggests many such spirits exist: "For the spirit that God gave us is no craven spirit, but one to inspire strength, love, and self-discipline" (II Tim 1:7 NEB). It is apparent in this rendering that God has sent a spirit entity whose purpose is to inspire strength, love, and self-discipline, not one of the lower spirits who inspire fear or timidity. In particular, we notice that the spirit is a thinking, acting entity in the service of God. It is not a mere mood or attitude in the mind of man, but a real entity existing outside of our minds. The word spirit "is never used in the New Testament of temper or disposition" (Vincent, *Vol. III,* p. 387).

If the spirit entity was sent by the Lord, it may be called "the Spirit of the Lord." This does not refer to the Lord Himself, Who is indeed a Spirit, but to one of the many spirits in His service. "By the Spirit of the Lord" (II Cor 3:18) is better translated as "from the Lord the Spirit." The Greek structure used here indicates the spirit proceeded from the Lord (Vincent, *Vol. III,* p. 310). In the same way "the Spirit of God" refers not to God, Who is Himself a Spirit, but to another spirit belonging to, or in the service of, God. The phrase "of God" refers to belonging to God as God's property (Vincent, *Vol. III,* p. 312). The activity of spirits sent from God is indicated by: "Now we have received, not the spirit of the world, but the Spirit who is from God, that we might know the things freely given to us by God" (I Cor 2:12 NAS).

It becomes apparent that God is active among His children by many spirits of God, or angels (see Heb 1:14), who serve as His agents. They brought instruction and guidance from above and were instrumental in teaching the early church and the Apostles. "Also be eager, of course, to enter into communication with God's spirits. Above all, strive to become instruments through which God's spirits speak to you in your mother tongue" (I Cor 14:1 GNT).

Spirits from God served as teachers who brought the truth to mankind. "For to us God revealed them through the Spirit" (I Cor 2:10 NAS). "Even so the thoughts of God no one knows except the Spirit of God" (I Cor 2:11 NAS). Paul taught in words taught to him by these spirits: "not in words taught by human wisdom, but in those taught by the Spirit" (I Cor 2:13 NAS). The literal meaning here is that the words were "communicated by a living Spirit" (Vincent, *Vol. III,* p. 197).

John makes it clear that "the Spirit of God" refers to any one of the multitudes of spirits sent from God. "Beloved, do not believe EVERY spirit, but test the SPIRITS to see whether THEY are from God" (I John 4:1 NAS) *(em add)*. Notice the plurality of spirits from God. "By this you know THE Spirit of God, EVERY spirit that confesses that Jesus Christ has come in the flesh is from God" (I John 4:2 NAS) *(em add)*. Hence, "THE Spirit of God" is "EVERY spirit" which is sent from Him. Paul makes the same point when he writes of "the ability to distinguish between spirits" (I Cor 12:10 NIV), and he identifies *any* spirit who declares Jesus is Lord as "the Spirit of God," or "the Holy Spirit" (I Cor 12:3 NIV) or "the Holy Ghost" (AKJ).

A spirit from God is a Holy spirit in contrast to the unholy spirits sent from Satan. This was expressed by a Holy spirit with great clarity to Pastor Greber:

Wherever the original Greek texts read 'a' spirit, one of many is meant. You therefore distort the meaning entirely by substituting: 'the' holy spirit . . . This does not mean that there is only one spirit of each kind, but is merely an instance in which the singular is employed in place of the plural. You have the same usage in your modern languages, for when you say to a sick person: 'I will get the doctor,' you do not mean to imply that there is only one physician in the world, and when you

speak of the farmer having had a prosperous year, you are referring to
all farmers collectively. So too you use the terms: 'the' workman, 'the'
lawyer, 'the' artist, you mean all those who are engaged in the respective callings.

When therefore Christ says: 'I will send the spirit of truth', He
means spirits of truth, for as you already know, the Divine spirits are
assigned to various callings according to their respective tasks. There
are spirits of protection, spirits of battle, spirits of strength, spirits of
wisdom and innumerable others. A spirit of truth has tasks of a very
different nature to perform than has a spirit of Michael's legions, and
hence possesses different qualifications. Neither one can take over the
work of the other. Every spirit has its definite calling, and is gifted
accordingly. Similarly, Lucifer has marshalled his hosts according to
their specific work. He too has his fighting forces, his spirits of lying,
of despondency, of avarice, pride, envy, revenge, lust, and of every
other vice. The different kinds of spirits, good or bad, are specialists in
their various callings and are well qualified to influence those on whom
they work, either for good or for evil within their respective provinces
(Greber, p. 371).

When the Bibles refer to one spirit they need to be understood in
this sense. For example, when it is said that, "There is one body
and one Spirit" (Eph 4:4), we know that there is not literally one
body—each of us has our own—any more than there is literally
one spirit. Both expressions are figurative, expressing the unity of
believers and of God's spirits. In the same way, "For by one Spirit
we were all baptized into one body" (I Cor 12:13 NAS) does not
literally refer to one spirit entity any more than it refers to one
literal fleshly body inhabited by all Christians together (see I Cor
12:14). Thus, "the Spirit" and "one Spirit" sometimes refer to the
entire plurality of spirits serving God.

According to the Scriptures, spirits sent from God communicated to the early church for the purpose of edifying the congregation. It is instructive to read expanded translations of some of
the references made to spirit communication.

"Thus also, as for yourselves, since you are those who are most
eagerly desirous of spirits (spiritual powers), by desiring them in
order that you may abound in them with a view to the building up
of the local assembly" (I Cor 12:17, Wuest). Wuest erroneously
inserts his *interpretation* "spiritual powers" here.

Part of the truth is translated away in, "So also you, since you
are zealous of spiritual gifts, seek to abound for the edification of

the church" (I Cor 14:12 NAS). Truth is restored by observing that the word translated "spiritual gifts" literally said "spirits." "Paul treats the different spiritual manifestations as if they represented a variety of spirits. To an observer of the unseemly revelries it would appear as if not one spirit, but different spirits, were the object of their zeal" (Vincent, p. 269). The rendition given by Paul is the correct one.

There remains the problem referred to in Corinthians (I Cor 12:10) of "distinguishing between the different prophetic utterances, whether they proceed from true or false spirits" (Vincent, p. 256). The popular Biblical translations lose much of the meaning of the tests for discerning of spirits. Therefore, we quote from two lesser known but more complete translations:

> Divinely-loved ones, stop believing every spirit. But put the spirits to the test for the purpose of approving them, and finding that they meet the specifications laid down, put your approval upon them, because many false prophets are gone out into the world. In this you know experientially the Spirit of God. Every spirit who agrees that Jesus Christ in the sphere of the flesh is come, is of God; and every spirit who does not confess this aforementioned Jesus [agree to the above teaching concerning Him], is not of God (from I John 4:1–3, Wuest, *In These Last Days*, pp. 160–161).

> With respect to spirit-communication, brothers, I wish you to have a clear understanding. You know that at the time when you were still heathens you entered into communication with the hideous spirits of the abyss as often as you were impelled to do so. I will therefore give you a rule by which you can distinguish between the spirits: No spirit from God who speaks through a medium will call Jesus accursed; and no spirit can speak of Jesus as his lord unless he belongs to the holy spirits (I Cor 12:1–3 GNT).

The word "spiritual" has the Scriptural meaning "of, or pertaining to, spirits". When Paul writes of a spiritual body he means precisely that: the body of a spirit. Today "spiritual" is more likely to be used in the sense of "religious" or "saintly." Such current meanings, if projected into the New Testament translations, gravely distort certain passages.

At this point we have begun to recover some of the meanings in the Scriptures which were lost or obscured by our misunderstanding of the literal meaning of "spirit" as a real entity rather than an emotion. Unfortunately, the English language has numerous idioms involving "spirit," such as "in good spirits," "in high spirits," "in a spirit of cooperation," "a high-spirited horse," "ran a spirited race," and others. These phrases are used to refer to moods, attitudes, and emotions. They mislead the mind when we attempt to read the equivalent phrase in the Bibles in that way. It is worth remembering that the English language did not exist then. We cannot take the current popular usage of such words and impute their meanings into the New Testament. Let us instead take the Gospel words with their original meanings and so understand the good news in the spirit in which it was given.

The soul is distinguished from the spirit in certain places, such as Hebrews (Heb 4:12 NAS). However, it is not defined. Human authors often characterize the soul as the source of the will and the seat of feelings, desires, affections, and memory. The soul may also be thought of as that power flowing through a spirit which animates it and powers its thought and memory. In any case, the spirit must necessarily contain a soul by virtue of its existence. Hence, spirit and soul are inseparable and we need make no further distinction between them in our discussions. Where one is, there is the other. Spirit and soul can be read as synonyms.

When Christ related a parable of a rich man in which God said to him, "You fool! This very night your soul is required of you" (Luke 12:20 NAS), the spirit of the man was also required of him, the soul being in the spirit body. We lose no meaning by exchanging the words "soul" and "spirit" here. Since the soul resides in the spirit and animates it, the spirit always continues to live even though the human dies.

Life and Death

The words "life" and "death" are used with two primary meanings in Biblical writings. They sometimes mean physical life and physical death in the same way they are used in everyday speech. Probably more often, however, they refer to spiritual life and spiritual death, especially when used by Paul in his Epistles.

Physical life is simply the condition in which the spirit of the person is in the body. Physical death is the departure of the spirit from the physical body.

In the moments before the physical death of Christ, He uttered

His last words, "My God, My God, why hast Thou forsaken Me?" (Matt 27:46; Mark 15:34), or, "It is finished" (John 19:30 NAS), or, "Father, into Thy hands I commit My Spirit" (Luke 23:46 NAS). Although the Gospel writers disagree about His words, they do agree that He quickly thereafter "breathed His last" (Mark 15:34; Luke 23:46 NAS) and at that instant released His spirit (Matt 27:50; John 19:30) from His physical body. Physical life ended when His spirit departed from His body. Nevertheless, Christ continued to exist as a Spirit.

Paul referred to physical death as departing from the physical body (Phil 1:22–23) and Peter wrote of it as "laying aside my earthly dwelling" (II Pet 1:14 NAS). As Stephen was being stoned to death he cried, "Lord Jesus, receive my spirit" (Acts 7:59 NAS) and his spirit left his body permanently. In the cases of Paul, Peter, and Stephen, their spirits continued to exist after leaving the body. Similarly, the spirits named Abraham, Isaac, and Jacob were continuing to exist in Heaven although their bodies were buried in the desert (Mark 12:26–27; Luke 20:37–38). When a certain beggar died, he was carried, as a spirit, by the angels (spirit agents) to be with Abraham (a spirit) in Heaven (God's spirit-world) (see Luke 16:22).

Physical life is simply that state in which the spirit is housed in the physical body. When Christ caused the daughter of Jairus to be raised from the physically dead, He commanded, "Child, arise. And her spirit returned, and she rose up immediately" (Luke 8:54–55 NAS) or, "In an instant her spirit returned into her body and she stood up" (Luke 8:55 GNT). Quite obviously her spirit had not ceased to exist. It was simply no longer in her body to animate it. We are not told from whence her spirit returned, only that she did.

The same phenomenon is reported in modern times, albeit without the visible presence of Christ. Many people have experienced brief periods of physical death and report having been fully aware in spirit of their continued existence. Such events are commonly referred to as "near-death experiences" or "out-of-body experiences." These experiences are consistent with the Scriptural accounts, which tell us that they do in fact happen, but which do not necessarily tell us what the people experienced while absent from the body. We will return to this topic in a later chapter. At this point we reiterate that physical life occurs when the human spirit is in the body; physical death occurs when the spirit leaves the body but continues to exist. Physical death does not imply that the spirit, or soul, is extinguished.

Spiritual life and spiritual death are quite a different matter. Neither term has any reference to continued existence or non-existence, to physical life or physical death. The terms refer, instead, to the relationship which a spirit has chosen between himself and God.

Every spirit is free to choose between Christ and Lucifer as his leader. If the choice is in favor of God through Christ, the person is said to be spiritually alive. The opposite choice is spiritual death. Spiritual death carries the idea of estrangement from God, separation from God, or divorcement from God, in much the same way as we use those terms in describing a marriage. The demonstration of the choice so made lies in the person's subsequent behavior. "You are slaves to the one whom you obey" (Rom 6:16 NIV). "If you wish to enter into life, keep the commandments" (Matt 19:17 NAS). Those people who have received Christ's message and believed it have "passed out of death into life" (John 5:24 NAS).

Paul wrote to Timothy that Jesus Christ had abolished death and brought life (II Tim 1:10), yet both Paul and Timothy were later deceased. Their deaths were only physical deaths, which Christ did not abolish. He abolished spiritual death, estrangement from God, and brought spiritual life, union with God, eventually to occur in His realm of Heaven. The continued existence of the spirit is not at issue here.

In the same vein, it is reported that God said to Adam and Eve, "in the day that you eat from it you shall surely die" (Gen 2:17 NAS). This verse is usually taken to mean that man would have physically lived forever had he not sinned. This interpretation appears to originate in man's age-old fear of physical death and his ignorance of the continued existence of his spirit. If this interpretation were true, then we would be required to believe that God placed His children on Earth, Satan's realm, with the intention of leaving us here forever, provided we lived perfect lives. This grotesque distortion of God's plan is removed when we realize that

God spoke of spiritual death, exile from Him, and not physical death.

That God was speaking of spiritual death is further borne out by the fact that Adam is reported to have lived perhaps nine hundred more years, although it was emphatically stated that "IN THAT DAY . . . thou shalt surely die" *(em add)*. That He meant spiritual death (divorcement from God) is an inescapable conclusion, since Adam, physically alive, was immediately exiled from Eden. Mankind was exiled from Eden until One would eventually come Who could reconcile the estranged parties, God and man. Genesis 2:17 could perhaps be translated more clearly as: "In the day that you eat of it, you will most assuredly be divorced from God."

Spiritual life and death are the issue in "For as in Adam all die, so in Christ all will be made alive" (I Cor 15:22 NIV). The meaning is that "as by following the example of Adam all have been divorced from God, in the same way by following Christ all shall be reconciled and reunited with God." There is no suggestion that Adam's descendants are to be punished for any mistakes other than their own. An entire chapter in Ezekiel is devoted to driving home the point that each person is responsible for his own acts (see Ezek 18).

Christ is He "that through death He might render powerless him who had the power of death, that is, the devil" (Heb 2:14 NAS). Compare with another translation, "Thus He was to be enabled to suffer the death of the body in order to wrest the power from him who rules over the spiritually dead, namely, the devil" (Heb 2:14 GNT).

Similarly, we find, "There is a way which seemeth right unto a man, but the end thereof are the ways of death" (Prov 14:12). An alternate translation could be: "There is a way which seems right to a man, but the result of following it is alienation from God." When Moses "placed life and death" before the Hebrews and urged them to choose life (Deut 30:19), he was not speaking of physical life, which they already had, nor of physical death, which they were all destined to face regardless. Moses was placing before them the choice between allegiance to God or alienation from God, "the blessing and the curse" (Deut 30:19 NAS). The choice was between spiritual life and spiritual death.

It sometimes happens that both the spiritual and physical sense of life and death are mixed in the same quotation. Paul wrote that "she who gives herself to wanton pleasure is dead even while she lives" (I Tim 5:6 NAS), which is to say that she is spiritually dead, or divorced from God, at the same time she is physically alive. She is one of the spiritually dead who is left to bury the physically dead, as in "let the dead bury their dead" (Matt 8:22). On occasion "dead" may also indicate unresponsiveness, as in being dead to sins (Rom 6:11; I Pet 2:24).

In a few instances, Life and Death are proper names for Christ and Lucifer, respectively. "And death and Hades delivered up the dead which were in them" (Rev 20:13 NAS) could be worded: "and Death [Satan] and Hell freed the spiritually dead who were in them." Similarly, "and death and Hades were thrown into the lake of fire" may be read as "the Prince of Death and his subjects were thrown into the lake of fire" (Rev 20:14 GNT).

The cause of spiritual death is the inherent nature of man. We are estranged from God to the extent that our individual natures differ from His nature, which in its very essence is love. "God is love; and he who continues in love remains united with God, and God with him [spiritual life]" (I John 4:16 GNT) *(em add)*. Departures we make from behavior based on love result in our alienation from God. Such departures are collectively called sin. "The soul who sins will die [be separated from God and His realm but continue to exist]" (Ezek 18:4 NAS) *(em add)*.

Sin

The consequences of sin are so great that we would do well to understand what the word means. Sin, in its various aspects, is represented by nine different Greek words in the New Testament. At times the words are translated as sin, transgression, or offense. Some of the meanings are far more delicate and subtle than the obvious sins of murder, theft, and wanton lust.

We list here some of the possible meanings abstracted from Wuest *(Studies in the Vocabulary of the New Testament)*. The full implications of the words are not given in this listing, as it is intended more as an overview than as a lexicon of the Greek.

Missing the Mark. The most common word used. As an archer. As a soldier who hurls his spear and misses the enemy.

Failing to Attain in a Field of Endeavor. As of a musician whose skills were not adequate for the performance he gave.

Failing to Hear. Hearing amiss. Inattentive or careless hearing of God's words.

Acting in Violation of the Law. Lawless. Without order. Breaking a known rule of life. Overstepping known bounds.

Falling Away from the Truth. Deviating from righteousness.

Falling Short of Doing Our Full Duty.

Failing to Carry Out a Command. Includes unintentional errors. Includes not knowing about the error.

Erring Through Ignorance. By not knowing the right way, or by not understanding.

In light of this listing, it is little wonder that no person has ever lived without transgressing. Furthermore, it is obvious that there is a wide range in the degree of seriousness of the errors. They range from murder, blasphemy, and premeditated evil to errors committed out of ignorance of the truth or committed in ignorance of their commission. Paul refers to these latter errors when he says, "I was shown mercy, because I acted ignorantly in unbelief" (I Tim 1:13 NAS). Christ spoke sternly to the prideful and arrogant hypocrites (see Luke 13:15), who, with premeditated intent, confronted Him (see Luke 12:56, 13:15). John the Baptist had called them "vipers" (see Matt 3:7), and Christ called them "tombs" (Matt 23:27 NAS). On the other hand, Christ freely forgave those very ones who crucified Him in their ignorance: "Father forgive them; for they do not know what they are doing" (Luke 23:34 NAS).

Separation from God entered the world due to sin and extended upon all men, for all have erred in one degree or another (Rom 5:12). Nevertheless, "the gift of God is eternal life [reunion with Him] through Jesus Christ our Lord" (Rom 6:23) *(em add).*

The guilt men often carry due to their mistakes is itself a

mistake, forgiveness having been promised by God upon confession and a change of heart (see I John 1:9). The man who
confesses his errors and works to correct his behavior, yet who still
carries guilt, certainly fails to correctly hear God's words, and falls
away from the truth, perhaps out of ignorance. These conditions
are among those listed as aspects of sin. Guilt therefore has no
place in the heart of a completed Christian. Neither does a companion of guilt: fear.

Fear surely misses the mark. Perhaps the most frequent command in the entire Bible is to have no fear. If the fear is fear of
God, then it misses the mark badly indeed.

Sin is often thought of as violation of any of the Ten Commandments. However, in the New Testament words we find a much
broader scope to the nature of our errors.

The warnings against sin are not God's efforts to force His
preferences on His children. God certainly has the sheer power to
have done that at any time. Instead, His commandments are
guidelines for teaching us how to live in harmony with others, a
necessity if we are eventually to dwell in the heavenly realms
without introducing disharmony. We are in training, in preparation for our future life. Sin, therefore, seems to be any act that
either eventually or immediately harms another soul, even including the act of withholding a good deed when it is within our
power to perform it. In general, any act contrary to God's law of
love may be viewed as some degree or other of sin. This concept
apparently includes all of the Old Testament and New Testament
instructions. Christ summarized all of these Scriptural instructions
in His commandments: "You shall love the Lord your God with all
your heart, and with all your soul, and with all your mind" (Matt
22:37 NAS), and "You shall love your neighbor as yourself" (Matt
22:38 NAS). "Do this, and you will live" (Luke 10:28 NAS).
According to Him, the entire Scripture hinges on these commandments (see Matt 22:40).

Parenthetically, let us remember that the love taught by Christ
may or may not involve romantic love, affectionate behavior,
warm feelings, or nice sensations. These may well be present, but
they are not the proof of our love. The proof is first our thought,
"for as a man thinketh in his heart, so is he" (Prov 23:7), and,

secondly, in how we act upon those thoughts. The one who keeps Christ's commandments, "he it is who loves Me" (John 14:21 NAS).

By way of analogy, we compare a person to a radio. Just as the radio can be tuned to various stations, so, too, can the person be in attunement with various spirit influences. Let us suppose that at the low frequencies on the left end of the radio dial we pick up Satan and his cohorts, while at the highest frequencies on the extreme right hand end we are in tune with God and His spirits. The more like Christ we become in our thoughts, the higher the frequencies we are attuned to, and the greater our access to His power and wisdom. The method of attunement is conscious unselfish love for God and our neighbor. The more we err and the more we think sinfully, the lower the frequencies we receive. The stations we receive most clearly are then on the far left side of the dial. We then hear Christ's message faintly, if at all, and with much static. Satan, however, comes in clearly. Thus, insofar as our natures differ from that of Christ, we are out of tune with Him. The task of raising our frequency is left up to us with the help of His spirits.

Returning to the subject of sin, let us note that the sin of apostasy is in a category by itself. Apostasy refers to abandonment or total desertion to God and His teachings. Quite naturally, if one voluntarily separates himself from God, he is then spiritually dead by the very definition of the term. Thus, the sin of apostasy is the "sin unto [spiritual] death." The Bible distinguishes between this sin and the errors of God's faithful, errors committed out of human weakness. John contrasted sin unto death and sin not unto death. "If anyone sees his brother committing a sin not leading to death, he shall ask and God will for him give life to those who commit sin not leading to death. There is a sin leading to death; I do not say that he should make request for this. All unrighteousness is sin, and there is a sin not leading to death" (I John 5:16–17 NAS). At first reading it might strike us as incomprehensible that we need not even pray for those who have committed a sin unto death.

The sense of these words can be explained by the example of a person who has taken an oath of allegiance as a citizen in our country. If he breaks the laws, he may be duly punished, but he does not lose his citizenship thereby. Although disciplined, he still remains a citizen under the juisdiction of his chosen government. If, however, our country is at war with another nation, and he deserts to the warring nation and joins with them, he loses his original citizenship. He is, from our point of view, essentially dead. He has committed the "sin unto death." No amount of pleading addressed to our government can help him, since he is no longer under its jurisdiction. He is subject to the ruler of the hostile nation to whom he transferred his allegiance. Applying this example to our relationship toward Christ, we acknowledge that we are citizens under His dominion, even if we daily commit trespasses and are duly chastened for them. Despite that, we do not cease to be His subjects. On the other hand, if we reject God by abandoning our belief in Him, or by living as though He did not exist, then we become quilty of desertion to the enemy in time of war. In His words, we would have committed the "sin unto death."

A final point is that the transgressions we have committed do not disqualify us for Heaven. We will never be flawless, for even the angels in Heaven err (Job 4:18 NAS). On the other hand, we can be, and probably must be, much better spirits than we are. It is not the stumbling and falling of those who believe in God and seek to please Him that bring forth spiritual death. The stumbling is through human weakness, and the falls are suffered on the road back to God. Just as our own children struggle to learn to walk, God's older children must struggle to learn to "walk in the spirit." It is this learning which is the process leading to salvation.

Saved and Lost

"And if it is with difficulty that the righteous is saved, what will become of the godless man and the sinner?" (I Peter 4:18 NAS). Countless words have addressed this question and the problem of how to attain salvation. Opinions and interpretations regarding the steps leading to salvation vary from church to church. Nevertheless, one of the points on which they agree is that salvation is a free gift from God. "It is to His grace alone that you owe your salvation after having adopted the faith. Your salvation is not what you deserve, then, but purely a gift of God. It is not the reward for your deeds, so that no one can boast of his salvation" (Eph 2:8–9 GNT). Opinions diverge quickly past this point.

Faith in Christ is necessary if one is to be saved. In the words of Paul and Silas, "Believe in the Lord Jesus Christ and you shall be saved" (Acts 16:31 NAS). This verse indicates salvation in the future tense, "you shall be saved," as something eventually resulting from trust in Christ. In the same way, Luke quotes Isaiah when writing that "all flesh shall see the salvation of God" (Luke 3:6 NAS). The reference is again to a future result in the verse: "Yet to all who received him, to those who believed in his name, he gave the right [power, AKJ] to become children of God" (John 1:12 NIV).

These verses do not suggest salvation is an immediate consequence of believing in Christ. Something is also required in the way of behavior. "For the grace of God has appeared, bringing salvation to all men, instructing us to deny ungodliness and worldly desires and to live sensibly, righteously, and godly in the present age" (Titus 2:11–12 NAS).

Although good deeds are not sufficient to win entry into Heaven for us (see Eph 2:8–9), they are at the same time necessary. "Faith without works is dead [separated from God]" (Jas 2:20) (em add). "You see that a man is justified [put right] by works, and not by faith alone" (Jas 2:24) (em add), or, more forcefully, "You see, then, that man pleases God with good deeds and not by faith alone" (Jas 2:24 GNT), although without faith it is impossible to please God (see Heb 11:6). The salvation process begins with accepting God through Christ, and continues by faith in Him evidenced by our deeds. As a result, our human way of thinking grows little by little into agreement with the nature of God. We achieve spiritual life thereby.

The final result of salvation and renion with God is truly a free gift of God, but He requires from us our best efforts to learn the lessons He teaches and to pass the tests He administers. Our eventual purification is then assured. "And I will bring the third part through the fire, refine them as silver is refined, and test them as gold is tested. They will call on My name, and I will answer them; I will say 'They are My people,' and they will say, 'The Lord is my God' " (Zech 13:9 NAS). The fire may grow hot indeed, but the refining produces purified spirits. Peter instructs us to rejoice at being tested by the fire of adversity (I Pet 1:6–7), because later on it produces "the outcome of your faith the salvation of your souls" (I Pet 1:9 NAS), "a salvation ready to be revealed in the last time" (I Pet 1:5 NAS).

The instructions from Paul to "work out your salvation with fear and trembling" (Phil 2:12 NAS) can be written as "work through your purification process on the way home to God with reverent awe and the trembling which may accompany it," and, he adds, "for it is God who is at work in you" (Phil 2:13 NAS).

Above all we strive to learn love and shun fear. As previously pointed out, Christ summarized the Old Testament commandments as the commandment to love. Peter stressed the fundamental importance of love, in view of our erring natures, when he wrote, "Above all keep fervent in your love for one another, because love covers a multitude of sins" (I Pet 4:8 NAS). Paul wrote to the faithful that the real "goal of our instruction is love from a pure heart and a good conscience and a sincere faith" (I Tim 1:5 NAS). The thirteenth chapter of Paul's first letter to the Corinthians explains at length that love is the spiritual gift of greatest value, to be sought above all others. Such love reconciles us through Christ to God's ways of thinking, defeating spiritual death and resulting in salvation.

We see, then, that salvation is presented in the Scriptures as a process, rather than as an immediate reward. Salvation is through the Savior, Whose victory won for us our release from spiritual death.

One may well wonder about the fate of people who refuse to learn God's lessons, but who believe in Christ. Are they ready for Heaven? One also wonders about the end in store for those who refuse to accept Christ until shortly before death. How can they be purified, seeing they have so little time remaining? The answers to these questions will become clear in later chapters.

The parable of the prodigal son is a Biblical example illustrating, among other things, salvation. The younger son took his share of the father's wealth and left home. He abandoned his father's house and jurisdiction and began living according to his own tastes. The son eventually squandered everything and came to ruin. Realizing that his own will was the cause of his wretched state, the son changed his attitude and set out on the road home. While he was still far away, his father ran to greet him. His father accepted his repentance with a homecoming feast, saying, "for this son of mine was dead, and has come to life again; he was lost, and has been found [saved, recovered]" (Luke 15:24 NAS) *(em add)*. Rephrased, this passage reads, "for this son of mine was alienated from me, and has come to be reconciled with me again; he was wandering away, and has been received back into my home." This parable vividly illustrates the common Biblical meanings of "life" and "death" as they describe our relationship with the heavenly Father. The parable further illustrates the salvation of the son as the homecoming of one who has learned from his errors and has changed his way of thinking. The son came to his senses on his own and freely desired to return to his loving father's house. In the same way, we set out on the homeward trek to our heavenly Father, enduring hardships, lessons, and tests along the way, but knowing that at last we shall be made fit to reenter His house. This is the process called salvation.

The son was said to be lost. Here, again, we have the familiar problem of a translation not having the same meaning as the original word. To the modern reader, a person is lost if we cannot locate him. That meaning is rarely the Biblical usage. On the contrary, the father of the prodigal may well have known where his son was at all times. We are not told that the son was lost in the usual sense. Instead, he was lost in the sense of having left his father's domain and of having gone astray. It is the leaving and going astray which are at issue here, not the knowledge of the whereabouts of the son.

We use "lost" in a variety of senses today. We may have lost track of time or have lost our place in a book. Perhaps our team lost a game. But all is not lost, for we still know where to find the time, our place in the book, or the game. We still know where they are. Similarly, a "lost" sinner has a known location, and "lost" Israel was taken to a known place. But the sinner and Israel both wandered away from God, as the prodigal left his own father. In that sense, they were "lost."

Christ said of His followers, "Those that Thou gavest me I have kept, and none of them is lost, but the son of perdition; that the scripture might be fulfilled" (John 17:12). The son of perdition, Judas Iscariot, did in fact stray from God and Christ, but his whereabouts were known.

"My people have become lost sheep; their shepherds have led them astray" (Jer 50:6 NAS). Nevertheless, the Lord said, "I will seek [come for] for lost, and bring back the scattered, bind up the broken, and strengthen the sick" (Ezek 34:16 NAS) *(em add)*. Many years later, He had no trouble finding His sheep for He said, "I was sent only to the lost sheep of the house of Israel" (Matt 15:24 NAS). "For the Son of Man has come to save [cleanse and call home, restore to spiritual life] that which was lost [wandered away from God, spiritually dead]" (Matt 18:11; Luke 19:9 NAS) *(em add)*. "For you were continually straying like sheep, but now you have returned to the Shepherd" (I Pet 2:25 NAS).

In summary, the term "lost" means virtually the same thing as "spirtually dead," and "the lost" the same as "the dead." Opposite in meaning to "lost" is "saved," "the saved" being those spiritually alive souls who are undergoing salvation, the purification process, with the assured end result of continued existence in the realm of Christ.

The humans God intended to use as His instruments for spreading His truth on Earth were the tribes collectively known as Israel. They were selected and set apart for the task of bringing salvation and spiritual life to all nations. Unfortunately, these "chosen people" strayed from obedience to His commandments and became lost. But their whereabouts were known.

Israelites and Jews

The process of salvation required human instruments to serve God in this earthly realm. For that service, He selected the descendents of Jacob, by way of keeping His promise to Abraham and others. "For you are a holy [set apart unto God] people to the Lord your God, the Lord your God has chosen you to be a people for His own possession [special treasure, NAS] out of all the peoples who are on the face of the earth because the Lord loved you and kept the oath which he swore to your forefathers" (Deut

7:6–7 NAS) *(em add)*. God changed Jacob's name to Israel. Israel's descendents then became known as Israelites, or simply as Israel.

The promises made to the man Israel were passed down to the nation, Israel, which sprang from him (see Deut 10:15). The nation was always to be a special instrument of God, "a kingdom of priests" (Ex 19:5), to serve "as a covenant to the people, as a light to the nations" (Isa 42:6 NAS), to remove spiritual blindness and bring freedom to Satan's captives (see Isa 42:7). " 'You are my witnesses' declares the Lord, 'And my servant whom I have chosen' " (Isa 43:10 NAS). The "chosen people" were chosen to carry out a specific mission. Should they faithfully follow God, they would receive, as a consequence of their faithfulness, great material possessions, good health, protection, and other blessings. However, these gifts were secondary to the purpose for which they were chosen.

Israel's obedience to God waivered for several centuries. The Israelites as a whole were unable, or unwilling, to retain faith in God. They were called deaf and blind (Isa 42:18–19) when David was king, and were still that way when Christ came much later.

Internal strife led to a division of the nation soon after the days of David and Solomon. Of the twelve tribes descended from the twelve sons of Jacob-Israel, ten rebelled and retained the name Israel. This new kingdom of Israel contained not only the ten tribes and their territories, but many of the people from the tribes of Judah and Benjamin. The remaining portions of Judah and Benjamin became known as Judah. Israel, the new kingdom, strayed far from God and was therefore "lost." Eventually, God divorced these lost tribes (see Jer 3:8) and gave them over into the hands of the Assyrians. The Assyrians conquered and deported these tribes from their homelands. They then repopulated the Israelite cities with new people, who later became known as Samaritans. We have here the origin of the phrase, "the lost tribes of Israel."

Although the English word "lost" misleads many readers into thinking that the location of the tribes was unknown, such is not the case. Both Biblical and archaeological records tell us where they were taken. Their surviving brethren, the nation of Judah in Jerusalem, knew quite well where they were. Ezekiel was even sent to the exiles (see Ezek 1:1, 2:3, 3:1). The Lord said to Ezekiel, "Go to the house of Israel and speak My words to them" (Ezek 3:4 NAS). The Lord continued with: "Go to the exiles, to the sons of your people, and speak to them and tell them, whether they listen or not, 'Thus says the Lord God' " (Ezek 3:11 NAS), and the spirit from God took Ezekiel to the exiles (see Ezek 3:12–15).

A portion of the tribe of Judah, in addition to some of those of Benjamin and Levi, remained unconquered in their territory in and around Jerusalem. They were collectively known as Judah. At that point in history the Biblical record shows a growing distinction between Judah and the exiled Israel, but on occasion the term Israel is used to mean the entire nation before it was divided. To further confuse matters, those of Judah finally came to view themselves as the survivors of the original clans of Jacob-Israel, adding yet a third usage of the term "Israel" by applying it to themselves.

Judah proved more faithless than exiled Israel. Little more than a hundred years passed after Israel's exile when the Lord gave Judah over to the Babylonians. When some of the Judahites finally returned to Jerusalem from Babylon and began rebuilding the temple, they were sometimes called by the shortened name "Jews." At that time, several centuries before Christ, a Jew was a returning captive from Babylon. Earlier still, he was a person from the southern half of the divided kingdom of Israel. In the earliest times, he was, in the literal sense, simply a descendent of the man Judah, or a member of the tribe of that name. The point is this: a Jew, or Judahite, is from a tribe of Israel and is therefore an Israelite. In contrast, an Israelite may or may not be a Jew, because he may or may not be descended from Judah. This distinction is relevant for understanding the older prophecies regarding Judah and Israel.

Later, by the time of Christ, the term Jew frequently referred to religious persuasion as it does today, rather than bloodline. Those people who worshipped God with the beliefs we now call Judaism could be called Jews, thus adding another meaning to the word with additional confusion resulting.

For example, Abraham was not a Jew, for he did not descend from Judah, who was not yet born. At the same time, Abraham worshipped the one true God worshipped by the later Judahites.

Joseph, the brother of Judah, was therefore not a Jew in the former sense (he was not a descendant of Judah), but was one in the latter sense (worship of the God of the Judahites). The Israelites were not Jews in the former sense, but were in the latter. A present-day convert to Judaism may be neither an Israelite nor a Judahite, but still become a Jew, if he inwardly becomes one (see Rom 2:29). Paul was a Jew of Tarsus, according to his religious faith, but was of the tribe of Benjamin instead of Judah (see Rom 11:1).

Names and designations change their meanings over periods of time. The Biblical record was written over a long time period. It is little wonder that interpretations of prophecies concerning Judah, the Jews, and Israel vary widely.

Israel never returned from the Assyrian deportation. The "chosen people" spread among the nations and ceased to exist as an Israelite nation. Judah, or at least a portion of it, returned from the Babylonian captivity and assumed the role of all of Israel. The Judahite fraction of the "chosen people" was utterly destroyed by the Romans a few decades after Christ. It would appear, then, that God had no group of people remaining on Earth who could serve as His chosen ones, to be a light and a witness unto the nations.

Who would obey the laws of the God of Israel and follow Israel's Messiah when He came? Who could be set apart from the world to serve Him?

Saints and the Church

Apostate Israel fell to the Assyrian invaders. The descendants of Jacob went as captives to lands north and west of their homeland in the Palestine area. They later escaped by the hundreds of thousands, according to ancient Assyrian records, and fled northward and westward. Some were joined later by a few of the Judahites captured by the Babylonians. Most of these Israelites continued northward and westward into all of Europe. Generations later, they had spread into all the countries of Galatia, Greece, Gaul (France), Iberia (Spain), Italy, Germany, and the British Isles. A small percentage of these people had returned to Palestine and lived there as Jews under Roman rule when the Messiah of Israel was incarnated as Jesus of Nazareth.

Many of the fugitives knew of their heritage as a special people of God. Many retained faith in Him during their centuries of exile. But most, perhaps, lost their heritage, their language, and their special identity, as generations of exile passed. Nevertheless, God kept track of the identities and locations of His sheep who had spiritually wandered away and who had been physically dispersed. The house of Israel was scattered among all nations "as grain is shaken in a seive, but not a kernel will fall to the ground" (Amos 9:9 NAS).

The Messiah (Hebrew), or the Christ (Greek), came for His people who had deserted God (the "lost"). He called upon them to follow Him on the road He opened back to the Father. Those who followed Him would be the "saved." "And it will come about that, in the place where it is said to them, 'You are not my people,' it will be said to them, 'You are the sons of the living God'" (Hosea 1:10 NAS).

Some of the Jews of Jerusalem followed the way of Christ, especially after His resurrection. Those people can be identified as the "good figs" (Jer 24) of the house of Judah, of whom it was written that they were to be His people, "and I will be their God" (Jer 24:7 NAS). The greater portion of the Jews rejected Jesus of Nazareth as the promised Messiah, thereby becoming those "bad figs" (Jer 24) who would become "a terror and an evil for all the kingdoms of the earth, as a reproach, a taunt and a curse in all places where I shall scatter them" (Jer 24:9 NAS). This terrible prophecy never applied to the main body of Israelites, whose location and identity became unknown even to themselves, but only to a portion of the Judahites. That particular portion of the house of Judah suffered the fulfillment, less than fifty years after Christ's ascensions, of the words: "And I will send the sword, the famine, and the pestilence upon them until they are destroyed from the land which I gave them and their forefathers" (Jer 24:10 NAS).

It would appear, then, that Israel's Messiah had no one to serve as His chosen servants, His chosen people. On the one hand, the Lord has referred to the Israelites Moses led out of Egypt as His only specially selected agents: "You only have I chosen among all the families of the earth" (Amos 3:2 NAS). On the other hand, He had divorced His original bride (see Jer 3:14), Israel, because of her unfaithfulness (see Jer 3:8–20). His chosen ones cannot be the Jews who rose up against Him, for to them it was given that "you will leave your name for a curse to My chosen ones, and the Lord God will slay you. But my servants will be called by another name" (Isa 65:15 NAS). This verse draws a stark contrast between the Jews and the chosen people, who will necessarily be called by some other name. In other words, those Jews were to be a curse to His chosen people, who were to be called by a different name, a name other than "Jews" or "chosen people." Yet the Lord had promised to call out His witnesses from among the Israelites, to "purify for Himself a people for His own possession, zealous for good deeds" (Titus 2:14 NAS).

Christ identified Himself as the good shepherd (John 10:1–21) Who had been sent only to the lost (apostate) sheep of the house of Israel. "I was sent only to the lost sheep of the house of Israel" (Matt 15:24 NAS). To these same sheep He later sent the Apostles: "go to the lost sheep of the house of Israel" (Matt 10:6 NAS). And so they went. Early church traditions hold that Thomas went to India; James to Spain; Peter and Paul to Britain, among other places; Joseph of Arimathea to Gaul and Britain in company with Lazarus, Mary Magdalene, and others; and so on. The traditions of different churches place various disciples of Christ in many places throughout Europe and the Near East. The travels of Paul, as recorded in part of the New Testament, are perhaps the best known of the travels of the first missionaries. The book of James is addressed "to the twelve tribes who are dispersed abroad" (Jas 1:1 NAS), not to the Jews of Palestine. We see that the good news of the kingdom of God was sent not only to Jerusalem, but also to those very places where the dispersed tribes of Israel were to be found. From those places Christ's disciples recruited followers for their Teacher.

In this manner did Christ call out His chosen ones from among the places where the descendants of the Israelites had settled. These converts were known as the "called out ones," in the Greek, translated into English as "the church." The church has the mission of serving as witnesses of God, of being lights to the world, and of bringing salvation by carrying His gospel, the New Testament description of the called out ones paralleling the Old Testament description of the chosen people. The church is, therefore, the great congregation of human spirits loyal to God under the rule of Christ. Whoever is in allegiance to His rule belongs to His church. The membership has nothing to do with worldly churches and manmade denominations, but refers to allegiance to Christ, for Whom "God has put everything under his rule and has made him the supreme head of the church" (Eph 1:22 GNT). His church is a church of the spirit, which knows of no priesthood or clergy, nor of any supreme earthly head. Among His church are people from every creed in the world.

The collection of chosen people, those "called out ones" for God, are called the church. The individuals comprising this church are "set apart ones," "consecrated ones," or "selected ones," those terms being the meaning of "saints." Accordingly, a saint is simply a person who is set apart from the worldly order to render service to God through Christ. The saint is necessarily, from the meaning of the word, a member of Christ's congregation, His church, whether or not he subscribes to any manmade creed.

There is no reference in the Scriptures authorizing the manmade honor of Sainthood. The custom of awarding this accolade is entirely manmade, God being no respecter of persons (see Acts 10:34; Rom 2:11; Eph 6:9). While we may rightly honor the faith and devotion of Peter, Paul, Mary, John, and many others, we at times mislead other followers of Christ by awarding the title of "Saint." These other Christians, however imperfect, are themselves "saints" in the Biblical meaning of the term. And all Christians are members of His "church" in the Biblical meaning of that word, despite differences in their beliefs and denominations.

The saints composing the church are chosen for special service in the world. Specific aspects of their mission have already been mentioned. Their mission, in its most general terms, is to serve as God's visible agents in preparing the hearts of mankind for the coming of the kingdom of God. This was the same mission entrusted to ancient Israel. In the fullness of time, "all Israel will be saved, just as it is written" (Rom 11:26 NAS).

The Last Days

The church has been chosen and called out by Christ to serve as His visible agents in the earthly realm. The saints of the church are assisted at every step by Christ's invisible agents from the spirit realm, the Holy spirits sent from God (see I John 4:1–2), who are sent to minister to the heirs of His salvation (see Heb 1:13–14). The heirs are "the nation whose God is the Lord, the people whom He has chosen for His own inheritance" (Psa 33:12 NAS), not a nation in the usual political sense, but in the spiritual sense of a collection of followers of Christ from many nationalities and denominations.

Upon completion of the mission of the church, the gospel will have been distributed to all parts of the globe. Israel will have been regathered from among the nations. Other predicted events, such as wars and famines, will have come to pass. The stage will then be set for the establishment of the rule of Christ on Earth. The coming of the kingdom of God and the return of Christ are mentioned some three hundred times or more in the New Testament alone (see Matt 24:30; Mark 13:26; Luke 17:24; John 14:3; I Thess 4:16; Jas 5:7; I Pet 5:4; Jude 4). The Apostles and early Christians believed His return was imminent (see Heb 10:37–38). Local groups of believers, "churches" in the common sense, have believed it and taught it for a great many years. But He has not yet returned.

Obviously, it is easier for men to understand Biblical prophecy after it has happened than before. Even the prophets and Apostles encountered this same difficulty. Peter implies (I Pet 1:10–13) that they searched the Holy writings in vain to discover what would happen before the millenial kingdom. Likewise, earnest students search the Scriptures today and arrive at an array of differing conclusions regarding the events of the end times. Yet there are many points of agreement.

It is usually agreed that the return of the Lord will be a public phenomenon: "and every eye shall see Him" (Rev 1:7 NAS). We are not told whether every eye will see Him simultaneously, as is usually assumed, or whether they will see Him over a period of time. Nor are we told the exact time to expect Him (see Matt 24:36–42), since even He did not know the time when He spoke of His return. Since the event could occur at any time (see Matt 25:13), and it will be sudden and unannounced (see I Thess 5:2–3), we are instructed to be in a state of readiness (see Matt 24:44).

Although the exact timing is unknown, certain events men-

tioned earlier must first occur in order to set the stage. Some of
these events are catastrophic. The famous Battle of Armageddon is
one. Another is the chaos in the sky when the elements melt with
extreme heat (see II Pet 3:10–13). We are sometimes led by these
predictions to expect the end of the world. But there is a contradiction here. The world cannot end and, at the same time, have the
kingdom of God established on it.

The contradiction is resolved by discarding the inaccurate translation of "world." More modern translations say that we look not
for the end of the Earth itself, but for the end of an age, of a period
of history, of a world order. Biblical references to a new Heaven
and a new Earth can have several meanings other than the total
removal of the planet Earth. We therefore look for the end of a
period of time of waiting.

The two-thousand-year waiting period will approach its end
accompanied by further revelations on the plan of salvation, things
"ready to be revealed in the last time" (I Pet 1:5). The meanings of
many Scriptural passages sealed up until the time of the end (see
Dan 12:4) will become clear. Demonic and supernatural activity
will greatly increase (see I Tim 4:1; Rev 9:1–21). Toward the end of
the age we can expect that "perilous times shall come" (II Tim 3:1
NAS).

It is in this setting that we find ourselves. We are in a time when
we have only a partial understanding of the Scriptures, and little or
no awareness of the Laws of nature (God) applying to the spiritual
realm. One believer speaks in tongues with the blessing of his
fellows, while another group teaches all such things are Satanic.
Still another group has not thought about it. People report having
died for a few minutes, having seen departed loved ones or others,
and having been sent back to their bodies. On occasion, Christians
say these people are blessed by a gift from God, while other
Christians claim the forces of the Deceiver are at work. The same
opposition of opinions can be found on many matters now taking
place. Is there life elsewhere in the universe? Is spiritism valid? Do
miracle healings occur?

In our poverty of spiritual knowledge we find ourselves un-
prepared to discern which forces are at work in the marvelous
occurrences of today. We are in a similar position to that of the

Pharisees and Sadducees who, by their incomplete and faulty understanding of what they read, failed to recognize that Jesus was, in fact, their Messiah. They then crucified Christ. Could not we also be blind to the fulfillment of prophecies in our own time?

We are at a time when marvelous things occur but are rejected as evil due to our misunderstandings. It may be that we, along with those who rejected Christ on His first visit, cannot recognize the signs of the times as being Divinely given. If so, then we would profit greatly from more knowledge of the nature of God's creation and of ourselves.

REFERENCES CITED

Greber, Johannes, *Communication with the Spirit World of God*

Vincent, Marvin R., *Word Studies in the New Testament, Vol. III, The Epistles of Paul*

Wuest, Kenneth S., *In These Last Days: Studies in the Greek Text of II Peter, I, II, III John and Jude for the English Reader*

Wuest, Kenneth S., *The New Testament, An Expanded Translation*

PART TWO

God's Creation

CHAPTER 5

Heavens

"My people are destroyed for lack of knowledge" (Hosea 4:6).

Long before Earth was created, Heaven already existed. Heaven was populated with multitudes of creatures we call angels. It was a place of boundless beauty and joy at a time when "the morning stars sang together, and all the sons of God shouted for joy" (Job 38:7). This kingdom was ruled by Christ, Who referred to it when He said, "My kingdom is not of this world" (John 18:36). Christ's followers look forward to someday living in His heavenly kingdom and participating in its beauty and joy. Yet, we seem to know little or nothing about what to expect there.

For example, we are accustomed to the image of multitudes of winged angels, halos glowing brightly, playing their harps and singing hallelujah. The redeemed are pictured as dressed in white, walking on streets of gold, singing praises to God, and worshipping their Creator day and night. In short, we are presented with a Christmas card Heaven, in which the majority of humankind would feel quite out of place. Let us see what the Scriptures reveal about Heaven. But first we should ask, "Which Heaven are we talking about?" The Scriptures mention several.

Seven distinct and separate levels of heavens were part of the beliefs of the Hebrews, although there seems to have been no definite idea of the conditions in the various levels. Several different heavens, or dimensions of existence, are implied by the

Christian Bibles of today. These Bibles contain numerous references to more than one Heaven:

> "By the word of the Lord were the heavens made; and all the host of
> them by the breath of his mouth" (Psa 33:6).
> "Give ear, O ye heavens, and I will speak" (Deut 32:1).
> "Thus the heavens and the earth were finished, and all the host of
> them" (Gen 2:1).
> Both Jesus (see Matt 4:17 and John the Baptist (see Matt 3:2)
> preached: "Repent, for the kingdom FROM THE HEAVENS [literal
> translation] is at hand" (em add).

God and Christ are sometimes reported as dwelling in the
highest heaven (see Psa 115:16 NIV) and at other times are said to
reside above the highest heaven:

> "That ascended up far above all heavens" (Eph 4:10).
> "Behold, the heaven and heaven of heavens cannot contain thee" (I
> Kings 8:27).
> "Seeing the heaven and heaven of heavens cannot contain him?" (II
> Chron 2:6).

The term, Heaven, is applied to the entire set of lower heavens
and the highest heaven when no distinction is necessary. The
existence of various, different heavens within Heaven is evident in
a statement made by Christ as He neared physical death on the
cross, "I tell you the truth, today you will be with me in paradise"
(Luke 23:43 NIV). Paradise cannot be the high level usually
thought of when we loosely use the word "Heaven," because
Christ did not ascend to there until the Ascension, forty days later
(see Acts 1:2–3). Another New Testament reference to multiple
dimensions in Heaven is contained in Paul's experience in which he
was taken up to the third heaven, but was not permitted to disclose
what he had seen there (see II Cor 12:2–4). We clearly see that there
are several heavens, although the details are lacking.

These heavens are all nearer to God than the Earth is, and are all
under the jurisdiction of Christ, to Whom God gave all power and
authority (see Matt 28:18). The conditions in these realms may
therefore be assumed to be pleasant, indeed. Although the details
are unclear, numerous clues are to be found in the Scriptures
which reveal to us some aspects of the conditions in the heavens.

Paradise is referred to as the "garden of God" (Ezek 28:13; Rev

2:7), and thus cannot be a barren desert. We find that the heavens, indeed, have many features in common with this physical universe in which we live, and in particular with the planet Earth. The heavens contain dwelling places (see John 14:2–4), rivers, streams, fields, and cities (see Psa 46:4–5 and others). In other words, the heavens are somewhat like Earth, but without the flaws (see Isa 55:9).

Such a description for the heavens was widely held among the early Jews and Christians, which means it was surely known by Jesus and the Apostles. The correctness of this description is apparently confirmed by the words of Christ, "If it were NOT so, I would have told you" (John 14:2) *(em add)*. Yet, although we can expect to see many recognizable things upon our arrival in Paradise, there is surely much that will be new and wonderfully astonishing, for "Eye hath not seen, nor ear heard, neither have entered into the heart of man, the things which God hath prepared for them that love Him" (I Cor 2:9).

Another point of familiarity with Earth life is that the things in Heaven are composed of matter. This matter must behave according to the laws of nature in order that plants and structures exist. In fact, the existence of such forms indicate that the laws of electricity, chemistry, gravity, physics, and nature, in general, apply in the higher dimensions of existence just as they do on Earth. The mere Scriptural references to flowing water already imply as much. It is not surprising that it should be so. The laws of nature are laws of God. We are becoming familiar with some of these laws while on Earth during our preparation and training for life in the next realms. Earth life would be a poor school, indeed, if it did not prepare its pupils for the life they will find after graduation.

However, experience with God's laws of nature and the knowledge of how that aspect of reality behaves is not, in itself, sufficient preparation for living in bliss. We must also learn to live in harmony with others. This is part of our training on Earth, and is the major thrust of Christianity. Above all lessons, this one is the most important in our being prepared to live in harmony with the other citizens of Heaven. But what of these other citizens? What are they like?

The inhabitants of the heavens are usually called angels. The

name "angel" calls up images of creatures bearing little resemblance to their Scriptural description. Indeed, the word "angel" conveys in itself no information whatever about the
appearance of the creature. "Angel" is often defined as meaning
"messenger," or, far better, "agent." The name describes the function of the creature, not the creature itself. In the same way, the
words soldier, mother, and friend do not tell of the appearance of
these people, nor even whether they are people, but describe their
function and suggest their relationship to us. An angel is a creature
who is functioning as an agent of God. God's agents are carrying
out His instructions. But what is this creature? The angel is a
spirit.

> "Are not all ANGELS ministering SPIRITS sent to serve those who
> will inherit salvation?" (Heb 1:14 NIV) *(em add)*.

Spirits are the inhabitants of God's heavens, which form a vast,
multi-dimensional spirit-world of God. God Himself is pure Spirit
(see John 4:24). Christ, the image of God, is a Spirit. The angels
are spirits, and we are spirits. None of these spirits fits the popular
myth that a spirit is a shapeless, formless, intelligence having no
body. The opposite is the case: spirits have bodies.

Spirit bodies are necessarily composed of a different condition
of substance than fleshly bodies, since they are invisible to us in
their usual condition. This different type of matter, this different
condition of substance, is the same as that matter of which the
aforementioned streams, plants, and structures of Heaven are
composed. The bodies of the spirit beings are variously called
"spiritual bodies," "celestial bodies," "glorified bodies," or "resurrection bodies" (see I Cor 15:40–44). The bodies of these spirits are
every bit as real, solid, and visible to each other in their dimension
as our bodies are to each other on Earth. Some of these spirits have
been seen when they materialized on Earth.

Angelic appearances reported in the Scriptures show that these
spirits walk, talk, eat, wear clothes, and generally resemble people
in every way. So great is their resemblance to humans that the
angels are sometimes referred to as men (Gen 18:1–15, 19:10–12,
32:24–30; Dan 9:21; Luke 24:4; Acts 1:10). We are told that these
Holy ones are sometimes among us, but that we mistake them for

ordinary people: "Let love of the brethen continue. Do not neglect to show hospitality to strangers, for by this some have entertained angels without knowing it" (Heb 13:1–2 NAS).

The Biblical description of angels has no resemblance to the usual conception of angels as pretty people with wings on their shoulders. This myth grew from the Biblical references to seraphim and cherubim. Seraphim are mentioned only in Isaiah in which we read of a vision he received (Isa 6:2–6). The seraphim were part of the vision, not claimed to be real beings. In any event, we have no further mention of seraphim in the Scriptures. On the other hand, cherubim are referred to on several occasions. Most of the verses involving cherubim describe statues of cherubim. Whereas the statues themselves have wings, it is not clear that the cherubim do. As we shall see in a later chapter, they do not. Thus, we conclude that angels are spirits having bodies resembling ours, with no wings.

The resemblance goes much deeper than external appearance. There must also be internal similarities. Humans can eat angel food (see Psa 78:24–25). Angels can eat human food, also, as the angels who materialized and visited with Abraham and Lot ate quite a variety of human foods (see Gen 18:1–22, 19:1–26). Even the Spirit, Christ, when He materialized from Heaven and appeared among the Apostles, ate fish. He had mentioned to them earlier that both food and wine exist in Heaven (see Psa 78:24–25; Mark 14:25). Since these spirits eat and drink, it follows that they must have internal organs of every necessary kind. It is as though these spirits of God's realms are more or less like flawless humans might be, if such existed. Yet angels are not flawless.

One shortcoming shared by both angels and man is that we both make mistakes (Job 4:18, 15:14). However good they may be, angels are not perfect. Nevertheless, they do display the most noble attributes. Among the virtues of angels, we find humility and gentleness displayed in their ministry to humans (see Matt 4:11; Heb 1:14). The angels are wise (see II Sam 14:20) and discerning of good and evil (see II Sam 14:17). They have extraordinary knowledge, but do not know everything. They do not know all the details of the plan of salvation, though they are especially interested in finding out (see I Pet 1:12). They worship and serve

God (see Psa 148:2), as man is expected to do. The angels of the spirit-world of God are, as one of them has said, our "fellow servants" (Rev 22:8–9). They excel in strength (see Psa 103:20), and will some day be sent to rescue God's elect (see Matt 24:31). At that time we shall also feel the great joy that they are capable of feeling (see Luke 15:10). Having examined the nature of angels, let us now turn our attention to their activities.

Angels perform many tasks in carrying out God's directives. They may be sent simply to bring messages, such as to the women at the tomb of Jesus (see Matt 28:5), or in response to prayer (see Dan 9:20–22). They may execute God's judgments (see II Sam 24:15–16; Acts 12:23). They may be sent to destroy, as in the destruction of Sodom (see Gen 19:13). Sometimes they are sent simply to bring instructions, as to Elijah (see I Kings 19:5–8), while on other occasions they bring protection and guidance (see Gen 24:7, 24:40; Psa 34:7).

An angel, in carrying out his or her mission as a ministering spirit, may apparently be given charge of groups of believers. In Revelation, messages are addressed to "the angel of each of the seven churches," or "to the Spirit of the seven churches," depending on the translation we read (see Rev 2 and 3). The relationship of the spirit (angel) to its church seems to be comparable to that of a parent to the children, or of a pastor to his flock.

The great diversity of activities implies some degree of organization in the spirit-world. In the spirit realm, God and Christ are at the top of the celestial chain of command. Further down, there are various degrees of rank and authority. For example, we read of angels, archangels, herald angels, princes, powers, authorities, thrones, dominions, and principalities. All of these exist among the spirits, though not all of them are necessarily in Heaven. The Scriptures give no details of the organizational structure past this.

In summary, we find in the Scriptures a great many similarities between angels and men. It is intended that, upon our arrival in the next dimension, we will be prepared to live in harmony, for it is said that man shall then be equal to the angels (see Luke 20:36). We have been made "a little lower than the angels" (Psa 8:5), in the same manner in which Christ Himself was also "made . . . for a little while lower than the angels" (Heb 2:6–9 NAS) during His earthly incarnation. Our future equality with the angels of Heaven apparently extends to the task of judgment, as "the Lord cometh with ten thousands of his saints, to execute judgment upon all" (Jude 14–15), and "Do ye not know that the saints shall judge the world?" (I Cor 6:2). However, it is written elsewhere: "when the Son of Man comes in His glory, and all the angels with Him" (Matt 25:31 NAS). There is apparently some connection between His saints, the believers in Him, and the angels. They have much in common.

The major differences between man and angel seem to be that we are in flesh on Earth, instead of in spirit bodies in Heaven, and that all mankind bears the stigma of "original sin" (I John 1:8 and others) which the Holy angels do not carry. The distinction between man and angel seems to be more of quality, or degree of spiritual purity, than one of species. We may well be puzzled over the close relationship the angels have with us, why they show so great a love for us, and why they so willingly aid and guard us along life's pathways (see Psa 91:11). Why do they show such delight when we show signs of improvement in our thought and behavior (see Luke 15:10)? "What is man, that thou art mindful of him?" (Psa 8:4). Let us leave this question for a later chapter and turn our attention to the revolt in Heaven.

It would seem out of reason that trouble of any serious kind could have occurred in God's domain, but it did. This was possible because God does not force His will on His creatures, but allows them to accept or reject His ways at their discretion and to learn by harvesting the results of their choices. Free will, the volition to choose according to their own tastes, was given to all of the angels. Whenever such freedom of choice exists, the possibility of error also exists. The heavenly spirits were capable of making errors in judgment (see Job 4:18, 15:15). With freedom of action, and the possibility of making mistakes, the angels had the chance of being led into great evil. As ages passed, evil did, in fact, result. Greed and arrogance grew in certain of the angels, led by the one we call Lucifer, or Satan (the adversary). Revolt broke out in Heaven as Satan and his dupes attempted to overthrow Christ, the One Whom God had annointed and given all authority. "And the angels which kept not their first estate, but left their own habitation" (Jude 6). By their desire to rule rather than be ruled, Satan and his followers committed the fatal error of rebellion against Christ.

Christ had already prepared His forces, Michael's legions, for such a contingency. "And there was war in heaven. Michael and his angels fought against the dragon [Satan], and the dragon and his angels fought back. But he was not strong enough, and they lost their place in heaven" (Rev 12:7–8 NIV) *(em add)*. Jesus recalled the great Fall with the words, "I beheld Satan as lightning fall from heaven" (Luke 10:18). One-third of the angels of Heaven sided with Lucifer in the revolt against Christ (Rev 12:4). In that tragic day, a third part of all the angels were cast out of Heaven into lower regions created for their exile. "God did not spare even the fallen angels, but drove them down into hell, into the caverns of darkness, where they will be kept until they turn their hearts to God again" (II Pet 2:4 GNT). These spirits were no longer to be found in the heavens. Until such time as the rebels should repent of their ways, they were to be "fettered in darkness with unbreakable chains, until the coming of that great day on which they will experience a change of heart" (Jude 6 GNT). Cut off from Heaven, out of contact with their friends, their families, and their God, these exiled angels were referred to as "the dead."

The "dead" were exiled from Heaven at the time of the Fall, a time which must have preceded the creation of man. To see this, we have only to notice that when Adam and Eve were led by Satan to disobey, Satan was at that time already evil and not a part of God's forces. Therefore, the angels, both good and evil, existed long before material creation, and the revolt itself had occurred and its outcome established before man and woman were placed on Earth.

The revolt was a time of anguish in the dimensions called Heaven. A great portion of the spirits were exiled into Hell, where they were powerless to escape. As a result of their freely made choice of how to live, they were given a place of their own where they could live with others of like mind and experience the results of their erroneous ways of thinking.

CHAPTER 6

------------------◇------------------

Hells

THE great revolt had taken place in Heaven. The rebellious angels were ejected from their home in Heaven and exiled to another place, an entirely different dimension where they could no longer cause harm in Heaven. They were no longer seen or heard in that realm and were referred to as "the dead." Those spirits who remained loyal to Christ retained their place in Heaven and were called "the living." The terms "living" and "dead" are used in the Scriptures in this sense quite frequently. They refer to whether a person holds allegiance to Christ or to Satan, not to whether that person is physically alive or physically dead. In a similar usage of these words, Christ, the leader of the "living," is called Life (see John 14:6), whereas Satan, the leader of the "dead," is called Death (see I Cor 15:26). These titles in the Bibles may occur with or without capital letters, depending on the beliefs of the translators.

The dead were separated from the living to be allowed to live according to their own desires and to reap the results of their thoughts. For this purpose a special realm was created. It is the place of confinement for the fallen spirits, where they are under the dominion of the Prince of Death (Rev 20:13–14 GNT). The realm ruled by Satan is known as Hell. Hell is usually thought of as a single location, but the Scriptures refer to several levels in Hell.

83

The various different dimensions, or levels, in Hell serve as places of confinement for the exiled spirits according to their degree of guilt in the revolt. Like Heaven, Hell is a collection of distinctly different regions. These regions are implied by the Scriptures by the use of the names *Sheol, Gehenna, Tartarus,* and *Hades,* but little is revealed about them. The bits of truth revealed in the Scriptures are, unfortunately, obscured by inconsistent translations and centuries of tradition based on errors. We sometimes find the names referring to the hells translated simply as "hell," or as "grave," "pit," "abyss," and others.

The Hebrew word *Sheol* is often translated in the Old Testament as "grave," which is, in fact, a legitimate meaning of the word in certain contexts. *Sheol* corresponds closely with the New Testament Greek word, *Hades,* which the Greeks thought of as the unseen world of departed spirits. Eventually, *Hades* became a common name for the lower spirit-world. *Hades* was used in the *Septuagint* as a translation of the word *Sheol.*

In the days when the King James Bible was translated, the English word "hell" meant a grave, a hole, or a pit. Englishmen buried potatoes in a hell to preserve them for winter. There is no suggestion of heat or fire in this usage.

Another Greek word translated as Hell is *Gehenna. Gehenna* is derived from an earlier Hebrew word meaning "valley of Hinnom," a narrow gorge southwest of Jerusalem. In this ravine, idolatrous rites and sacrifices once occurred. Children were sacrificed to the god, Molech, until King Josiah of ancient Judah ended these practices. The valley of Hinnom was later used as a dumping ground for garbage, dead animals, and other waste from Jerusalem. Bodies of criminals were also thrown there. Smoldering fires smoked there continuously amid the stench and decay.

The third region of the hells mentioned in the New Testament is *Tartarus.* This term is used in the Greek only in II Peter 2:4. It was the place to which Satan and his angels were banished. *Tartarus* was described by the ancient Greek writer Homer as lying as far below *Hades* as *Hades* lay below Earth. It was thought of as a bottomless pit into which Zeus, of Greek mythology, imprisoned those who resisted him.

The rebellious dead in the hells find themselves in dire conditions, indeed. They are still "sons of God" (Job 1:6), but they are prodigal sons who have deserted Him. Only a few clues have been revealed about the conditions these spirits endure. They are compared with prisoners gathered in a pit (see Isa 24:22). They are described as being in prison (see I Pet 3:19; Rev 20:3), in gloomy dungeons (see II Pet 2:4 NIV), or chained in darkness (see Jude 6). Certain sinful men have "blackest darkness" reserved for them (see II Pet 2:17 NIV).

Under such conditions the captive spirits naturally experience great sorrow (see II Sam 22:6; Psa 18:5, 116:3), pain and troubles (Psa 116:3), and tears and grinding of teeth (see Matt 13:40–42). The fallen spirits must endure these agonies without knowing the true cause of their condition, for they do not have the knowledge of the truth (see Eccl 9:5) and have no remembrance of their former glory (see Psa 6:5; Eccl 1:11). Hence, it is figuratively said that the dead know nothing (see Eccl 9:5 NIV) (see also Isa 8:19–20 NIV). The miserable conditions in the hells are symbolically referred to as the fires of Hell.

The symbol of fire as an agent of purification or destruction is widely used in the Scriptures, as is the literal word fire. The fire of Hell is figurative, as is shown by the use of that word in other places in the Scriptures. For example, God's words are like a burning fire (see Jer 20:9, 23:29), yet they are not for injury but for healing. God Himself is spoken of as a consuming fire (see Deut 4:24; Heb 12:29), and His anger and wrath are pictured as fire (see Deut 32:22; Psa 89:46; Jer 15:14; Ezek 22:31, 38:19). We will all be baptized with fire (see Matt 3:11), yet none shall be harmed by this figurative fire. Fire in these verses is clearly symbolic. It is the same fire which was to melt Jerusalem (see Jer 9:7; Ezek 22:18–22), where melting can only be in a symbolic sense. In another case, Israel (the house of Jacob) is called a fire which shall destroy the house of Esau, described as stubble (see Obad 18).

It is said that sin is a fire that produces destruction (see Job 31:12) and that wickedness burns like a flame (see Isa 9:18), yet in neither case is literal fire in evidence. The lips of evil men are likened to a burning fire (see Prov 16:27), while an uncontrolled tongue is a fire which "defileth the whole body . . . and it is set on fire of hell" (Jas 3:6). However, no literal fire issues from the tongue or lips.

The Scriptures further state that "people shall labour in the very fire" (Habb 2:13). In this connection, the slavery of the Hebrews in Egypt was described as a time when they were in a furnace of iron (see Deut 4:20). When David mourned that the pains of Hell had gotton hold of him he was sad and troubled, not on fire (see Psa 116:3).

The king of Tyre had already been, in symbol, burned up and reduced entirely to ashes (see Ezek 28:11–19 NAS) at the very moment he was the king and was receiving God's message brought by Ezekiel.

We see that fire as a literal flame is not used in these connections. The use of literal fire in Hell would be totally contradictory to the nature of our God, the essence of Whose nature is love (see I John 4:7–8). Jesus points out that everyone will, in fact, be salted with fire (see Mark 9:49), and then quite remarkably adds, "Salt [fire] is good" (Mark 9:50) *(em add)*. What good can come from the fire of anguish and sorrow?

Salt was used as an agent of ritual purification. Sacrifices were sprinkled with salt before being presented to God on the altar. In a similar way, the purpose of the fire of suffering is to purify the thoughts of the spirits enduring it. The penalty is not for the sake of revenge by God, nor of punishment for its own sake. God's nature is love, and even the hardships of the hells are designed for the improvement of the incarcerated spirits. Little by little, each spirit, at his own rate, and according to his own volition, learns by reaping the results of his way of thinking. It is the same as with humans, who learn from the consequences of their own choices and thereby grow toward purity.

God's laws for our behavior, therefore, are not arbitrary guidelines laid down according to the tastes of the Creator. They are simply instructions which, if followed, lead to a life of harmony and love for God and our fellow man. His rules of behavior are designed for our good, not His. He is immune from harm. His laws are guidelines for finding joy and internal peace. We must follow them on faith that they are the true way to happiness. We may accept them and live them, or we may violate them and reap what we have sown. We eventually discover that God's way of love is the only way that results in a life fit for Heaven. The spirits in the hells are undergoing training of this same type. The fire of bitter experience is the tool for their teaching. The fire is not quenched until the learning is achieved. Thus it is written, "Behold, I have refined you, but not as silver; I have tested you in the furnace of affliction" (Isa 48:10 NAS).

God proves us as silver is tested for purity by melting it (see Psa 66:10). We are, in fact, now in God's symbolic refining pot for silver and His furnace for gold, wherein God assays the desires of our hearts (see Prov 17:3). The impurities in these melted metals are the dross which floats to the surface where it can be skimmed off, leaving the purified metal behind.

> And I will bring the third part through the fire, and will refine them as silver is refined, and will try them as gold is tried: they shall call on my name, and I will hear them (Zech 13:9).

Many are the people, indeed, who have been brought to call on God only by their suffering. But the end result is: "That the trial of your faith, being much more precious than of gold that perisheth, though it be tried with fire, might be found unto praise and honour and glory at the appearing of Jesus Christ" (I Pet 1:7).

The spirits confined to Satan's symbolic prisons, the hells, are therefore in a reform school of sorts. But what possible purpose could be served by an improvement in their attitudes, if their confinement were eternal? If there were no possibility of escape from the hells, it would be sadistic cruelty to instill in them a yearning for escape. It would have been a taunting and cruel Christ Who descended into Hell after His crucifixion and preached the message of salvation to the spirits imprisoned there (see I Pet 3:19), if these same spirits had been doomed to eternal imprisonment. That cannot be. (Note that these spirits to whom He preached were the same people who were disobedient in the days of Noah. They were in Satan's regions called "prisons," not in an earthly prison. Christ did not appear in any earthly prison, or at any place on Earth, for that matter, until Easter morning after the crucifixion. He was nowhere to be found on Earth.)

Only one conclusion exists: God plans to free the captives. The length of time they must spend in Hell cannot, therefore, be infinite. There is no eternal stay in Hell.

Eternal punishment is a misconception so barbaric that it has driven many human souls away from Christianity. Other thinking Christians invent the most absurd rationalizations in their attempts to reconcile the diabolic doctrine of eternal, real fire with the loving nature of God, Who promises never to leave us. One denomination interprets eternal punishment to mean punishment by the Eternal One. Other groups of believers try other escapes from what the Scriptures seem to say. Most Christian churches teach the eternal Hell which they believe their Bible proclaims.

Therein lies the root of the problem. As we have seen in an earlier chapter, there is no such thing as "the" Bible, but many Bibles. There are no original manuscripts, but hundreds of disparate copies. Most of all, there are a great many ways in which these copies of manuscripts can be, and have been, translated imperfectly by honest men.

The Greek word translated "eternal" does not truly mean everlasting. It may, indeed, indicate a long period of time but, on occasion, it was used in the Greek to indicate as short a time as a man's life. The essence of the word is that it is a time period of *indefinite* length, not *eternal* length. In certain places where the Greek word occurred, it was nonsensical to translate it "eternal" or, in the noun form, "eternity." It was then translated as "world," or as "age," because "eternal" made no sense. This is the case in, "[God] Hath in these last days spoken unto us by his Son . . . by whom also he made the WORLDS" (Heb 1:2) *(em add)*. The word "eternities" would make no sense here. The same problem arises in: "Through faith we understand that the WORLDS were framed by the word of God" (Heb 11:3) *(em add)*, where "eternities" would be nonsensical.

We conclude that, though a superficial reading of Bibles depicts Hell as eternal, it is not true. Several Biblical references verify this conclusion. The "everlasting chains" of Jude 6 are to last only until "the judgment of the great day," not everlastingly. This translation causes the verse to contradict itself. A clearer translation is: "For God did not spare even the fallen angels, but drove them down into hell, into the caverns of darkness, where they will be kept until they turn their hearts to God again" (II Pet 2:4 GNT). We are further told of a time when the dead will be released from Hell (see Rev 20:13), albeit for judgment according to their works. Souls are spoken of as being delivered from Hell (see Psa 86:13) or brought up from Hell *(Sheol)* (see I Sam 2:6 NAS). Certain erring humans were to be shut up in Satan's prison "and after many days shall they be visited" (Isa 24:22). They were confined and were visited by Christ when He descended (see I Pet 3:19). Other references to spirits being brought out of *Sheol,* or the pit, or Satan's dungeons, are found in Job 33:30; Psa 30:3, 86:13, 102:20; and Isa 42:7, 61:1.

The doctrine of eternal Hell has been used as a bludgeon to subdue Christians and to threaten non-Christians. Its claim to authenticity rests far more on centuries of tradition than on the Scriptures. Nor was it universally accepted in the formative years of the Christian doctrines.

Writing soon after the year 400 A.D., Saint Augustine, in *The Eight Questions of Dulcitus,* argues against those who believe Hell to be eternal with the words, "They wish, in fact, to maintain that punishment endures as eternal as reward. But, in answer to them the judgment of the Gospel is prescribed which reads: 'Thou shalt not go out from thence till thou repay the last farthing' [see Matt 5:26]. In the end, therefore, when the debt has been paid, one can go forth." Even though Saint Augustine argues clearly and forcefully in this passage that Hell is not eternal, he writes in his treatise on patience *(De Patientia),* "For, it is good for a man to believe he will have to suffer eternal punishment if he denies Christ, and for him to endure and make light of any punishment whatsoever for that faith." In other words, St. Augustine judges it good to raise the false specter of eternal punishment in order to frighten Christians into stronger faith, even though he, himself, repudiated that very doctrine. Many religious teachers followed the same strategy. Now, centuries later, the teachers themselves have come to believe the falsehood.

We cannot rationally conclude that the One Who preached to the spirits trapped in torment and Who has "the keys of hell and of death" (Rev 1:18) will leave His erring children there. Surely He intends to use the keys. "I will ransom them from the power of the grave; I will redeem them from death" (Hosea 13:14). But the redemption had to wait until the coming of the Redeemer.

In summary, the fallen spirits are confined to Hell, a word referring to a group of levels, or hells, under the jurisdiction of Satan. The abysmal conditions there include pain, anguish, and sorrow, but not literal fire. The cause of these conditions is the attitude of the confined spirits and their leader. The result of these conditions is improvement in the attitude of the spirits. This improvement is necessary because their release is planned. The length of their confinement is not eternal, but indefinite.

After the Fall from Heaven, Creation was divided into higher dimensions still under the rule of Christ, and lower dimensions under the rule of Satan. The higher dimensions are collectively called Heaven, while the lower ones are collectively called Hell. The angels were divided into the "living," those who remained loyal to Christ, and the "dead" who are bound to Satan. The dead could progress to higher hells, accordingly, as their attitudes improve, but they could not escape Satan's dominion, being totally unfit to enter Heaven again. The spirits were able to progress upward until they finally arrived in Hell's highest dimension, the physical universe. The particular place in the highest dimension of Hell that is of the most vital interest to us is the planet Earth.

We have already seen that Satan and his angels were cast from Heaven into Hell. If we locate some of those exiled spirits, then we may be certain that we have located a region in the hells. We are told that Satan "was cast unto the earth" (Rev 12:13), that "he was thrown down to the earth, and his angels were thrown down with him" (Rev 12:9 NAS). The Earth and the physical universe are, then, one of the hells. Since Christian humans go upward upon physical death and arrive in one of the heavens, not a higher dimension of Hell, the physical universe must be the highest, and therefore least unpleasant, of the hells. Furthermore, the fact that we do not remain eternally on Earth is additional proof that Hell is not eternal.

From another point of view, observe that Satan is "the prince of the power of the air" (Eph 2:2), or, more emphatically, "the god of this world" (II Cor 4:4). The "whole world lies in the power of the evil one" (I John 5:19 NAS). Since the dimensions under Satan's rule are collectively called Hell, the Earth is, therefore, necessarily in one of those hells. Man's escape from Earth has been made possible by Christ's victory. But "What is man, that thou art mindful of him? . . . For thou hast made him a little lower than the angels" (Psa 8:4–5).

CHAPTER 7

◆

The Nature of Man

G OD ejected Satan and his deceived followers from Heaven.
They were injected into lower dimensions called Hell.
The hellish dimensions were created to serve as places of
confinement for these spiritually dead. In the highest dimension of
the hells, the physical universe we know, Earth serves as a prison
for certain of the fallen angels.

The fallen spirits exiled to the prison, Earth, include the demons. Demons are discarnate spirits of Satan. Discarnate spirits
are spirits who do not have fleshly bodies of ordinary matter like
ours. Instead, they have spirit bodies invisible to us, as are all other
spirits. These discarnate beings are subjects of Satan. They are in
the highest level of his kingdom, having been cast down to Earth
with him (see Rev 12:9). The ruler of the demons is Satan, who
rules in the kingdom created for him and his erring followers. God
created the kingdom for him and placed him and his adherents
there. God, the ultimate power and authority, maintains their
existence and allows their demonic activity. We may not fully
understand why God allows demonic forces to mislead and plague
man, but we can trust that even this aspect of creation is according
to His overall strategy for recalling the fallen spirits, as we shall see
in the following chapters. "For as the heavens are higher than the
earth, so are my ways higher than your ways, and my thoughts
than your thoughts" (Isa 55:9).

The evil spirits are not distinguished from one another by name
in the Biblical texts. An evil spirit may be referred to by a phrase
descriptive of its function, such as "the spirit of greed," or "the

spirit of pride." It is not implied that only one such spirit exists. On another occasion, a demon may be referred to as "the spirit of the antichrist," which is to say, "a spirit in the service of Satan, the enemy of Christ." Sometimes, any such spirit is called simply "the antichrist," never meaning that there is only one such spirit opposed to Christ. Evil spirits are sometimes simply given the generic name, Satan, being called after the one whom they follow. Thus, Christ asks, "And if Satan cast out Satan . . . how shall then his kingdom stand?" (Matt 12:26).

God has allowed Satan great freedom of action and power to implement his desires. If it were not so, Satan could not roam about "as a roaring lion . . . seeking whom he may devour" (I Pet 5:8), for God is God over all, including Hell: "Thou believest that there is one God; thou doest well: the devils also believe, and tremble" (Jas 2:19). When Satan "the accuser of our brethren . . . accused them before our God day and night" (Rev 12:10), it could only be because God had granted Satan the right to be heard. When Satan slandered Job before God, it could only be that God allowed Satan the opportunity. What is more, God then gave permission for Satan to persecute Job. Where is God's fairness in that?

On another occasion, Satan requested permission from God to sift the Apostles "as wheat" (Luke 22:31). Upon Christ's arrest, the Apostles abandoned Him in fear. Judas had betrayed Him, Peter denied knowing Him, and the others fled from His side. Why did God permit Satan and his spirit agents to assault the Apostles?

That God has given Satan the power to cause havoc among men, even among those men who try to follow God, seems to be unfair. Is God unjust to His children? The answer to this question is obvious, once we recognize our role in creation.

All of creation is divided into only two domains: the heavens and the hells. All angels under Christ in the heavens are spirits who are loyal to Him. All spirits under Satan in the hells are spirits who sided with Satan in the revolt against Christ. Human spirits are in a region of Hell. We are, therefore, numbered among the enemies of Christ.

In view of the close bonds and uncanny resemblances between God's angels and man, it might seem terribly unfair that His angels are in Heaven under Christ, while we are confined to Earth under Satan. And where, we might ask, are the angels who were thrown from Heaven down to Earth for rebelling against Christ (see Rev 12:4, 12:9, 12:13)? To answer this question, we need only look in a mirror. We are fallen angels. As such, we are fallen spirits who long ago voluntarily became subjects of Satan. He is within his God-given rights in influencing us. We are reaping the results of our participation in the heavenly revolt against Christ. God is fair, and, like it or not, we are reaping what we have sown.

There are a number of Biblical references to our existence prior to being incarnated for this present life of learning and testing. Here are a few examples:

"BEFORE I FORMED THEE IN THE BELLY I KNEW THEE; and before thou camest forth out of the womb I sanctified thee, and I ordained thee a prophet unto the nations" (Jer 1:5) *(em add)*.

"Where were you when I laid the foundation of the earth? Tell Me, if you have understanding" (Job 38:4 NAS). "YOU KNOW, FOR YOU WERE BORN THEN, AND THE NUMBER OF YOUR DAYS IS GREAT!" (Job 38:21 NAS) *(em add)*.

"Thou knowest me through and through . . . how I was secretly kneaded into shape and patterned in the depths of the earth" (Psa 139:14–15 NEB).

"The spirit shall RETURN unto God who gave it" (Eccl 12:7) *(em add)*.

"We proclaim . . . a plan . . . which God established BEFORE TIME BEGAN IN ORDER TO LEAD US BACK TO GLORY" (I Cor 2:7 GNT) *(em add)*.

"In hope of eternal life, which God, that cannot lie, promised BEFORE THE WORLD BEGAN" (Titus 1:2) *(em add)*.

"Who hath saved us . . . according to his own purpose and grace, which was given us in Christ Jesus BEFORE THE WORLD BEGAN" (II Tim 1:9) *(em add)*.

"Brethren beloved of the Lord, because God hath FROM THE BEGINNING chosen you" (II Thess 2:13) *(em add)*.

"According as he hath chosen us in him BEFORE THE FOUNDATION OF THE WORLD" (Eph 1:4) *(em add)*.

"For God is able to graft them in AGAIN" (Rom 11:23 NAS) *(em add)*.

"Do you not know? Have you not heard? Has it not been declared to you FROM THE BEGINNING? Have you not understood FROM THE FOUNDATIONS OF THE EARTH?" (Isa 40:21 NAS) *(em add)*.

These verses, and others, repeatedly mention plans made and people known, before material creation ever took place. They indicate that our existence was already established by then, and that the fall from Heaven had already occurred.

The animal species known as man has appeared on Earth only in the last moment of geological history. Billions of years have elapsed in the development of the physical universe, the Earth itself being several billion years old. The spirits now incarnated in human bodies on Earth languished in Satan's lower dimensions of existence for untold amounts of time awaiting the opportunity to be incarnated in human form. Although the length of stay in Hell was not eternal, it was dreadfully long. Thus, we read that we are incarnated from below (see John 8:23).

The exiled spirits could not escape from Hell, not even from the highest level, before Christ made it possible. Physical death did not release a human spirit to Heaven before that time. The human (physical) body returned to the ground from which its substance came, while the human spirit remained captive in one or the other of the dimensions of the hells.

"Then I shall bring you down with those who go down to the pit, to the people of old, and I shall make you dwell in the lower parts of the earth . . . with those who go down to the pit" (Ezek 26:20 NAS).

"I cast him down to hell [Sheol, NAS] with them that descend into the pit" (Ezek 31:16).

"They also went down into hell [Sheol, NAS] with him unto them that be slain with the sword" (Ezek 31:17).

"The grave [Sheol, NAS] below is all astir to meet you at your coming; it rouses THE SPIRITS OF THE DEPARTED TO GREET YOU" (Isa 14:9 NIV) (spoken to the King of Babylon, *em add*).

The wicked will return to Sheol [Hell, AKJ], even all the nations who forget God" (Psa 9:17 NAS).

In this translation, it is evident that, if these people are to *return* to *Sheol,* they must first have arisen from there.

In the days of the Apostles, many people understood that we could have sinned before this life. Recall the question, "Who sinned, this man or his parents, that he should be BORN blind?" (John 9:2 NAS) *(em add)*. In order for his blindness to be due to his own sin, he would have had to commit the sin *before* his birth. Jesus did not contradict this assumption, but simply responded to the real point of the question.

It is said that Christ "reconciled mankind with God." For a reconciliation to occur, there must have been a prior disagreement between friends. For purposes of a reconciliation, Christ was temporarily caused to be a little lower than the angels (see Heb 2:9), in precisely the situation as those whom He came to rescue (see Heb 2:6–7).

God, in His love, does not leave the fallen forever in the pit. The spirits are eventually brought up to an earthly incarnation for their spiritual growth. On Earth, they may learn about Christ and find a chance to believe in Him. "Lo, all these things worketh God oftentimes with man, to BRING BACK HIS SOUL FROM THE PIT, TO BE ENLIGHTENED WITH THE LIGHT OF THE LIVING" (Job 33:29–30) *(em add)*.

Christ alludes to the incarnation of fallen spirits from Hell with the words, "You are from below" (John 8:23 NAS), and "Your father is the devil" (John 8:44 NEB). The Psalms often refer to the incarnation of David from below:

> For great is thy mercy toward me: and thou hast delivered my soul from the lowest hell (Psa 86:13).
> O Lord, thou hast brought up my soul from the grave [Sheol] (Psa 30:3) *(em add)*.
> My substance [literally, bones] was not hid from thee, when I was made in secret, and curiously wrought in the lowest parts of the earth (Psa 139:15) *(em add)*.

We may be confident that these verses are correctly interpreted as meaning coming up from Hell, because the same mode of expression is used in the verses referring to the raising of Christ from Hell, into which He descended. It is precisely this point which Luke is supporting (see Acts 2:27–31, 13:35), when he invokes the sixteenth Psalm as his proof: "Thou wilt not abandon my soul to Sheol" [or, Hades, Acts 2:27 NAS]; "Neither wilt Thou allow Thy Holy One to undergo decay" (Psa 16:10 NAS).

John (John 2:17 NAS) applies another Psalm to Jesus, quoting: "Zeal for Thy house will consume me" (see Psa 69:9 NAS). In that same Psalm, we also read that the pit shall "not shut its mouth on me" (Psa 69:15 NAS), which therefore must also refer to Christ. John (John 2:22) alludes to other Scriptures which Christ's resurrection from the realm of the dead caused disciples to believe, but he does not list them for us.

In addition David was, like us, one of the fallen spirits. Since David lived before the time of Christ's victory, he did not enter Heaven upon his physical death. Escape from Satan's domain was not possible until Christ opened the door to Heaven for us. "For David is not ascended into the heavens" (Acts 2:34).

As we have seen, Earth is populated by fallen spirits working their way up from the pit. However, there have been exceptions to this rule. If incarnation from below is possible, then incarnation from above is equally possible. Certain spirits have incarnated from Heaven to help in bringing salvation to man. Christ is the foremost among these incarnated heavenly spirits. It is unnecessary to prove to Christian readers that Christ existed prior to man and that He incarnated from above. We cite only, "[Christ] Who verily was foreordained BEFORE THE FOUNDATION OF THE WORLD" (I Pet 1:20) *(em add)*, and "YOU ARE FROM BELOW, I AM FROM ABOVE" (John 8:23 NAS) *(em add)*.

Christ was preceded by other incarnated spirits who helped prepare the way for His coming. The verse, "no man hath ascended up to heaven, but he that came down from heaven, even the Son of man" (John 3:13) applies to everyone, though some translators render this verse so that it seems to refer exclusively to Christ. In other words, at the time of Christ, no person ascended to Heaven at death unless he had come from there, this including Christ. Salvation had not yet been achieved for the fallen. Hence, any spirit prior to Christ who ascended to Heaven must have come down from Heaven.

Accordingly, Abraham was one of the spirits incarnated from above. He was later described by Christ as being in Heaven (see Luke 16:23), implying that He must have come from there. Enoch (see Gen 5:24; Heb 11:5) and Elijah (see II Kings 2:11) were both taken into Heaven even though Christ had not yet achieved the redemption of man. These two agents of Christ had, therefore, incarnated from Heaven. Moses and Elijah (Elias) appeared to Christ on the mountain (see Matt 17:3; Mark 9:4; Luke 9:30). Moses must, therefore, have come down with Elijah from Heaven. To have been in Heaven with Elijah, Moses must first have come from there. The Apostle Paul reported visiting Heaven (see II Cor 12:2). The Apostle, then, was probably also a spirit from above. In Paul's case, however, this conclusion could be debated, since his visit to Heaven occurred after Christ's victory.

As we see, Earth is a battleground for the souls of men, wherein discarnate spirits from above, God's spirits, and those from below, influence man for good or for evil, and wherein certain spirits from Heaven have incarnated to work on behalf of Christ. The people of earth are intermingled followers and adversaries of Christ: the "living" and the "dead."

Man is therefore a spirit. It is not that we have a spirit, as is commonly said, it is that we *are* spirits. We differ from the discarnate spirits in that we are incarnate. "Incarnate" means "in flesh." We are incarnate spirits as distinguished from the discarnate spirits, but we are spirits in Satan's realm, nonetheless. We participated in the revolt against Christ ages ago in Heaven. That participation is the guilt which every human bears from birth. That is the original sin of which we are all guilty. We were confined to Satan's kingdom due to guilt incurred, personally, by actions freely taken. It cannot be that we are being blamed for a mistake made by Adam.

The idea that God perennially punishes every person because of Adam's mistakes seems totally unfair. And so it should. It is not a Scriptural concept at all. The Bibles stresses many times that each of us is personally responsible for our errors, that the son shall not "bear the iniquity of the father" (Ezek 18:14–32 explains this at length), and that "the soul that sinneth, it shall die," i.e., be divorced from God (Ezek 18:4). We acquired our original sin "from Adam," not by inheriting his blame, but "from Adam" in the sense of having followed his example. This is the sense in which "as in Adam all die, even so in Christ shall all be made alive" (I Cor 15:22). That is to say, all shall be made alive by following Christ and His example. Furthermore, we must have followed Adam's example before this earthly life because we were born already in disobedience (see Psa 51:5).

The question of "original sin" now can be seen to have an easy answer. The original sin was rebellion in Heaven against Christ. All people bear this sin from birth, since it was that very sin which caused us to be born here at all. We are fallen spirits incarnated into flesh bodies.

Every church of all Christian denominations tells us that to enter Heaven we must accept Christ as our Lord. But why is this a requirement? Why not simply lead a good life? The answer is obvious. Since our personal rejection of Christ as Lord in the Holy spirit-world was the cause of our expulsion, our acceptance of Christ as Lord is logically required for readmission to His kingdom. Since our original sin was our choosing sides with Satan over Christ in the great revolt in Heaven, then our choosing Christ as Lord in this life sets this error straight. It is surely fair that citizenship be granted only to those whose allegiance is to the rightfully appointed Ruler.

It may be argued that our lack of memory of previous existence shows we did not exist then. However, if God finished creating all things on the symbolic sixth day and rested on the seventh, we human spirits must have been created before the seventh day and not thereafter. Otherwise, God is still creating human spirits, and, what is more, creating them flawed and sinful from birth and placing them under the dominion of Satan. This idea makes a mockery of the skill and love of the Creator. No, our spirits were created eons ago, before the fall from Heaven. Obviously the dead on Earth to whom Jesus spoke remembered nothing of their former existence. "The gospel was preached EVEN TO THOSE WHO ARE NOW DEAD" (I Pet 4:6 NIV) *(em add)*. It appears that God in His mercy has made memories of former joy inaccessible to the spirits who cannot yet repossess that joy.

In the same vein, lack of memory is not claimed to prove nonexistence when we encounter it in other contexts. Can we remember even a single event from the first year of life? We cannot. Yet, it is perfectly clear that we did, in fact, exist during that year. We are accustomed to other memory lapses. Do we remember our existence while asleep? A third part of our lives are spent in sleep, but all of those accumulated years are a total blank in our memories, except for occasional dreams. Yet, who would dare claim we did not exist while asleep?

The spirits confined to the hells, mercifully, have no memory of their previous existence in Heaven. These spirits are the spiritually dead, the apostates, to whom the Scriptures refer: "the dead know not any thing" (Ecc 9:5). "For in death there is no remembrance of thee: in the grave [Sheol] who shall give thee thanks" (Psa 6:5) *(em add).* The King of Tyre had no memory of his participation in the Fall. He had once been a cherub before the revolt in Heaven. This wingless, fallen cherub was addressed by God:

YOU WERE . . . A . . . CHERUB . . .
I drove you in disgrace from the mount of God,
and I EXPELLED YOU, O guardian cherub . . .
I THREW YOU TO THE EARTH . . . You have come to a
horrible end (Ezek 28:11–19 NIV) *(em add).*

Similarly, the King of Babylon had no memory of his earliest days in Heaven. Isaiah brought this message from God to the King of Babylon:

HOW YOU HAVE FALLEN FROM HEAVEN,
O morning star, son of the dawn!
YOU HAVE BEEN CAST DOWN TO THE EARTH,
you who once laid low the nations!
You said in your heart,
I will ascend to heaven . . .
BUT YOU ARE BROUGHT DOWN TO THE GRAVE [Sheol],
TO THE DEPTHS OF THE PIT (Isa 14:12–15 NIV) *(em add).*

It is unfortunate that certain translations render "O morning star" as "O Lucifer," thereby distorting the entire meaning of this passage. The message is clearly addressed to the King of Babylon (Isa 14:4), not to Lucifer. In addition, it had to be, literally, the King of Babylon who would be denied burial (Isa 14:19–20), not Lucifer.

We conclude that our lack of memory of any portion of our existence has no relevance to whether we existed during the time forgotten. We existed long before our present incarnation.

In agreement with what we have already said about Earth, it is seen here to be part of "the grave" *(Sheol),* also called "the pit." That is, Earth is located in one of the hells.

We are fallen angels. Our lack of memory of our tragic guilt in the revolt is evidence of great mercy on the part of God. He allows each of His fallen children to prove his fitness to reenter Heaven by means of the tests of Earth life. He gives each of His erring children a chance for a fresh start, unburdened by conscious memories of his previous behavior.

The idea that mankind originated in Heaven disagrees with the

usual teachings involving Adam, Eve, and the Garden of Eden.
Let us digress and deal with this disagreement. The creation story,
as usually recounted, is drawn from the first two chapters of
Genesis. The Genesis story was passed down verbally for many
centuries before it was committed to writing. The written version
was recopied many times before becoming the copies available to
us. These copies underwent the interpretative, and sometimes
ambiguous, process of translation before they arrived in the form
we read in English. We can be certain that a translation does not
contain precisely all the meanings and implications of the original
writings. This fact is known by any person who knows two or
more languages. Although we do not know the extent of such
errors, we can deduce that they are serious. Even if we were to
assume that the creation story of the first book of the Bible was
originally sent directly from God, we cannot assume that we have
it in an uncontaminated form at this late date. Claims that God
prevented the introduction of errors are mere assertions lacking
proof. On the contrary Jeremiah quotes God as saying that all His
communications up to Jeremiah's time had been seriously altered:

> How can you say, 'We are wise,
> and the law of the Lord is with us?'
> But behold, the lying pen of the scribes
> has made it into a life (Jer 8:8 NAS).

God makes a strong indictment, indeed, of the Scriptures then
available to Jeremiah. Those sacred scrolls included Genesis. We,
therefore, interpret the first parts of Genesis with caution, knowing that they do not measure up to God's standards of accuracy.

An example of the apparent problem with accuracy is found in
the creation story told in the first two chapters of Genesis. These
two chapters are not in agreement about what happens. The first
chapter of Genesis relates that creation required six days, followed
by a day of rest for the Creator. Chapter 2 lacks any division into
time periods. In the first chapter, God is said to have created
evening and morning, day and night, on the first day, even though
the sun which produces day and night did not exist until the fourth
day. The saga then relates that God formed the plants on the third
day (verses 11–12), which would mean they were required to sur-

vive without sunlight. On the next two days, the lower animals were first formed, then the higher ones, and finally men and women (verses 27–28).

In the second chapter of Genesis, the creation proceeds quite differently. There were no shrubs or plants of any kind (see Gen 2:5) when God formed man (verse 7). The story does not divulge where this man was kept until God planted a garden spot in Eden in which to put him (verse 8). In contrast to the first chapter of Genesis, where humankind in general were called into existence (Gen 1:26–27), the man is said to have been alone. Quite naturally he was lonely, having already endured a period of time without even a green plant for company, and now finding himself without animals or other people. Animals had not yet been formed (see Gen 2:18–20), although we were previously told that they were created before Adam (see Gen 1:20–25). The other people mentioned in the first creation story are nowhere to be found, so God formed a woman to be Adam's "help meet" as His crowning act of creation.

Another problem concerns the location of the Garden of Eden. As given in Genesis (Gen 2:10–14 NAS), four rivers originate in Eden. The rivers are the Tigris, Euphrates, Pishon, and Gihon. These rivers are known today in the near east, but Bible scholars are unable to locate Eden there. In addition, the Biblical description of the location of Eden does not match the maps. Perhaps a more direct approach for locating Eden is for us to ignore the theorizing of the scholars and to use common sense. Let us look at the clues found in the Bibles.

Eden is said to be a lush paradise which man cannot enter. Entrance to Eden is prohibited by cherubim with flaming swords. Man was driven from Eden and not allowed to return. But explorers have never come upon a lush, yet uninhabited, paradise in the near east, nor anywhere else. No person has ever encountered a supernatural force preventing his entry into any region on Earth. No man has ever encountered cherubim with flaming swords blocking the entrance to any place on Earth. There are, however, places that are not on Earth. The Scriptures give certain clues.

First we note that man in Eden had not yet been completely severed from God. Thus the Adam and Eve story must refer to a time *before Earth was formed,* for Earth is one of the places created as part of Satan's realms after our separation from God. The inhabitants of Eden are symbolically referred to by Ezekiel as trees. They were in Eden (see Ezek 31:8–18), the "garden of God" (verse 9), before being cast down to Hell (verse 16), also called the "nether parts of the earth" (verse 18), a common description in ancient times. We see, then, that the inhabitants of Eden were not *on* Earth, in one of the hells, but were cast down *to* Earth. The only beings who were ever cast to Earth were Satan and those spirits he misled, including Adam and Eve.

The Bibles clearly refer to Adam and Eve allegorically, for many other inhabitants are mentioned in this passage in Ezekiel. These souls were exiled from a paradise wherein grew the "tree of life" (Gen 3:22). Whatever is represented by the symbolic tree of life, the tree cannot be on Earth, because the tree is in Eden, and Eden has not been found on Earth. If we can locate the tree of life, then we will have located Eden.

The tree of life is in the paradise of God to which Christians ascend upon leaving Earth life, as is explictly stated in: "To him who overcomes, I will give the right to eat from THE TREE OF LIFE, WHICH IS IN THE PARADISE OF GOD" (Rev 2:7 NIV) *(em add).* If the tree is both in Eden, guarded by angels, and also in the paradise to which we shall ascend, then Eden must be in this paradise. Accordingly, Eden, and the entire Adam and Eve story, refer by allegory and symbolism to the fall from Heaven in ways not clearly understood by the churches. This location for Eden is transparently clear in the message of God to the King of Tyre, "YOU WERE IN EDEN, THE GARDEN OF GOD . . . YOU WERE . . . A GUARDIAN CHERUB . . . I THREW YOU TO THE EARTH" (see Ezek 28:13–18 NIV) *(em add).* From this we see that the King of Tyre was an angel thrown down from Eden to Earth. The King of Tyre was like the rest of us in that respect.

For an authoritative explanation of the creation and fall of the spirits, the reader can consult the historic book by Johannes Greber entitled *Communication with the Spirit World of God,* available from the Johannes Greber Memorial Foundation, 139 Hillside Avenue, Teaneck, NJ 07666.

In Summary, we have found that the fallen angels on Earth are the discarnates, the demons; and the incarnates, the people. We are all here for the same cause. We are all spirits carrying the stain of the "original sin" of rebellion against Christ in our former home, Heaven. We have been confined to Satan's domains for long ages, lacking a way to escape, and lacking the knowledge of our true condition. The One against Whom we revolted came for us and obtained our redemption. Acceptance of the Redeemer as our King (Lord) is a necessary and reasonable condition for returning to His kingdom.

It is not the only condition, however, because even Satan and his angels recognize the sovereignty of God "and tremble" (Jas 2:19). There is more required. We must also be cured of our faulty ways of thinking. In short, we must repent, that is: change our way of thinking. We must achieve sufficient purity of thought to qualify for Heaven as our home. The purity of thought must be reflected in our deeds. To that end, we must be born again.

◇

CHAPTER 8

Born Again

"EXCEPT a man be born again, he cannot see the kingdom of God" (John 3:3). The "new birth" is held to be essential for admission into Heaven after this life on Earth. However, interpretations vary as to the exact meaning of what is called the "born-again experience."

One interpretation of being born again is that of mending one's ways, turning over a new leaf, or starting afresh with a new viewpoint on life. Consequently, the rebirth might be understood as a reformation, a repentance, or a starting over again. Another interpretation of the rebirth is that of suddenly becoming "religious," a term equally as vague as the term rebirth. Therefore, it is sometimes taught that a person is reborn if he joins a church, receives baptism, and perhaps begins to behave in other ways like his fellow church members. Some interpreters conclude that the rebirth consists of a radical change of heart accompanied by some manifestation of Divine power. Indeed, it is sometimes claimed that the sign of "speaking in tongues" (see Acts 2:4) must accompany the experience in order for it to be valid, and that without such an experience a person is not truly assured of a happy afterlife. We have here one of those many doctrines about which no consensus has been reached, despite much discussion and thought. The situation recalls to our attention that, "God, when he made man, made him straightforward, but man invents endless subtleties of his own" (Eccl 7:29 NEB).

In order to clarify this confusion of ideas, let us examine the Scripture references from which the various interpretations are drawn. The prime source is the third chapter of John. In John 3, we read that a learned, scholarly, devout Pharisee named Nicodemus approached Jesus at night with a statement that he believed Jesus was sent from God. The Scriptural account at this point has a peculiar skip in subject matter, as though something has been omitted from the story. Jesus seems to respond to a question not recorded when He replies, "Except a man be born again, he cannot see the kingdom of God" (John 3:3).

Nicodemus reacted with apparent astonishment, thinking that Christ had said a physical rebirth would be necessary. "How can a man be born when he is old?" Nicodemus asked. "Surely he cannot enter a second time into his mother's womb to be born!" (verse 4 NIV). We, in turn, might be astonished that Nicodemus could so misunderstand Christ's words. Nicodemus was, after all, an educated man, and a member of the Sanhedrin. He was surely aware of Jesus' teachings, for he was a secret disciple who later assisted in burying Christ's physical remains.

"Nicodemus answered and said to Him, 'How can these things be?'" (John 3:9 NAS), to which Christ reponded, "What! . . . Is this famous teacher of Israel ignorant of such things? (John 3:10 NEB). The difficulty in conveying a new understanding of a familiar concept to the scholarly Nicodemus, already steeped in dogma and doctrine, is painfully clear in the poignant question posed by Christ in verse 12 (NAS): "If I told you earthly things and you do not believe, how shall you believe if I tell you heavenly things?"

Christ's choice of words was purposeful. He testified that, "I did not speak on My own initiative, but the Father Himself . . . has given Me commandment, what to say, and what to speak" (John 12:49 NAS), and "Whatever I say is just what the Father has told me to say" (John 12:50 NIV). "The word which you hear is not Mine, but the Father's who sent Me" (John 14:24 NAS). The words "born again" which Jesus used in talking with Nicodemus, as relayed to us by the Greek manuscripts, were the words meaning a literal, physical rebirth. The verb used is translated as physical birth in numerous places in the New Testament. The adverb used, *anothen,* translated as "again," refers in the Greek to the repetition of an act, with special reference to a return to the beginning point and a repetition from the very outset onward. Thus, Nicodemus certainly understood Christ to mean reincarnation, because that is reportedly what He said. His astonishment is akin to his saying to Christ: "Do you mean this is *really* so?!"

Let us consider other translations of these words of Christ to Nicodemus. In some instances, the adverb translated "again" in John 3:3 is translated as "from above." The Biblical phrase "born from above" is therefore an alternate translation used instead of "reborn in the physical body." The phrases "born of the Spirit," "born of God," and "born from above," all admit the possibility of being incarnated from a higher realm than Earth, a spirit realm "above" Earth in its nearness to god. Christ, having incarnated from the highest such realm, declared that He was from above and that His earthly adversaries were from below. Pre-existence, if not repeated incarnation, is implied here for all people.

In discussing reincarnation, the Greeks sometimes used a specific word for it: *paliggenesia.* Pythagoras, Plato, and other Greek writers had used this term to refer to the "transmigration of souls," That is, to the rebirth of souls into other bodies. *Paliggenesia* was therefore a well-known term a long time before its New Testament usage, where it is usually translated as "regeneration." It occurs in the letter to Titus, where Paul the Pharisee explained that a man is made fit for Heaven "by the washing of regeneration" (Titus 3:5), so translated. This rendering hides the meaning of the Greek terms, which may be brought out as "by [by means of] the washing [the purifying and cleansing bath] of reincarnation"*(em add).* Accordingly, one is made fit for Heaven by means of repeated life experiences until the lessons are learned and purity of sould is achieved.

The other occurrence of *paliggenesia* in the New Testament is in Matthew 19:28, where its meaning is completely lost in most translations. A vestige of its meaning is retained in at least the following version: "Truly I say to you, that you who have followed Me, in the REGENERATION [*paliggenesia*] when the Son of Man will sit on His glorious throne, you also shall sit upon twelve thrones, judging the twelve tribes of Israel" (Matt 19:28 NAS) *(em add).* If we read this remarkable passage without prior doctrinal bias, we see in it Christ's statement that upon the establishment of His throne and kingdom at His return, the Apostles will be reincarnated and serve as judges of the twelve tribes. If this is, in fact, His meaning, then His present-day followers will have to rethink certain doctrines. Even one observation alone, that Judas Iscariot was one of the Apostles to whom Christ was speaking, gives rise to rethinking certain accepted beliefs.

The possibility of reincarnation opens new vistas of meaning for a great number of other Biblical passages. "The Lord killeth, and maketh alive: he bringeth down to the grave, AND BRINGETH UP" (I Sam 2:6) *(em add).* Is this a reference to reincarnation? Regarding the regathering of the Israelites, Ezekiel wrote: "And [I] shall put my spirit in YOU, and YE shall live, and I shall place YOU in YOUR own land: then shall YE know that I the Lord have spoken it, and performed it" (Ezek 37:14) *(em add).* "I will open YOUR graves, and cause YOU to come up out of YOUR graves, and bring YOU into the land of Israel" (Ezek 37:12) *(em add).* "Then I will set over them one shepherd, My servant David, and he will feed them; he will feed them himself and be their shepherd. And I, the Lord, will be their God, and My servant David will be prince among them; I, the Lord, have spoken" (Ezek 34:23–24 NAS. Repeated in Ezek 37:24–25 and Jer 30:9). "Behold, he cometh with clouds; and every eye shall see him, AND THEY ALSO WHICH PIERCED HIM" (Rev 1:7) *(em add).*

In the translating of *paliggenesia* and *anothen,* we have one of those cases where doctrinal beliefs seem to have preceded understanding of the Scriptures. Some scholars of the Greek have remarked in their expositions that these words took on new and expanded meanings in their New Testament usages, different from their meanings in secular writings. That remarkable state of affairs would mean that we could not necessarily determine the meanings of Biblical words from their everyday, contemporary usage. Although such ambiguities occasionally occur, and although we must undergo a "regeneration" ["renewing," as in Rom 12:2] to reach spiritual maturity, it is probable that we must also undergo reincarnation. Translation includes interpretation.

The usual objection Christianity offers to reincarnation finds its basis in the verse, "it is appointed unto men once to die, but after this the judgment" (Heb 9:27). Upon superficial reading, the verse would seem to settle this issue. If this verse has the meaning usually ascribed to it, then Lazarus, whom Jesus brought back to physical life, must still be alive somewhere in the world, and well over two thousand years old by now. Otherwise, he must have died again, and thereby died twice in contradiction to the above Scripture. Naturally, the same can be said for the daughter of Jairus and for many others who were brought back to life. Are they still alive? If not, then they died more than once, and the usual interpretation of the verse fails. On the other hand, the Bibles state that neither Enoch nor Elijah died even once. They were transferred directly into Heaven, so the usual reading of this verse from Hebrews fails again. Clearly, the accepted interpretation of Heb 9:27, as referring to physical life and death, is incorrect. To understand this verse, we must recall that "death" in the Bible usually does not mean "deceased." Instead, it means divorced from God, separated and removed from God and His kingdom, exiled and estranged from God. And so it is true that mankind did, indeed, suffer once this death of separation from God's heavenly kingdom, and was stranded on Earth without hope of escape until the coming of the Savior.

Returning to the fundamental point, we note that "incarnate" simply means "in flesh." Christians agree that Christ was an incarnated Spirit Who existed prior to His incarnation. Other, lesser, spirits also existed prior to their earthly lives. David made references to having been brought up from below (see Psa 30:3), while Isaiah (Isa 49:1, 5), Jeremiah (Jer 1:5), and Paul (see Gal 1:11–17), all aver that they were known to God and their missions were assigned before they were born in human bodies. John the Baptist was a man "sent from God" (John 1:6), Who is in Heaven, which reveals that he was a spirit who had incarnated from above.

"Reincarnation" means "in flesh again." The reference, then, is to a spirit, such as a human spirit, being put into a fleshly body again. It is well established that Christ was an incarnated Spirit. The question before us is simply whether a spirit is ever incarnated more than once. In this question, there is no reference at all to any change in the species of the spirit. There is neither scientific nor

Scriptural evidence for the popular myth that one might return to another Earth life as an animal of some sort. On the contrary, we are human spirits, and humans we remain.

On this train of thought, consider John 9:1–3 (NIV): "Rabbi, who sinned, this man or his parents, that he was born blind?" Clearly, for the man to have been born blind, any sin for which he was atoning must have been committed prior to that lifetime. The assumption that this was possible was obviously accepted by the disciples asking the question. Otherwise, their question would not have arisen at all. In Christ's response, He did not alter their point of view, but simply responded that, in this case, neither the man nor his parents were guilty, that the purpose of the blindness was to reflect the work of God by the restoration of sight. It would be difficult to explain why Christ did not correct His disciples' point of view if it was in error. We therefore presume that He understood their point of view and agreed with its validity.

On another occasion, the Jews had sent priests and Levites to John the Baptist to inquire of his identity. They asked if he was Elijah, or the Messiah, or a prophet (see John 1:19–25). Such a question would have been completely pointless had the questioners not seriously believed that an affirmative answer were possible. Since the questioners were Pharisees (verse 24), their act shows that the belief in reincarnation existed among at least some of the Pharisees.

Josephus, the ancient historian of the Jews, tells us how the chief schools of Jewish religious belief regarded immortality. In *The Antiquities of the Jews,* he states that the Pharisees believed the soul to be immortal, and that virtuous persons have the power to revive and live again on Earth. We note that both Nicodemus and the later Apostle, Paul, were Pharisees. The Jewish Josephus sheds more light on early beliefs in the return of the soul in *The Jewish Wars,* where he writes, "Do you not know that those who depart out of this life obtain a most holy place in heaven, from whence, in the evolution of the ages, they are again sent into pure bodies?" Other, modern, writers have pointed out that reincarnationist ideas are so deeply written into the esoteric Jewish literature that those Jews who follow the kabbalistic way make reincarnation sound almost like an essential part of the faith.

The Pharisees and the Sadducees often came under stinging condemnation from the mouth of Jesus, yet the third Jewish sect, the Essenes, escaped His criticism. Further, the Essene teachings, which have since been discovered in certain Dead Sea Scrolls, bear strong resemblances to the teachings of both Jesus and John the Baptist. These facts have led some scholars to conjecture that both Christ and John the Baptist were Essenes, since they were known to be Jews. Some investigators have further concluded that a form of reincarnation was an Essene belief. It is not completely clear what the Essenes taught, but a passage in Josephus' *The Jewish Wars* reports they taught preexistence, at the very least.

It is further obvious that many of the people, priests, and Scribes believed in reincarnation. They seem to have taken it for granted. Some of them thought that Jesus was one of the prophets returned (see Mark 8:27–28), while others thought He was the Prophet (perhaps Moses reincarnated, or perhaps the prophet predicted in Deut 18:15,18). Still others considered that Jesus might have been Elijah or one of the prophets of old (see Mark 6:14–16, 8:27–28; Luke 9:18–20). Herod suspected Jesus might have been John the Baptist revived from the deceased. Jesus, of course, knew of the speculating among the people. He asked His Apostles who they thought He was, at which question Peter responded that He was the Messiah sent from God (see Mark 8:28 NEB). Conspicuously, Jesus paid attention to their speculations as to His identity and offered no correction to the possibility that He was a reincarnated prophet. If He let a widespread erroneous belief among His very Apostles pass by uncorrected, a great deal of theological gymnastics is required to explain why. Far simpler is it to take His lack of comment as tacit agreement to the commonly held belief that reincarnations do occur.

Reincarnation was not an entirely alien doctrine in the time or place of Christ's mission on Earth. Although reincarnation is often associated with India, the belief is so widespread that it cannot even be claimed to have had it roots there. Reincarnation was also well known to the Romans, for a number of Roman poets refer to it. In the British Islands to the northwest, and in Gaul, reincarnation formed part of the mystic lore of the Druids. The ancient Greeks had long known of the idea, as witnessed by Pythagoras' and Plato's writings regarding the "transmigration of souls." Plato, along with Plutarch and Herodotus, attributed the belief in reincarnation to the ancient Egyptians. The famous scripture of the Egyptians, *The Book of the Dead,* presents a version of reincarnation.

There were other religious movements extant at the time of Christ which taught reincarnation, such as the Alexandrian Neoplatonic school of thought and Persian Mithraism. Those Persians wise in divine matters, who were called Magi, held as a primary doctrine that which was called the transmigration of souls. It could be speculated that the Magi who came from the East to honor the newborn King Jesus might have believed Him to be some great person reincarnated. Certainly, the common people entertained that notion. Thus, we see that Jerusalem at the time of Christ was surrounded by nations, many of whose ancient religions had taught some form of reincarnation for centuries. Moreover, the idea was common where Nicodemus lived. We are reminded that it is, therefore, natural that Nicodemus thought Christ referred to reincarnation when He spoke of a physical rebirth.

The coming of the Saviour had been anticipated for centuries, but it was not clear to the people of Jesus' day that He was truly the promised Messiah. They knew he was a greatly anointed man, and they speculated that He might be one of the prophets reborn. But most believed He could not be the Christ. The central objection was that Jesus could not be the Messiah because Elijah had not yet returned as prophesied. "Behold, I will send you Elijah the prophet before the coming of the great and dreadful day of the Lord: and he shall turn the heart of the fathers to the children, and the heart of the children to their fathers, lest I come and smite the earth with a curse" (Malachi 4:5–6). No doubt this unfulfilled prophecy caused much consternation among the Pharisees and Sadducees, and even more among the Apostles who were committing their lives to Jesus.

When Peter, James, and John were with Jesus on the mountain they saw Him converse with Moses and Elijah. The Voice from the bright cloud identified Jesus to them, saying, "This is my beloved Son, in whom I am well pleased; hear ye him." These

Apostles then understood that Jesus was in fact the Messiah, but the revelation troubled them greatly. On the way down the mountain, they tried to reconcile the Messiahship of Jesus of Nazareth with the prediction that Elijah had to first return. Unable to do so, they addressed the question to Jesus. It was in response to their question that Jesus identified John the Baptist as Elijah in person (see Matt 17:1–13). Matthew records, "And his disciples asked him, saying, 'Why then say the scribes that Elias must first come?' And Jesus answered and said unto them, 'Elias truly shall first come, and restore all things, But I say unto you, that Elias is come already, and they knew him not, but have done unto him whatsoever they listed [desired]. Likewise shall also the Son of Man suffer of them. Then the disciples understood that He spake unto them of John the Baptist" (Matt 17:10–13) *(em add)*. Here Jesus emphasized that the true identity of John the Baptist as Elijah had gone unrecognized by his persecutors. (John the Baptist had already been beheaded, thus freeing the spirit, who reappeared from above in his previous identity as Elijah.)

The identification Christ made of John the Baptist with Elijah is usually avoided by interpretations of Luke's words that "he shall go before him in the spirit and power of Elias [Elijah], to turn the hearts of the fathers to the children, and the disobedient to the wisdom of the just; to make ready a people prepared for the Lord" (Luke 1:17) *(em add)*. Apparently the interpreters are unaware that that idiom, "in the spirit of," did not mean the same then as the English idiom does today. It meant simply that the identity of the spirit in control was in fact Elijah. This is the same usage whereby the Bible says "in the Holy Spirit," to convey the meaning that the Holy Spirit is the identity of the spirit in charge.

John the Baptist retained no memory of his previous mission under the name Elijah. When asked if he were Elijah or one of the prophets, he replied that he was the "voice of one crying in the wilderness" (John 1:23). Yet, Christ identified him as the spirit previously known as Elijah.

It is a weak rebuttal to assert, as is often done, that John the Baptist was a "type" of Elijah. Malachi specifically says that Elijah himself shall return, not someone like Elijah, and so the Jews believed. "Behold, I am going to send you Elijah the prophet before the coming of the great and terrible day of the Lord." (Mal 4:5 NAS). In contrast, when the Old Testament wishes to express a "type" it manages to do so, such as when it refers to Moses as a "type" for the Messiah to come, with the words, "the Lord thy God raise up unto thee a Prophet from the midst of thee, of thy brethren, like unto me [Moses]; unto him ye shall hearken" (Deut 18:15) *(em add)*.

We are left with the completely unambiguous statement of Christ Himself: "And if you care to accept it, he himself is Elijah, who was to come. He who has ears to hear, let him hear" (Matt 11:15 NAS).

Let us find the ears to hear with and consider the enormous weight of the statement. Even today, many honest people cannot accept that Jesus is the Messiah because Elijah must return before the Messiah comes. They need wait no longer for Elijah. He has already returned, in person. And if John the Baptist was not actually Elijah, as Jesus claimed, *then Jesus of Nazareth could not have been the Messiah*.

The early Christian church was well aware that Jesus was the Messiah, and portions of the early church were aware of the Scriptural basis for reincarnation. Justin Martyr, in the first century, taught that human souls inhabit more than one body in the course of their pilgrimage on Earth. Origen, an influential Christian writer some two hundred years after Christ, taught a version of reincarnation, as did another church leader, Clement of Alexandria (Bishop of Alexandria). Numerous other writers in the first few centuries promulgated their versions of reincarnation. Sketches of their ideas, as well as evidence of suppression of the doctrine of reincarnation, are presented in some of the more scholarly books on the subject of reincarnation. St. Jerome, the distinguished scholar of Hebrew and Greek who first translated the Bible into Latin, explicitly stated that reincarnation was, from the earliest days of the Church, held as a secret doctrine not suitable to be imparted to the masses. Reincarnation is, therefore, by no means a doctrine foreign to Christianity. It is unnecessary to choose between Christianity and reincarnation. Neither need be rejected because of the other.

Suppose we have been incarnated into human life from a lower or higher realm than Earth. If so, then we obviously have little or no recall of our previous existence. However, this is no rebuttal to reincarnation. We are accustomed to having no remembrance of parts of our existence, yet we pay it no attention. As already noted, we sleep approximately one-third of our lives, yet remember nothing except a few dreams. If we accept those dreams as evidence of personal existence, then perhaps we should seriously consider the recollections of people who claim to remember events from past lives, as investigated in several current books. St. Augustine in his *Confessions* struggled with the problem of memory: "Tell me, Lord, tell me, did my infancy succeed another age of mine that died before it? Was it that which I spent within my mother's womb? And what before that life again, O God my Joy, was I anywhere or in any body? For this, I have none to tell me, neither father nor mother, or experience of others, nor mine own memory." As expected, "There is no remembrance of former things; neither shall there be any remembrance of things that are to come with those that shall come after" (Eccl 1:11).

If the doctrine of reincarnation is indeed a Christian truth, as it appears to be, then many statements in the Bibles take on much clearer meanings and more forceful relevance. For example, it is stated quite clearly that one will indeed reap what he sows, that the debts must be "paid [to] to the last farthing" (Matt 5:26 NEB). The payment is payment in kind, for "If anyone is destined for captivity, to captivity he goes; if anyone kills with the sword, with the sword he must be killed. HERE IS THE PERSEVERANCE AND THE FAITH OF THE SAINTS" (Rev 13:10 NAS) *(em add)*. Is it any wonder that in such knowledge is the "perseverance and faith of the saints?" What could instill perseverance and sincere effort better than the sober realization that God cannot be tricked into awarding access to Heaven to an evil person? (What an advantage to the adversary that reincarnation has been replaced with today's doctrinal definition of "born again.")

Salvation is promised to all who believe in Christ, but that entry into Heaven is possible only after Christ has made us fit for that realm by the cleansing fire of repeated Earth lives. Thus it is, that "every one shall be salted with fire." Yet, "Salt is good" (Mark 9:49–50). The fire of reaping what we sow brings with it the blessing that we learn and grow, and eventually reject our erring ways by virtue of our having experienced the results of those ways. The resulting change of heart is then not superficial but genuine. The knowledge and wisdom so gained are then not borrowed, but are our own possession to treasure.

The purpose of reincarnation appears to be the education of the soul. The course of study may well be difficult and the lessons hard-won. The student soul cannot permanently graduate unless he adequately passes his tests, and he cannot pass the tests unless he takes them. As a result, suicide, a direct violation of God's law, is a tragic error. It is an act to be shunned at all costs. Not only must the lessons temporarily avoided still be learned in some future life, and the same tests passed, but the spirit must also learn the additional lesson of persevering in God's school for souls: Earth life. "He that overcometh will I make a pillar in the temple of my God, and HE SHALL GO NO MORE OUT" (Rev 3:12) (em add).

To be taught that an act or thought is harmful convinces few of us, although for a time we might refrain from it. The conviction that it is harmful becomes firm, however, when we are allowed to suffer the consequences of our acts and ways of thinking. By no other way than experience is the point truly driven home. "For the sorrow that is according to the will of God produces a repentance without regret, leading to salvation" (II Cor. 7:10 NAS). The responsibility for ourselves lies, then, with us. With the guidance and love of God's spirits, we are required to work out our own salvation with reverent awe and trembling (see Phil 2:12).

It is not true that a correct understanding of the doctrine of reincarnation leads one to play havoc now and make it up later. A correct understanding of it has just the opposite effect. It is a sobering realization to know with certainty that the evil sown in a present life must surely be reaped in a future one, that truly we shall reap what we sow. Indeed, we are doing precisely that in our present lives. On the other hand, the doctrine that a last minute deathbed confession is sufficient to gain entry into Heaven has seduced multitudes into living profligate lives. God forgives the truly repentant soul, it is true, but then He corrects its defects. Otherwise, that soul is not fit for Heaven.

"If we confess our sins, He is faithful and righteous to forgive us our sins and to cleanse us from all unrighteousness" (I John 1:9 NAS). The cleansing can require another life, another "salting with fire," if the present life has been unsatisfactory. A man of a totally depraved nature might be forgiven, but his nature remains unchanged. He is by no means ready for Heaven until his nature improves.

"Make no mistake about this: God is not be be fooled; a man reaps what he sows. If he sows seed in the field of his lower nature, he will reap from it a harvest of corruption, but if he sows in the field of the Spirit, the Spirit will bring him a harvest of eternal life" (Gal 6:7–8 NEB).

———————◇———————

CHAPTER 9

Resurrection of the Dead

THE Scriptures have shown us that we are spirits whom God divorced and exiled from our original homes in Heaven. The heavenly spirits were frequently called gods in the days of the prophets. Thus, it is said of man, "Ye are gods" (Psa 82:6), this statement being affirmed later by Christ (see John 10:34). The Hebrew word *"elohim"* is translated here as "gods." It is the same word used in the Scriptures when it is written that we are created in the image, or likeness, of the gods (see Gen 1:26–27, 5:1, 9:6). We therefore look like these heavenly spirits, as indeed we should, since we are from among them, having been made temporarily "a little lower than the angels [*elohim*, gods]" (Psa 8:5) *(em add)*.

Consequently, we are incarnated spirits. The figure of speech that "we have a spirit" conveys a false impression. Instead, we *are* spirits, as indicated by "there is a spirit in man" (Job 32:8). What we have, as well, are physical bodies. It is this spirit/soul which gives physical life to the fleshly body it inhabits, for "the body without the spirit is [physically] dead" (Jas 2:26) *(em add)*.

The body of a spirit is called by various names. Some of the names are "spiritual body," "celestial body," "ghost," "angel," "apparition," and "phantom." Paul contrasts the physical body with the spiritual body in "It is sown a perishable body, it is raised an imperishable body" (I Cor 15:42 NAS). This points out that the physical body is perishable. It decays and decomposes into the dust from which it came. The spiritual body, the body composed of spirit substance, is the imperishable body which goes heavenward. "For a spirit hath not [physical] flesh and bones, as ye see me have" (Luke 24:39) *(em add)*. These words of Christ were spoken to the Apostles when He appeared among them after He had risen from the kingdom of the dead. Paul further explains that "it is sown a natural body, it is raised a spiritual body. If there is a natural body, there is also a spiritual body" (I Cor 15:44 NAS). The separation of the spirit body from the flesh body is what we call physical death. Again, "the body without the spirit is [physically] dead."

A commonplace analogy serves to clarify this idea. If we look at a gloved hand, we see only the glove. Since the glove can move, wiggle its fingers, and flex its palm, we might conclude that the glove is a living thing. However, it is really the hand inside the glove which gives the glove its motive power and directs its actions. The hand is the real living thing, not the glove. If the hand is withdrawn, the glove can no longer move about. It is emptied of its source of power and motion. This separation of the hand from the glove corresponds to physical death. But the hand still exists— free at last. Comparing the glove with our physical body and the hand with our spirit, we easily understand that physical death is simply the withdrawal of the spirit.

As a further illustration, consider the Scriptural account of the daughter of Jairus. When she died, her spirit simply left her body. When Christ called her back to life "her spirit came again, and she arose straightway" (Luke 8:55).

The departure of the spirit from the physical body at decease is indicated several places in the Scriptures. When nearing His physical death, Christ quoted Psalms 31:5 when He uttered, "into thy hands I commend my spirit" (Luke 23:46). Soon thereafter His Spirit left His body and He "gave up the ghost [His Spirit]" (Luke 23:46; John 19:30) *(em add)*. When Ananias and his wife abruptly died, they were said to have given up their ghosts (spirits) (see Acts 5:5–10). When Stephen was near death from stoning he cried, "Lord Jesus, receive my spirit" (Acts 7:59). King Herod was smitten by an angel of the Lord and "he . . . gave up the ghost" (Acts 12:23).

We emphasize that the physical body does not ascend into

Heaven. It is left behind to "return to the earth as it was: and the spirit shall return unto God" (Eccl 12:7). It is the spirit, in its spirit body, which ascends to Heaven, whose inhabitants are likewise spirits, just as the Father, the Son, and the angels are also spirits (see John 4:24, Heb 1:14).

When the beggar Lazarus died, "and was carried [in his spirit body] by the angels [other spirits in spirit bodies] into Abraham's bosom" (Luke 16:22) *(em add),* his physical body remained on Earth. When Abraham was rejoicing to see Christ's day (John 8:56), his physical body had long since been buried in a cave in Machpelah (see Gen 25:9–10). Isaac and Jacob, along with Abraham, have been raised from the dead (Mark 12:26; Luke 20:37) and are alive in the kingdom of God (see Luke 13:28), although their physical bodies lie buried with Abraham's in Machpelah (see Gen 49:29–32, 50:13). Moses and Elijah appeared to Christ on the mountain (see Matt 17:3 NAS) in their spiritual bodies, for the physical body of Moses, at least, had been in the ground for centuries "in a valley in the land of Moab, over against Beth-peor" (Deut 34:6). The thief on the cross went, in spirit, with Christ's Spirit to Paradise, but his earthly body did not vanish from the cross—nor did the body of Christ. The body of Jesus was placed in a tomb, even though His Spirit had already ascended to Paradise.

Paul said that to be present with the Lord in Heaven, he would have to "be absent from the [physical] body" (II Cor 5:8) *(em add).* Paul was in the flesh but desired to be only in his spirit body when he wrote, "For I am in a strait betwixt two, having a desire to depart, and to be with Christ; which is far better: Nevertheless to abide in the flesh is more needful for you" (Phil 1:23–24).

The physical body housing a spirit has sometimes been compared to a tabernacle. Peter writes of his impending death when he must shortly "put off this my tabernacle" (II Pet 1:14). Paul writes that "we that are in this tabernacle do groan" (II Cor 5:4), but that "we know that if our earthly house of this tabernacle were dissolved, we have a building of God, an house not made with hands, eternal in the heavens" (II Cor 5:1). There is no doubt that both Paul and Peter are now with the Lord in their spiritual bodies, even though thousands of people visit the reputed graves of their physical bodies every year.

Examples such as these could be repeated many times over,

showing that the physical body returns to Earth while the spiritual body ascends to Heaven. We need merely attend a funeral, look at a cemetery, or consider the results of a crematorium to know that "[physical] flesh and blood cannot inherit the kingdom of God" (I Cor 15:50) *(em add)*.

The common meanings of the words "life" and "death" are, as earlier noted, not the usual meanings in the Bibles. On the contrary, life and death in the Bibles usually refer to "spiritual life" and "spiritual death." This is especially true in the writings of the Apostle Paul. A person is said to be "alive," "spiritually alive," "living," or "quickened" if he has chosen allegiance to Christ over Satan. Beginning at that moment of decision, a person is numbered among Christ's subjects. From the point of view of God's spirit-world, he had been "spiritually dead" ever since the Fall (see Rom 5:12; Rev 12:9). At the very moment he chooses to ally with Christ, he becomes "alive" again.

If a person elects not to choose Christ over Satan, then he remains numbered among the (spiritually) dead. A person may not have made a conscious choice between Christ and Satan. Nevertheless, he has chosen sides according to his behavior, for "you are the servants of him whom you obey" (Rom 6:16 GNT). Therefore, a spirit is living or dead according to its allegiance, whether or not it is in the physical body.

To further illustrate spiritual death, let us draw upon our common medical experiences. Suppose that a man receives an injection of anaesthetic in his shoulder, so that all feeling is lost in one arm. The arm hangs limply. It does not respond to the man's will. The arm still belongs to him, but, though his blood still flows through its veins, it will not respond to him. We say the arm is numb or "dead." This arm has been "deadened" by an anaesthetic and no longer obeys the will of its master. Spiritual death is similar to this. The anaesthetic, in this instance, is disobedience to God's law of love. The spiritually dead do not obey the will of God, their Master. Their voluntary disobedience and rebellion is the "sin unto [spiritual] death" (Rom 6:16) *(em add)*, because it results in separation from God (spiritual death). Those spirits who behave in this way are referred to as "the dead."

Spiritual death, therefore, means "estranged from God," "divorced from God," or "separated from God," in much the same way we use those terms when talking about a wonderful marriage torn apart when one of the partners deserts the other. The one who was deserted may issue a divorce, as God did to the Israelites (see Jer 3:8). While spiritual death is often defined as separation from God, physical death is separation of the spirit body from the physical body. The complete breaking of the connecting bond between the spirit body and the physical body is the physical death process alluded to in Ecclesiastes as breaking "the silver cord" (Eccl 12:6).

There are situations, however, in which the spirit does not completely disengage from the physical body upon leaving it. The body and the spirit can remain tenuously connected. The weakened connection supplies a greatly diminished power flow from the spirit into the body, and results in a trance, a deep sleep, or a coma. This rare condition allows the spirit to be outside of the body. This condition was referred to in the Greek as a state of ecstasy, literally being *ek-stasis* in the Greek, meaning "out of and beside one's self." The meaning of the word has obviously changed over the intervening centuries.

Another means by which the Scriptures refer to being outside the body is by the phrase "in the spirit." This phrase emphasizes the contrast with being "in the flesh." In modern times we call this phenomenon an "out-of-body experience." Verifiable instances of this phenomenon are so rare that it is understandable that our language has lost the original meanings of "ecstasy" and "in the spirit." In the language of today these terms merely refer to moods or emotions. It was not so in the New Testament days. Unfortunately, people of today read "to be with you in spirit" to mean "I'll be thinking about you," which is an entirely different statement.

When John received the Revelation of Jesus Christ, he was "in the Spirit on the Lord's day" (Rev 1:10), not merely thinking about the Lord. When John was carried in the spirit (see Rev 17:3) into the wilderness, he left his physical body behind.

It is apparent that, aside from receiving visions or revelations while out-of-body, a human spirit may at times journey to another location. One of the clearest Biblical examples of the body being in one place, while the spirit journeys elsewhere, is given by Paul when he reports that he was sometimes with the Corinthians without their knowing it:

> For I verily, as absent in body, but present in spirit, have judged already, as though I were present, concerning him that hath so done this deed, in the name of our Lord Jesus Christ, when ye are gathered together, and my spirit, with the power of our Lord Jesus Christ (I Cor 5:3–4).

The meaning of Paul's statement is even clearer in other translations:

> Even though I am not physically present, I am with you in spirit. And I have already passed judgment on the one who did this, just as if I were present. When you are assembled in the name of our Lord Jesus and I am with you in spirit (I Cor 5:3–4 NIV), and,
>
> I, who am present with you in spirit if not in body, have passed judgment upon this man who has offended so outrageously, exactly as if I were there in person (I Cor 5:3–4 GNT).

To the Colossians Paul writes, "For even though I am absent in body, nevertheless I am with you in spirit, rejoicing to see your good discipline" (Col 2:5 NAS), or, "For although I am absent from you in body, my spirit is with you" (Col 2:5 GNT).

Hence, Paul, prior to writing letters to the congregations at Colossae and Corinth, had visited them in spirit while his body was elsewhere. Paul had another well known out-of-body experience in which he was taken to a higher dimension, when he was "caught up to the third heaven," at which time he could not tell "whether in the body, or out of the body" (II Cor 12:2–4). The reason for his uncertainty is that the spirit body in Heaven is like the physical body in all respects, as we have already discussed. The body and the environment are every bit as real and solid in that realm as they are to us in this dimension.

A spirit, out of body, may be so nearly detached from that body that it no longer sustains respiration or brain activity. The body is then physically dead for all intents, though the spirit can return. If the spirit does return, the body revives. This phenomenon is called a near-death-experience in current literature. We see that this experience is essentially the same as an out-of-body experience. Numerous examples of this occurrence have been published in several recent books.

Frequently, a person who has died for a few minutes, and then revived, has a consoling and exhilarating experience to relate. He typically tells of having been met by deceased loved ones, or even by angels, and of having experienced overwhelming peace and joy while in a place of great beauty. As we have seen, this experience is in agreement with what we expect from the Scriptures. As regards this resurrection, it is conspicuous that the person finds himself still aware and "alive," and still in a body, and that the departed loved ones who greet him are in the same state. They are not sleeping in the earth awaiting the resurrection of their pitiful flesh on some future day. That particular body has been vacated and is of no further use whatever.

Funeral services are preached daily in which we hear phrases such as "she has gone to be with Jesus." A few moments later the bereaved family hears a Scripture reading purported to predict a future resurrection of the flesh. These claims cannot both be true, seeing that they contradict each other. Such a blatant lapse in logic can do little to bring hope to the bereaved. Her resurrection, or her raising to a higher dimension, took place "in the twinkling of an eye" (I Cor 15:52) at the moment she departed from the physical body.

It is obvious, then, that Jesus was never at any time in the tomb where Joseph and Nicodemus had placed His physical remains. Jesus, the Spirit, ascended to Paradise immediately upon His release from the physical body (see Luke 23:43), and from there He descended as a Spirit to the lower dimensions of Hell where He ministered to the penitent spirits (see I Pet 3:18–20) and conquered the belligerent ones (see Col 2:15 GNT). Christ never walked out of the tomb, as is commonly believed, for the simple reason that He was never in it. The tomb was empty when the women arrived, and Christ materialized while they were present. This materialization from a higher dimension was no different from that of Gabriel or of the high spirits who visited with Abraham and Lot. His body had simply been dematerialized by God's spirit agents in the same way that the bodies of Enoch and Elijah had been dematerialized. His body was not intended to undergo decay (see Psa 16:10), and, in common with the body of Moses, it was not intended that His corpse should survive to become an object of veneration. Further, His appearances during the next forty days were materializations. We note His appearance to the disciples in the closed room and His dematerialization, where there were no available doors for His departure (see John 20:19–26).

The Apostles and the people had witnessed the bringing back to life of several people at Christ's command. In view of their experiences, it is remarkable that the Apostles did not understand what Jesus meant by being "raised from the dead." They puzzled and wondered among themselves as to what He meant by it. "And they kept that saying with themselves, questioning one with another what the rising from the dead should mean" (Mark 9:10), but they were afraid to ask Him what He meant by it (see Mark 9:31–32). The Jews were equally confounded by Jesus' words about death (see John 8:51–53). Quite obviously, Christ was not referring to the renewing of physical life, a phenomenon totally familiar both to His Apostles and to the Jews.

A clue to His meaning lies in the wording of the New Testament. Although there is no record of what He said in the Aramaic language, the remembrances handed down to us in the Greek New Testament show that He often referred to being "raised up out of," or "out from among," the dead. That is, He, the Spirit Jesus, was raised up from among the apostate spirits in the lower dimensions. The dead included those apostate spirits dwelling in human bodies (see John 5:25; I Tim 5:6), and spirits then trapped in the lower dimensions. It is interesting to note that, when Christ descended and preached to certain of those spirits, their physical remains were still on Earth (see I Pet 3:19–20). The physical body neither descends nor ascends, only the spiritual body. It is from among these dead that Christ was resurrected, being "raised up" to a higher dimension of existence, in His spiritual body. The same resurrection is promised to all who follow Him. The resurrection of the dead is, therefore, the return of the spiritually dead, who had been exiled in Hell, to the higher dimensions.

Christ was the first to descend to the spiritually dead in Hell and to ascend from there. As such, He is called the "firstborn from the dead" (Col. 1:18). His was the first such ascension from the dead, to which Paul refers: "Now this expression, 'He ascended,' what does it mean except that He also had descended into the lower parts of the earth?" (Eph 4:9 NAS). This fact is also indicated by the words, "having been buried with Him in baptism, in which you were also raised up with Him through faith in the working of God, who raised Him from the dead" (Col 2:12 NAS). By having given Christ their allegiance, the Colossians were already viewed as having been raised from the dead, although their departure from Earth had not yet taken place.

The "resurrection of the dead," or, "from the dead," or, "out from among the dead," has, therefore, not the slightest reference to the reanimating of a physical body, nor to the transporting of a fleshly body into Heaven. "Now I say this, brethren, that flesh and blood cannot inherit the kingdom of God; nor does the perishable inherit the imperishable" (I Cor 15:50 NAS).

The catechisms in the early centuries of this era did not speak of the resurrection of the *flesh,* but of the resurrection of the *dead.* The doctrine that the physical bodies of the deceased would some day be reassembled and transported heavenward is of later invention.

The Biblical case for the resurrection of the spirit body, and only the spirit body, is strong indeed. On the other hand, there are certain Scripture verses which specifically state the physical body shall be raised. We have here simply another instance in which tampering hands have contaminated the Scriptures so that they contradict themselves. An example of this tampering is in Matthew, where it is recorded that at the moment Jesus gave up His Spirit, an earthquake occurred which cast bodies out of their tombs hewn in the rocky hillside. The original report is said to have been: "The veil in the temple was rent in two from the top to the bottom; and the earth did quake; and the rocks were rent; and the tombs were opened; and many bodies of those who had fallen asleep were cast forth. Many, who had come from the holy city, did see the bodies lying there" (Greber, p. 348). Many years later, when the resurrection of the flesh had become an axiom of the Christian faith, the verse had evolved to read, "The bodies of those who had fallen asleep were raised." Then the phrase was added, "and coming out of the tombs after His resurrection they entered the holy city and appeared to many" (Matt 27:53 NAS), so that Christ might still be thought of as the first to be raised from the dead, although simple logic shows that it fails at that purpose. Are we to believe that the bodies were reanimated at the moment of

Christ's crucifixion and that their tombs were opened (see Matt 27:52), and at the same time believe that these revitalized corpses sat quietly, and unnoticed, in their open tombs for three more days before emerging? Had they been revived as claimed, that event could scarcely have escaped the notice of the Gospel writers, and of Paul, and even of the Romans and the Jews, so great a miracle would it have been. It is conspicuous that neither Mark, Luke, John, Peter, nor Paul ever mentions this alleged mass revival anywhere in the New Testament. In point of fact, neither did the writer of Matthew.

Another example of a mistranslation made with an implicit belief in the resurrection of the flesh is found in Job. The passage in questions reads, " 'I know that my Redeemer lives and at last he will stand upon the earth. Then shall I see God, though my skin is destroyed and MY BODY WITHOUT FLESH' . . . (Job 19:25–26)" (Greber, p. 386). These words are distorted into the opposite meaning by the King James translation: "and though after my skin worms destroy this body, YET IN MY FLESH SHALL I SEE GOD" (Job 19:25–26) *(em add)*.

There are still other passages where the Bible translations clearly state that the flesh shall be raised, despite the statements that same Book makes to the contrary. In this event, we might bear in mind that observation can be superior to theological deduction. When the Bibles refer to the four corners of the Earth, but we observe that the Earth has no corners, we conclude that the expression is not literally true. When the Bibles refer to the sun as moving about us, yet we observe that the Earth rotates instead, we conclude that the statement is figurative, or symbolic, or a product of human belief, but not literally accurate. If any New Testament writings can be construed to indicate physical resurrection, the reader may be wary that the early church revisers were strongly pro-resurrection, and that documents were adjusted and altered in places to match church doctrine. Also, translations are, to an extent, interpretations. In addition, some of the writings are intrinsically unclear. Since resurrection of the flesh is inconsistent with many of the Biblical passages regarding the afterlife, and in disagreement with observation, we have no honest choice but to follow Paul's example and discard it as inaccurate.

Paul was apparently as difficult to understand in his day as he is in ours. Peter remarks that there are things in Paul's letters which are "hard to understand, which the untaught and unstable distort, as they do also the rest of his writings" (II Pet 3:15–16 NAS, using footnote from NEB) (The phrase "in his writings" is almost universally translated as "in the Scriptures," the implied motive of the translators being to classify Paul's letters as Scripture). As regards the resurrection of the spirit body, Paul had attempted to convey the truth to his converts, but they were as slow to grasp it as the Apostles themselves had been. The Corinthians had debated among themselves as to whether the flesh rose again, and seem to have believed that it did. Despite Christ's warning against calling anyone a fool (see Matt 5:22), Paul's frustration is evident as he tries to correct the Corinthians with the words, "But someone will say, 'How are the dead raised? And with what kind of body do they come?' You Fool!" (I Cor 15:35–36 NAS). Paul devotes the next several lines to drawing the distinction between the physical body and the body we will have as a spirit. Then he emphasizes: "So also is the resurrection of the dead. It is sown a perishable body, it is raised an imperishable body" (I Cor 15:42 NAS), and "it is sown a natural body, it is raised a spiritual body. If there is a natural body, there is also a spiritual body." (I Cor 15:44 NAS). He concludes his comparison of the flesh and spirit bodies with the statement that, "Flesh and blood cannot inherit the kingdom of God; nor does the perishable inherit the imperishable" (I cor 15:50 NAS). Paul effectively rebuts the idea of resurrection of the flesh. He does not reveal how he coped with Old Testament statements to the contrary.

In summary, Paul's refutation of the belief in fleshly resurrection is clearly and forcefully presented in some modern translations, such as:

But, some one will ask, how do the dead rise? What kind of a body do they have? Foolish man! Just consider the earthly seed that you sow in the ground. Must it not first perish in the earth before new life sprouts from it? . . . There are celestial bodies and terrestrial bodies . . . SO IS IT WITH THE RESURRECTION OF THE DEAD. That which is sown perishes; that which grows out of it does not perish . . . THAT WHICH SPRINGS INTO LIFE IS A SPIRITUAL

BODY . . . Let me impress upon you this one thing, brothers: earthly flesh and blood cannot inherit the kingdom of God . . . None of us will remain in the kingdom of the spiritually dead for ever, but WE SHALL ALL UNDERGO THE TRANSFORMATION INTO THE SPIRITUAL BODY. (from I Cor 15:35–52 GNT) *(em add)*.

What could be clearer?

REFERENCE CITED

Greber, Johannes, *Communication with the Spirit World of God: Its Laws and Purpose*

PART THREE

Reconciliation

◇

CHAPTER 10

Preparation for Salvation

"Where there is no vision, the people perish" (Prov 29:18).

Gᴏᴅ is a spirit and every living thing created by God is a spirit. The Spirit we call Christ is the highest Spirit of God, in every way God's most perfect image. Paul calls Him "the image of the invisible God, the firstborn of every creature" (Col 1:15). The revolt in Heaven was against this Son of God.

The ringleader in the revolt in God's spirit-kingdom was Lucifer, the "Light-bearer," the second son of God, and after Christ, the highest and fairest spirit in Creation. What was his aim? He was ambitious: he wanted to be the supreme ruler, being unwilling to occupy a second place, subordinate to a superior. He wanted to step into Christ's place and to reign in His stead (Greber, p. 271).

In view of their freedom of action, which was the highest gift conferred upon the spirits by the Creator, it was possible for them to refuse obedience to the laws of the King whom God had set over them, for the words of the Bible: 'Even on his heavenly servants he cannot rely; his very angels he convicts of error,' (Job 4:18) and 'Even on his angels God cannot rely, the very heavens are stained to Him' (Job 15:15) are true of every created spirit, save only of the first Son of God. And yet, the spirits are holy so long as they recognize the authority over them of God and of Christ, and do not by apostasy, secede from God's kingdom" (Greber, p. 270).

Unhappily, the defection of a large part of the spirit-world from God came about through rebellion against Christ, the Regent appointed by God. When the uprising came to a head, God cast the rebellious spirits from Heaven into an altogether different dimension of space and time.

> The mocking remark said by the Bible to have been uttered by the Lord on this occasion is also the reverse of the truth. By the Scriptural account, God, at the moment when countless hosts of His children were being driven into the unspeakable woe of utter exile from His kingdom, exclaimed: "Behold, the man is become as one of us, to know good and evil; and now, lest he put forth his hand, and take also of the tree of life, and eat, and live forever, therefore Jehovah sent him forth from the Garden of Eden . . ." (Gen 3:22). These are the words of a fiend, not those of an infinitely benign God, and as a matter of fact they were spoken by Satan in mockery of the deluded spirits. On the contrary, God wished that even after their fall, those spirits would reach out after the tree of life, in obedience to His will and in an effort to return unto Him (Greber, p. 287).

God is not willing that any should perish. He wants all to come to repentance and eternal life (Luke 9:56; II Pet 3:9–10). "This is good and acceptable in the sight of God our Savior, who desires all men to be saved and to come to the knowledge of the truth" (I Tim 2:3 NAS). It was for the very purpose of leading all souls back to God that the material universe was created, including the earth and everything on it. We human spirits cannot truly imagine the ages that have elapsed from the days of the fall of the spirits to the time when the first fallen spirit was fit to be incarnated in human shape. "One day is with the Lord as a thousand years, and a thousand years as one day" (II Pet 3:8).

The creation of the physical universe in this dimension was no easy task. Far from being a magical six day process, as the allegorical reports in Genesis suggest, the material universe came into being some ten to twenty billion years ago. Many lines of scientific evidence point to the beginning of the universe as being a colossal explosion from which matter and energy sprayed in all directions. Here again, we have no magic at work, but the natural laws laid down by the Creator, with every such law of nature in this dimension having its counterpart in the spirit spheres.

It appears that God formed the physical universe by the same agency He uses in other endeavors, namely, His spirits—the unfallen, faithful spirits. Genesis begins with: "In the beginning (of the universe), the *elohim* (gods) created the heavens and the earth" *(em add)*. *Elohim* in the original Hebrew, is translated as God and interpreted as the Trinity, a later invention of the early Christian church. This interpretation fails utterly when we read, in reference to man, that "Thou [God] hast made him a little lower than the *elohim*" (Psa 8:5) *(em add),* where translators feel constrained to insert "gods" or "the angels" for *elohim*. However, the gods, or the angels, are, as we have seen in earlier chapters, simply our spirit brothers, sisters, parents, and children, who remained loyal to God. The Psalms specifically identify such spirits as *elohim* in, "I said, 'You are gods [*elohim*], and all of you are sons of the Most High'" (Psa 82:6 NAS), *(em add)*. Jesus confirmed this view of the *elohim* in using it to defend Himself against the charge of blasphemy (see John 10:34–35) when He quoted from the same Psalms used here, although we received His remarks in Greek rather than Hebrew. Therefore, it was the spirits of God (see Gen 1:2) who directed the formation of the galaxies, stars, planets, and, eventually, all living things. And, therefore, it is that our physical bodies were designed in the likeness of the *elohim* (see Gen 1:26–27, 5:1, 9:6), both male and female.

The love, patience, and dedication of the spirits who labored to carry out God's creative decrees during billions of years is unfathomable to the minds of the fallen spirits. Working under Christ, His agents have served Him loyally and long. Saint Paul writes in his Epistle to the Colossians: "For by him [Christ] were all things created, that are in heaven, and that are in the earth, visible and invisible, whether they be thrones, or dominions, or principalities, or powers: all things were created by him, and for him: and he is before all things, and by him all things consist" (Col 1:16–17) *(em add)*.

> God did not create the world at one stroke. God is the great Architect who, with strict observance of laws conceived with infinite wisdom, builds up little things into large ones, simple things into complex, and, out of a single seed, produces the tree with its millions of seeds; who builds up the family, not by calling into existence parents and children simultaneously, but by first creating the parents and endowing them with the power of reproduction, so that in time the family may grow through the birth of the offspring, and that, out of this family new ones may arise without limit (Greber, p. 266).

God's omnipotence and wisdom are nowhere more evident to thoughtful minds than in the coming into the world of a new human life. Human understanding has failed to grasp the Divine secret of how fallen spirits are incorporated into bodies produced by procreation, in conformity with laws God has conceived with infinite wisdom. We truly do not understand how these processes come about any more than we understand the other processes of nature going on all around us, although we see them daily with our own eyes.

The supreme problem Heaven confronted was that of bringing the beloved fallen spirits back. The plan of salvation required the creation of a physical universe in a different dimension of existence, and the outfitting of it with planets and living things. That phase finished, man was placed on the scene for training, testing, and rehabilitation, according to his own free choice in his thoughts and attitudes. Even at that, there was no hope of salvation until a Redeemer would rescue the spirits from the power of Satan. Where no hope of salvation exists, the will to achieve it is absent, and where the will is lacking, no effort is made by the hopeless to prepare for salvation.

Mankind, as a whole, made little improvement. Man's way of thinking was continually evil, with few exceptions. Noah was one such exception. The story of Noah may or may not be literally true as related in Genesis, and Ararat may or may not be the mountain known to us by that name today. A similar story of Gilgamesh was some two thousand years old before the experiences of Noah were committed to writing. Despite the uncertainties we encounter with the story of the Flood, it is clear that man strayed so far into error that the Lord found it necessary to virtually start over with a handful of His followers. Those people who were destroyed returned to the pit, there to await another chance at incarnation, and "after many days shall they be visited" (Isa 24:22). (Christ later visited these same spirits who "had once been disobedient, in the days of Noah" (I Pet 3:20 GNT).

A great deal had to be done to prepare the people for the Redeemer, without Whose victory no human spirit could ascend from this dimension.

This was the frontier of Lucifer's jurisdiction, and before the Redemption, this was the point beyond which no spirit was allowed to pass. Being lawfully Lucifer's subjects, none could escape from his rule, since he was unwilling to waive his right of sovereignty even in the case of those spirits which had repented of their misdeeds and longed to return to God's kingdom. The surrender of this right had to be forced upon him by a Redeemer, prior to Whose coming all human spirits would be obliged to remain in the human sphere, either as corporeally existent human beings, or as spirits in a sphere of the same level as that of mankind. Beyond this lay the great gulf dividing Lucifer's kingdom from that of God. To bridge this gulf, a victory over Lucifer must be achieved. (Greber, p. 292).

In preparation for the coming of the Redeemer, certain of His loyal spirits underwent incarnation to serve among mankind. Once in a material body, these spirits, as all other people, were unable to recall their former glory and splendor. They were aware only of their existence at the moment, having no recollection of any previous state of existence. God had granted permission to these spirits from Heaven

> to be born as human beings, in order that they might help others to attain the true faith in God and thus prepare themselves for redemption. Of these spirits which lived in human form were Enoch, Abraham, Isaac, Jacob, Moses, Joshua, Caleb, most of the prophets, Mary, the Mother of Jesus, and many others whose names do not figure in the original Scriptural documents. After their death on earth, these spirits returned to God's kingdom, since, having taken no part in the secession from God, they had not fallen under Lucifer's jurisdiction (Greber, p. 292).

It is at great risk that any celestial spirit incarnates on Earth, for the spirit is "emptied" thereby, even as Christ "emptied Himself" to become man (Phil 2:7 NAS). The spirit loses its knowledge, memories, and powers in the process of incarnation. As such, the person begins life ignorant and vulnerable. His ignorance is difficult to overcome, for where on Earth shall he find the truth? At the same time, he is vulnerable to the onslaughts of Satan's lying spirits. The spirit then lives as a human in Satan's kingdom with no advantage over other men, except for his innately purer soul. Even so, the danger of falling prey to the enemy is ever present.

One such spirit was Abraham, a man of unshakable loyalty to God. Christ communicated with him, at times through His spirits, at times directly. Abraham's dedication to God was put to a severe test, as is the case of all those to whom God thinks of entrusting a particularly important mission (In this context we recall Jesus' forty days of testing in the wilderness before His mission began). Abraham was told to sacrifice his beloved son Isaac. He was determined to follow the Lord's instructions and would have done so, had not God intervened by His angel at the last moment. Severely tested though he was, Abraham proved faithful and was rewarded with God's promise: "By Myself I have sworn, . . . because you have done this thing, and have not withheld your son, your only son, indeed I will greatly bless you, and I will greatly multiply your seed as the stars of the heavens, and as the sand which is on the seashore; and your seed shall possess the gate of their enemies. And in your seed all the nations of the earth shall be blessed, because you have obeyed My voice" (Gen 22:16–18 NAS). Abraham's seed was spiritual and would ultimately embrace all the fallen spirits, in the sense that his faith and devotion to God would eventually extend to all those who had forsaken Him. Many nations (see Gen 17:1–5) would result from him and his descendants would spread in all directions (see Gen 28:14).

Abraham's son Ishmael, by the slave Hagar, was to be the ancestor of a great nation (see Gen 17:20), often believed to be the Arab people. But Isaac, the only begotten son from Sarah, was to inherit all the covenents God made with Abraham. "My covenant I will establish with Isaac" (Gen 17:21 NAS). Isaac had two sons, Jacob and Esau. The promises of God were passed to Jacob, whom God renamed "Israel." Israel, in turn, had twelve sons, Joseph being his firstborn from Israel's chosen wife. At that point the covenant promises made to Abraham were divided.

The kingly office, the line of royal power, went to the son Judah, to culminate many years later in Christ. The promises of great power, wealth, and possessions of lands and people was given to Joseph: "But the birthright was Joseph's" (I Chron 5:2). At the end of his life, Israel blessed Ephraim and Manasseh, the two sons of Joseph born in Egypt. They were to carry the name of Israel and of Abraham and of Isaac, and were to "grow into a multitude in the midst of the earth" (see Gen 48:14–20). Manasseh was to produce a great nation, with Ephraim's descendants becoming a company, or family, of nations (verse 19). There is no specific mention here of where those nations were to be, what they were to be called, or when they were to be formed.

Judah later sired twin sons by his widowed daughter-in-law, Tamar. In a difficult delivery, the arm of Zarah emerged before his twin. He was tagged with a red string by the midwife to signify that he was the firstborn to whom Judah's birthright would pass. As it turned out, his twin brother Pharez was born first, and became more well-known in the subsequent history of the nation of Israel. Zarah and Pharez later parted ways. Pharez remained in the Near East, with the Pharisees later carrying his name. Zarah, on the other hand, left the area with his followers. Sketchy, but plausible, archaeological evidence indicates that Zarah's company and their offspring went northwest to Greece; then to Italy, Spain and the British Isles, leaving traces of their passing generations along the way. The "thin red line" of Zarah carried with them the birthright from Judah, to become a royal house for the kings of Israel.

Even in those distant days, the nation of Israel awaited the Messiah, the special one seed promised to Abraham. The concept of a Messiah is an old one, also in evidence among what we would now call the Persians and Assyrians. The early Egyptians looked for a Messiah, as did the later Druids in the British Isles. Messianism is found among the earliest Egyptians a thousand years before its appearance among the Hebrews. When we go far back into Egyptian history, we find a belief in one god, and find that the Egyptian sacred writings refer to the resurrection of the body and the coming of a Messiah (Breasted). In these earliest days, the theological view throughout Babylonia was of a heaven for the righteous whom the gods might choose (Langdon). Nearer to Egypt were the Phoenicians, so named for their descent from Enoch, where *Pa-Hanok* in Egyptian meant "house of Enoch." The *Ras Shamru* tablets from the coast of Phoenicia around 1500 B.C. show that, despite their Bel and idol worship, the Phoenicians believed in a supreme diety. On these tablets is found the name Yah—the Yahweh, or Jehovah, of the Old Testament.

Time was not then right for the Redeemer. More had to be done in the preparation for salvation. The descendants of Israel had been

God's choice to be His instrument for bringing morsels of truth to a spiritually starving world. They, unfortunately, were not equal to the task. Their faith in God waivered. They fell into idolatry and the worship of other gods, such worship frequently being referred to in the Old Testament as adultery. As a result of their desertion of God, He sent the Hebrews into captivity in the land of Egypt. There they served as slaves to a highly developed people. The Egyptians had some commerce with Europe, and even China (Barthel, p. 96). Traces of Egyptian influence in that era are also found in Britain, where mining and smelting operations had already been carried out for over a thousand years (Mackenzie). Britain already had its Druidic religion, while Hinduism was already an old religion in India.

In time, the Lord set about to release the children of Israel from their bondage. For that purpose, He chose another incarnated high spirit, known to us as Moses. Moses succeeded, by the mighty power of God, in leading the Hebrews out of Egypt. The Israelites, carrying the embalmed body of Joseph with them, crossed the Sea of Reeds, or possibly the Red Sea, and headed for the promised land, to "the land which he sware unto our fathers" (Deut 6:23; see also Deut 8:1, 9:5). Once again, God undertook the training of the Israelites as free people, although, in their hearts, they had brought idols and other gods with them from Egypt (see Acts 7:41–43).

It is interesting to note that Moses was not a Jew. That is to say, he was not from the tribe of Judah. He was a Levite, from the priestly tribe of Levi. Although he worshipped the highest God, Yahweh, that is quite a different matter from being of the tribe of Judah. Other nations and kings had done the same, and neither were they Jews.

No one is quite sure how many Hebrews followed Moses in the Exodus. Two to three million Hebrews is a common estimate. However, the old Hebrew system of writing numbers lends itself easily to scribal errors quite as much as epic tales, such as this one, lend themselves to embellishment. It is likely that a corrected reading of the Scriptures gives as few as six hundred families following Moses. If so, then the Biblical statement that the Hebrews had only two midwives with them makes sense, but their deliverance is no less miraculous than before. It further explains why Egyptian records make no mention of the Exodus, an omission difficult to account for if millions of slaves, perhaps outnumbering the Egyptians themselves, were involved, as is usually taught. Nor did all the Hebrews necessarily follow Moses. There is good reason to believe that others of the Hebrews left northward by ship, some of them arriving at the Hebrew coastal settlements along southern Europe and in the British Isles. These lands were well known, both to the seafaring Egyptians and to their slaves. However, there is no Biblical mention of these escapees.

In the promised land, the people quickly reverted to idolatry. Even while Moses was on Mt. Sinai, also called Mount Horeb, the Israelites made idols and worshipped them. Moses returned with the famous Ten Commandments. These commandments are essentially the same as the Code of Hammurabi. An ancient carving still exists picturing Hammurabi sitting opposite his highest god, the sun god Shamash, who is placing the tablets of the law into the king's hands. Perhaps God was also at work with this Babylonian king some four hundred years before Moses. In any event, we know that God later used the Babylonian king Nebuchadnezzar, referring to him as "My servant" in the book of Daniel. Certainly God works among all nations, not just among His Israelites.

Despite the many supernatural signs given to the wandering Hebrews, they were not faithful to the Highest God. At one time He was ready to cast them aside and raise up a new special nation from Moses. Moses protested and was able to obtain God's pardon for the Israelites (see Num 14:11–38). In the end, the Lord relented and patiently stood by the Israelites for many more years as they awaited their Messiah, the deliverer to come. The Messiah would have a mission similar to that of Moses in many ways. "I will raise up a prophet from among their countrymen like you [Moses], and I will put My words in his mouth, and he shall speak to them all that I command him. And it shall come about that whoever will not listen to My words which he shall speak in My name, I Myself will require it of him" (Deut 18:18–19 NAS) *(em add)*.

For a period of time, Israel was a theocracy in which judges were the visible instruments of the rule of God. But the Israelites grew to desire a king, that they might be like the other nations (see I Sam 8:19–20). God granted this and gave them Saul as their first king about 1000 B.C., roughly a hundred years after Brutus of Troy had founded London on the island of Britain.

After the death of Saul, David became king of Israel, although at first only the tribe of Judah accepted him. The other tribes had allegiance to a son of Saul. The Lord established a perpetual covenant with David, that there would always be a king over Israel from the line of David, and thus from Judah. Solomon, the son of David, followed his father as king.

During the reign of Solomon, the Phoenicians, with the tribe of Dan in their midst, were the legendary seafarers of the world. They had idols and local gods of their own, but at first they had only one god (Haberman). Philo of Byblus, the Greek, quoted Sanchoniathon from around 1000 B.C. as writing that the Phoenician diety was Elioun, apparently the *Elohim* of the Hebrews, and that he was called Hypsistos, or "most high." The golden age of Phoenix coincided with the golden age of Solomon (Breasted). The Phoenicians had sailed along all the Mediterranean coasts of Europe. In the Atlantic they had ventured as far south as the tip of Africa and north past the British Isles. The Phoenician language, the Punic, was the commercial language of the day (Rawlinson). There was a close connection between the early Britons, with their Hebrew outposts, and the House of Enoch, the tribe of Dan, and the Phoenicians.

The Hebrew and Phoenician words *ish* and *ishi* mean "man, my man, men." The Hebrew word for covenant is *Bryth,* or *Berith,* with the "h" being silent. "British," then, means nothing less than "the covenant people," and Brit-ain means "covenant land." Ancient Welsh speaks of the British as *Bryth-Y-Brithan,* meaning "covenanters of the land of the covenant." It has also been proposed that the British Isles acquired their name from Brutus of Troy (Waddell). Scholars seem to have no definitive answer to the origin of the name of the islands, but their connection with the Hebrews is strongly indicated, and monuments, inscriptions, coins, and the like, show that a large portion of the people of those islands were Phoenicians (Waddell).

When Solomon set about to build the fabulous temple of God,

he had trade routes to all the sources of metals and materials needed for the project. He was well acquainted with the "islands in the west." Herodotus, writing in the fifth century B.C., about the time the Old Testament was committed to writing, referred to the metal trade with the "Isles of the West," calling the British Isles the "Cassiterides," or "Tin Islands." Pytheas (353–323 B.C.) also wrote about the tin trade with Britain. The tin mines of Cornwall in Britain were still the source of the world's supply of tin in the time of Christ (Capt, p. 25). The importance of tin, of course, was its use as an alloying metal with the copper from Cyprus to make brass. Zinc, lead, gold, and silver were also mined in the same region of Britain.

These islands were still referred to much later by similar descriptions as in the above. Eusebius, Bishop of Caesarea (c. 320 A.D.), noted that "the apostles passed beyond the ocean to the isles called the Brittanic isles." These islands were mentioned as the "British Isles which are beyond the sea (the Mediterranean), and which lie in the ocean" by Chrysostom, Patriarch of Constantinople (c. 402 A.D.). Since Crete, Cyprus, Malta, and other nearby islands in the Mediterranean had familiar names a few centuries before the Christian era, Biblical references not using their proper names, but using instead "the isles" or "the ends of the earth," as Britain was thought to be, probably refer to the British Isles. This possibility opens deeper understandings of such passages as: "Be silent before me, YOU ISLANDS! Let the nations renew their strength!" (Isa 41:1 NIV) *(em add)*. "THE ISLANDS have seen it and fear; the ENDS OF THE EARTH tremble" (Isa 41:5 NIV) *(em add)*. "Sing to the Lord a new song, his praise from THE ENDS OF THE EARTH, you who go down to the sea, and all that is in it, YOU ISLANDS, and all who live in them" (ISA 42:10 NIV) *(em add)*. "Let them give glory to the Lord and proclaim his praise IN THE ISLANDS" (Isa 42:12 NIV) *(em add)*. "Surely THE ISLANDS (coastlands, NAS) look to me; in the lead are the ships of Tarshish, bringing your sons from afar, with their silver and gold" (Isa 60:9 NIV) *(em add)*. Tarshish was a close descendant of Noah. Some ancient maps have Tarshish, or Tartesus, as the name of southern Spain or Iberia. Iberia, itself, means "land of Hebrews." At least one map calls the British Isles "Tarshish." In the Bibles, Tarshish seems to indicate Israel's colonies in the islands to the west. Tarshish was also the Phoenician word for "smelter" or "furnace," suggesting the location of a source of metals for Solomon's kingdom. Solomon's navy, the ships of Tarshish, returned every three years from a joint voyage with the fleet of Hiram, King of Tyre (I Kings 10:22). Spain was a fairly routine voyage for the Phoenicians, and they also visited Britain. According to Pliny, "the whole of the Roman Empire was supplied with metals and tin from Britannia." Greece, too, "was supplied with tin and sundry metals from the same source" at least as early as 907 B.C. Solomon, therefore, had a readily available source for the tin and copper used in making the bronze (translated incorrectly as "brass" in AKJ) for his temple: copper from Cyprus, for which the island is named, and tin from Britain.

The Phoenicians had a covenant with their Most High God. The Covenant Phoenicians, the Barat, or Brit, Phoenicians, pictured a symbolic woman, Barat-ana, as ruling over the seas they traversed (Waddell). Barat-ana ruled the waves, as Britannia ruled the waves nearly three thousand years later.

Solomon's successor, Rehoboam, sent his agent Adoram to collect the exorbitant tribute the king demanded (see I Kings 12:18). The people stoned Adoram (see I Kings 12:16–19). A stone found near Gibraltar tells of a Phoenician named Adoram who was sent by Solomon to collect tribute from ancient Spain. Proof is lacking that this was the same Adoram, but it is apparent that Solomon and the other Israelite kings required tribute from even the most distant Hebrew settlements and that they knew where to find them. Eber, or Heber, means "colonizer," and the Hebrews bearing his name were aptly labeled.

There is no doubt, then, that the Islands and coastlands in the west surely contained some Israelites. "Keep silence before me, O islands . . . thou, Israel, art my servant, Jacob whom I have chosen, the seed of Abraham my friend" (Isa 41:1, 41:8). "Hear the word of the Lord, O ye nations, and declare it in the isles afar off" (Jer 31:10).

Israel, the incarnated fallen spirits whom the Lord chose as His special servants, were unable or unwilling to remain loyal to Him, or to remain united as a nation. Israel had troubles enough under

David. Under Solomon, they were heavily troubled with the burdensome taxes Solomon required for his lavish empire and the building of the great temple. The people drifted further into worshipping foreign gods, as did their king. When Solomon died, Rehoboam ascended to the throne. Rehoboam increased the tax burden and was even more oppressive than his father. God had said that the kingdom of Israel would be taken from Solomon because of his idolatry, and it came to pass under Rehoboam. One tribe, Judah, was to remain under Rehoboam so that the royal line promised to David would continue (see I Kings 11:11–13). The other tribes, now called Israel, chose their own king "and made him king over all Israel: there was none that followed the house of David, but the tribe of Judah only" (I Kings 12:20), although we see in the next verse that Benjamin, or a part of Benjamin, joined with Judah (verse 21).

The causes and outcome of the internal strife in Israel were similar to those between England and her American colonies, in which taxation without representation was a major issue leading to the separation of the United Colonies, with a president of their own choosing, from England, with its king by royal succession. The parallel continued when the armies of Rehoboam attempted to subdue Israel and prevent their independence. The war to restore the kingdom was stopped by Divine intervention. Thus said the Lord through Shemaiah the prophet, "you must not go up and fight against your relatives the sons of Israel . . . for this thing has come from Me" (I Kings 12:24 NAS).

At that point the pledges of God to Jacob (Israel) divided between two nations. The line of royalty remained in Judah with the house of David. The birthright went away from Jerusalem with the nation of Israel under the rule of an Ephraimite named Jeroboam. It is these two distinct branches of the original twelve-tribed Israel which we now follow.

Israel, the northern kingdom, proved unfaithful to her husband, the Lord. Her adultery consisted in forsaking the One Who had brought her as a young bride out of Egypt and Who had kept His vows. "And they have played the harlot, departing from their god" (Hosea 4:12 NAS). This is not to overlook their sexual adultery, but to emphasize their infidelity to the God of their youth. After nearly three hundred years of patience, Israel's Husband reluctantly set them free from their marriage. "How can I give you up, O Ephraim? How can I surrender you, O Israel?" (Hosea 11:8 NAS). He sent Israel away because of her adultery, "For she is not my wife, and I am not her husband" (Hosea 2:2 NAS). God divorced Israel (see Jer 3:8). The sufferings Israel would endure were intended to result, in time, in her longing to return to her Husband. Israel would "wail like a virgin [young woman] girded with sackcloth for the bridegroom of her youth" (Joel 1:8 NAS) *(em add)*. At such time as Israel came to her senses, the Lord would take her back. "You will call Me Ishi (my Man, or Husband in this context) and will no longer call Me Baali (my Master)" (Hosea 2:16 NAS) *(em add)*. "And I will betroth you to Me forever . . . And I will betroth you to Me in faithfulness. Then you will know the Lord" (Hosea 2:19–20 NAS). The bride of Christ had much suffering and wandering to experience before she could be reconciled, but the time would come when, "as the bridegroom rejoices over the bride, so your God will rejoice over you" (Isa 62:5 NAS). The wedding vows were to be someday reenacted: "And I will say to those who were not My people, 'You are My people!' And they will say, 'Thou art my God!' " (Hosea 2:23 NAS).

"They will not return to the land of Egypt; but Assyria—he will be their king, because they refused to return to Me" (Hosea 11:5 NAS). The Assyrians swept down from the north onto their prey, Israel. Over a period of some fifty years, the Assyrians conquered virtually all of Israel except part of Judah in Jerusalem. Israel was captured and deported, where they would "abide many days without a king" (Hosea 3:4). "The Lord was very angry with Israel and removed them from his presence. Only the tribe of Judah was left." (II Kings 17:18 *et seq.* NIV). Archaeological findings give the Assyrian account of their conquest of Israel. One Assyrian obelisk reads, "Sargon, king of Assyria, came up against the city of Samaria [the capitol of the northern kingdom, Israel] and against the tribes of Beth-Kymri and carried away into captivity 27,250 families." Beth-Kymri in Assyrian means the "house of Omri," the Israelite king mentioned in the Old Testament (see I Kings 16:16–30). Sennacherib's own record of his campaign against the Israelites, translated from the Taylor prism (c. 700 B.C.), reads,

As for Hezekiah, who did not submit to my yoke, 46 of his strong walled cities, as well as the small cities in their neighborhood . . . by escalade and by bringing up seige engines, by attacking and storming on foot, by mines, tunnels, and breaches, I took 200,150 people, great and small, male and female, horses, mules, asses, camels, cattle, and sheep without number, I brought away from them and counted as spoil. Himself, like a caged bird, I shut up in Jerusalem his royal city (Luckenbill).

The Assyrians led the captive Israelites away, repopulating the land of Samaria with people from various non-Israelite origins. (The descendants of these aliens were still despised by the Jews as the Samaritans of Jesus' time). Assyrian tablets from that time say that the Israelites escaped in vast numbers, with the Assyrian army in pursuit. It obviously made no sense for the Israelites, lacking adequate weapons and supplies, to attempt to return to their homeland. If they did, they would have to drive out the foreigners from the cities of Samaria while defending their rear from the pursuing Assyrian armies. The only practical choice was to flee to the north, and then west, to the desolate heritages prophesied for them. Assyrian army outpost records from that time report that the army pursued Israel into the upper Euphrates district, where large numbers of them escaped to the shores of the Black Sea.

Another, possibly a lesser, reason for the path Israel took was that they had fellow Hebrews in numerous settlements along the Mediterranean and in Britain. Rome, founded by Latinus, a man with Hebrew blood, was then only fifty years old, while London was some four hundred years old. Ptolemy, in writing of the inhabitants of the western isles of Britian, says that, "They were peopled by descendants of the Hebrew race, who were skilled in smelting operations and excelled in working metals." On his map of the world, Ptolemy has Britain named Javan, who was a son of Japheth and a grandson of Noah. Perhaps, then, there was not only the driving force of the Assyrians behind them, but also the prospects of the new lands before them, which propelled Israel through Europe.

Israel's friends and enemies had various names for Israel, in the same way that a nation today has different names in different languages. The Phoenicians referred to their Israelite relatives as the Beth-Sak, meaning "house of Isaac," fulfilling the prophecy that they would carry the name of Isaac (Gen 21:12). They are called house of Isaac by Amos (Amos 7:16). By other people the Hebrews were called other names, among them Habiru, H'Abiri, and Abiri. The name "house of Isaac" could be found as Saga, Sakai, or Saka, meaning "sons of Sac [Isaac]." These, and other names, are traceable northward, and westward across Europe and into the British Isles. Further, there are plentiful tombstones and other physical evidence along the way, showing the migrations of these people who sprang onto the European continent from the Caucasus Mountain area between the Black Sea and the Caspian Sea. These Caucasians gradually evolved into the powerful conquering tribes of early Europe. Eventually, the house of Omri became the Khumri, then the Gimira and Iskuza (house of Isaac). The meanderings of the different splinter groups from dispersed Israel are detailed in several current books (Capt, and others).

Hundreds of graves found in Crimea have Hebrew-Phoenician inscriptions. As an example, a man named Buki died at about the time of the birth of Christ. His epitaph reads: "This is the grave of Buki son of Itchak [Isaac], the priest, may his rest be in Eden at the time of the salvation of Israel. He died in the year 702 of our exile." Another tombstone dated nearly a thousand years after that of Buki reads,

> To one of the faithful in Israel, Abraham-Ben-man-Sinchal of Kertch, in the year of exile 1682 [c. 961 A.D.], when the envoys of the prince of Rosh Meschech came from Kiev to our Master Chefar Prince David Halet, and Haba and Gozen, to which place Tiglath-Pileser [Sargon of Assyria] had exiled the sons of Reuben and Gad and held the tribe of Manasseh, and from which they have been scattered through the entire East, even as far as China.

The conclusion is that the Cimry, Celts, Saxons, Gauls, Galatians, and certain other tribes which settled in Europe and Britain, are descendants of the Israelite tribes, with admixtures of unknown amounts of other ethnic groups. This conclusion satisfies Biblical prophecies concerning Israel, as well as agreeing with a very large body of archaeological evidence. It is not without debate, however.

Many of the exiles finally arrived at the islands of Britain, most of them by then having lost their original language, traditions, and identity as Israelite descendants. In Britain they encountered many people of their same ancestry, who had also largely lost their origins. The encounters were therefore usually far from peaceful. Some of the exiles traveled slowly, their distant offspring reaching their ultimate destinations many centuries later. Others moved more quickly, there being a Biblical reference to the ten tribes going northwest from Assyria to a distant uninhabited land in only a year and a half (see II Esdras 13:39–46 NEB). Still other Israelites did not wait for the Assyrians to capture them. The tribe of Dan, among the Phoenicians, had access to large numbers of seaworthy boats, and a whole generation of time in which to build more, as the Assyrians crept down from the north.

The Danites therefore had the means and the skills to flee aboard ships from the Assyrian invaders. Perhaps some of them escaped to their distant relatives and Hebrew outposts in Greece and Italy. Probably some of them went to Iberia ("Hebrew land"), which became Hispania, and later on, Spain. Most likely, the bulk of the Danites who escaped sailed to the British Isles, where the arch Druid wore a breastplate of judgment set with twelve stones (as in Ex 28:15–21), where stone circles were used in religious rites (as in Josh 4:19–21), and where altars were constructed with unhewn stones (as in Ex 20:25). Although Paganism had somewhat corrupted the Druidic faith, they still worshipped one God who had left them a set of commandments essentially the same as the Ten Commandments. And they awaited a great healer, a savior of the world, whom they called Hesu, or Yesu (Capt, *Druidism;* Roberts). The similarities between early British Druidism and the religion of Moses are apparent, suggesting that the Druidic beliefs in fact came to Britain by way of Egypt, as some authors have speculated.

Ireland, as well as Britain, was well-known among the Israelites of the time. Ireland was formerly known as Hibernia, still another variant of "Hebrew land." Irish annals record that about the year 700 B.C., when the Assyrians were devouring Israel, thousands of a powerful people arrived in ships and established themselves in Ireland. Those people were called the "Tuatha de Danaans," translated as the "Tribe of Dan." Even the most distant isles, therefore, looked for the Messiah of Israel: "the isles shall wait for his law" (Isa 42:4). But the time was not yet right.

Israel had been dispersed and scattered through the world to cure her of her apostasy. Judah remained behind, but did not remain faithful. God sent the same kind of warnings to Judah that He had sent to Israel. God had intended to spare Judah even though Israel had proved unreliable (Hosea 1:6). Yet even after Israel, "her treacherous sister Judah did not fear; but she went and was a harlot also," worshipping idols made of stone and wood (Jer 3:8–9 NAS). God labeled Judah this way: "You adulteress wife, who takes strangers instead of her husband" (Ezek 16:32 NAS). "Though you, Israel, play the harlot, Do not let Judah become guilty" (Hosea 4:15 NAS). Adultery remains the valid ground for divorce in the New Testament. The Lord divorced Judah and sent her into exile in Babylon.

There is an interesting parallel between the exile of all of the Israelites from the promised land due to their following other gods, and the exile of the spirits from Heaven, brought about by their following Lucifer instead of Christ. In both cases, the first cause was the spirits' change of allegiance from Christ to another spirit leader. In both cases, deterioration of attitudes and behavior followed as a consequence. In both cases God patiently and lovingly counseled the apostate spirits, warned them of the results of their choice, and urged them to return to Him. The final outcome was due to the choice the spirits freely made: to go their own way. In both cases, the Father sent His prodigal children away, requiring them to learn from the results of their errors. In one case, the exile was from Palestine into Assyrian and Babylonian hands. In the other case, it was from Heaven into the hands of Satan in the lower dimensions. Fortunately, God has a plan in action which will heal the breach in both situations.

Unfaithful Judah showed herself more guilty in the sight of God than adulterous Israel (see Jer 3:6–11). Judah's captivity in Babylon is familiar to every reader and little need be said here. We note, however, that many of the poor of the land were left in Judea, while the elite, the craftsmen, and the artisans were taken to Babylon (see II Kings 24:14). In addition to being slaves, some of the captives were used as entertainers (see Psa 137). A significant

point here is that during the Babylonian captivity the first manuscripts of the Old Testament were set down (Barthel, p. 229), so
that the Judahites no longer had to rely on oral tradition to
preserve and transmit the Scriptures. Another important factor is
that Cyrus, when he later overcame Babylon, issued an order of
religious tolerance. The Jews were then able to worship their own
God without fear of persecution while, at the same time, their
Scriptures were preserved for posterity in written form.

Cyrus aided the Judahites by sending them to rebuild the temple
at his expense (see Ezra 6:4). However, there was a certain amount
of difficulty in persuading the people to return to Jerusalem (see
Neh 11:1–2). Josephus tells us that "only the lowest of the low, the
poor in health, in knowledge, and in ancestry, the very outcasts,
the refuse of the nation," returned to Judea. He adds that "Jew" is
derived from "Yehudim," meaning "the remnant of Judah."
Scholars estimate that only one in ten of the men of Judah returned
from Babylonia. Most of them were, by then, second or third
generation Babylonians, in a sense, and no longer able to speak
their former Hebrew language. By the end of the Babylonian
captivity, they were speaking Aramaic. The generation that returned had forgotten their fathers' language to the extent that Ezra
had to translate the books of Moses for them. Judah, then, like
Israel before her, did not return from exile, except for a very few
stragglers. Therefore, almost all of Israel and all of Judah had been
removed from their homelands and dispersed throughout the nations.

In that period of history, the world experienced a great influx of
powerful spiritual leadership from Buddah in India, and from
Confucius and Lao-Tze in China, these leaders being preceded by
Zoroaster in Persia. The Jews had Ezekiel, Daniel, and Jeremiah.

Jeremiah was the grandfather of King Zedekiah of Judah (see II
Kings 24:18). Jeremiah prophesied not only to Judah, but at one
time was sent to the north to the exiles of Israel (see Jer 3:11–12), to
whom also a great portion of the words through Ezekiel and
Daniel were addressed. Jeremiah was one of those high spirits
whose incarnation was to help prepare the way for the coming of
the Saviour. "Before I formed you in the womb I knew you, and
before you were born I consecrated you; I have appointed you a

prophet to the nations" (Jer 1:5 NAS). In that respect, Jeremiah is reminiscent of Isaiah, whom the Lord formed "in the womb to be his servant to bring Jacob back to him and gather Israel to himself" (Isa 49:5 NIV).

Jeremiah encountered other prophets who prophesied in the name of the Lord, but who were under the influence of lower spirits (see Jer 28). Jeremiah himself could not always tell whether the word he received was from the Lord (see Jer 32:6–8). (At a much later date, Paul had a similar problem with discernment, as he ends his remarks to the Corinthians regarding women with the words, "and I THINK that I also have the Spirit of God" (I Cor 7:40 NAS) *(em add).*) Jeremiah was sent as a prophet to the nations, not only to Judah. He apparently traveled most of the known world to carry God's message to His people, judging from the extensive list of countries he gives (see Jer 25:18–26). According to that list, God intended for Jeremiah to address even the "isles which are beyond the sea" (Jer 25:22). A conspicuous fact is that the prophet Jeremiah was familiar with the nations where the exiled Israelites and early Hebrews were to be found. He was furthermore Divinely commissioned to preach to those nations. Nebuchadnezzar, King of Babylon, in fact freed Jeremiah, supplied him with money to go to Mizpah, and gave him free reign to travel anywhere.

Jeremiah's mission was more specific than to be a prophet to the nations: "See, I have appointed you this day over the nations and over the kingdoms, to pluck up and to break down, to destroy and to overthrow, to build and to plant" (Jer 1:10 NAS). What was it that Jeremiah was to pluck up and to plant? "Thus says the Lord, 'Behold, what I have built I am about to tear down, and what I have planted I am about to uproot, that is, the whole land" (Jer 45:4 NAS). The whole nation was being uprooted, to be replanted elsewhere. God was moving His nation, and Jeremiah had been appointed as His agent. The kingdom of Judah and the royal lineage promised to David forever was being transplanted. The human instrument which God would use was Jeremiah.

Let us recall, at this point, that when David was king over Israel, the Lord promised that the throne of David would never end, that someone from his royal bloodline would always sit upon the throne. This promise was a binding promise from God, an unconditional covenant not dependent upon the behavior of the Israelites or anyone else. "Thus saith the Lord: IF ye can break my covenant of the day, and my covenant of the night, and that there should not be day and night in their season, THEN may also my covenant be broken with David my servant, that he should not have a son to reign upon his throne" (Jer 33:20–21) *(em add)*. This promise is repeated in other verses, such as when God made with David "an EVERLASTING COVENANT, ordered in all things, and sure" (II Sam 23:1–5) *(em add)*. And in speaking to David through Nathan the prophet, He says: "thine house and thy kingdom shall be established FOR EVER before thee: thy throne shall be established FOR EVER" (see II Sam 7:1–17) *(em add)*. Again it was said, "Thus saith the Lord; IF my covenant be not with day and night, and if I have not appointed the ordinances of heaven and earth; THEN will I cast away the seed of Jacob, and David my servant, so that I will not take ANY OF HIS SEED to be rulers over the seed of Abraham, Isaac, and Jacob" (Jer 33:25–26) *(em add)*. Thus it was stressed repeatedly that this covenant would surely be kept, that the kingly line descending from David would always have an heir upon a throne. "The sceptre shall not depart from Judah" (Gen 49:10).

At the same time, the Lord said of the son of Jehoiakim, King of Judah, "no man of his seed shall prosper, sitting upon the throne of David, and ruling any more in Judah" (Jer 22:30), that is, in the geographical area of Judea. The resolution to this apparent paradox lies in the realization that the throne could be moved from the land of Judea to other descendants of Judah living in other places.

The Chaldeans (Babylonians) took Judah in stages between about 604 B.C. and 585 B.C. Zedekiah, then king of Judah, was captured. Nebuchadnezzar had all of Zedekiah's sons slain before their father's eyes. Zedekiah was then blinded and taken to Babylon where he died in prison (see Jer 52:10–11). It appeared that the royal bloodline of King David ended there, and that the unconditional and binding promises of God to David were broken. Various scholars have made efforts to reconcile the promises with the facts, usually by "interpreting away" the promises, or by taking them in some "symbolic" sense. These efforts seem futile, however. Either the unbreakable covenant with David was broken, or the throne of David still exists today. Where in today's world is a royal line traceable all the way back to David? The answer is found in Jeremiah's mission.

After Babylon captured Judah, Jeremiah prophesied among the small remnant of conquered people left behind. He later left Jerusalem against his better judgment to flee with others into Egypt: "all the remnant of Judah . . . men, and women, and children, AND THE KING'S DAUGHTERS, . . . and JEREMIAH the prophet, and BARUCH . . . So they came into the land of Egypt." (Jer 43:5–7) *(em add).* Jeremiah took with him his trusted scribe, Baruch. The travelers went as far as Tahpanhes in Egypt, where the rest of the party once more sacrificed to idols in hopes of easing their persecution. They believed their calamities were due to their deserting the religion and the idols of their forefathers and kings. They resumed their sacrifices, after which God destroyed even this remnant of Judah (Jer 44:17–19). But Jeremiah, Baruch, and the daughters of King Zedekiah of Judah remained alive in Egypt. Here ends the Biblical record of the throne of David. The last link in David's royal line ends in Egypt with Zedekiah's daughters. The throne has certainly been uprooted. The next step is to replant it.

The line of David had been taken into Egypt in the form of Zedekiah's daughters. This is in complete agreement with the seventeenth chapter of Ezekiel, in which the transplanting is predicted symbolically and the symbolism explained. The passage states that a tender young twig (daughter) of the highest branch of the cedar (Zedekiah) is to be *transplanted and flourish* in some other place (Ezek 17:22). With Zedekiah, his sons, and all the noblemen of Judah slain, the lineage of David could only be perpetuated through a daughter. "If a man dies and has no son, then you shall transfer his inheritance to his daughter" (Num 27:8 NAS). Zedekiah did, indeed, have daughters (see Jer 41:10), who were certainly known to their great-grandfather, Jeremiah (see Jer 52:1). And he escorted them to Egypt, where the Biblical record of Jeremiah and the Davidic crown ends.

We next pick up the trail with early Irish history. Irish historians are familiar with the legend that around 580 B.C. a noted patriarch arrived at Ulster. The elderly, white-haired man was accompanied by a companion named Simon Brach (also spelled Breck, Berech, and Berach) and a young princess named Tea Tephi, or possibly Tamar Tephi. She was said to be the daughter of an eastern king. In Irish tradition this great prophet is known as the Ollam Fodhla (or Fola). Ollam denotes hidden knowledge in Hebrew, while Fola in Hebrew means "amazing, or wonderful," or in Celtic, "revealer." The name would apply to a Hebrew prophet who revealed wonderful knowledge to the people. Other ancient traditions indicate that the traveling group that arrived in Ulster included a son of the king of Ireland, who had been in Jerusalem at the time of the seige, and his wife and a young son. Perhaps this accounts for one of Zedekiah's other daughters.

According to Irish traditions, the Hebrew prophet found the Irish people worshiping serpents and a god named Bel, presumably the same as the Babylonian god of the same name, arguably the same as the Phoenician god, Baal. The prophet converted Eochaidh, the local king, and his court to the worship of Jehovah, and eradicated serpent and Bel worship from Ireland. The Ollam Fodhla established a "school of wisdom," known as the "Mur-Ollamain" at the royal residence, which later came to be called "Tara," a word derived from the Hebrew-Phoenician word "Torah," meaning "the Law." The Hebrew patriarch, Jeremiah, if such he was, is said to have brought certain revered objects with him: a harp or lyre, an ark, and a stone, the so-called "stone of destiny," or "Lia-Phail." The ark of the covenant disappeared from Solomon's temple at about the same time (Barthel, p. 125), never to be seen again. The Apocryphal book of Maccabees records that Jeremiah hid the ark in a cave on Mount Pisgah (II Maccabees 2:4–6 NEB).

For over two thousand years the national emblem of Ireland has been the harp of Tara with its guardian angel. Only the stone still survives. It is said to be the stone mounted in the base of the old coronation chair in Westminster Abbey since 1298 A.D. It is further claimed that all who have reigned in Ireland, Scotland, or England since Tamar Tephi have been crowned upon that stone. The stone is about 26 inches by 16 inches by 11 inches in size, a reddish sandstone like some found near the Dead Sea, but unlike any found in England. A plaque beside the stone describes it as "Jacob's pillar-stone" (see Gen 28:18), although there are other legends for it.

Tephi is reputedly buried beneath the sacred mound (bothel in Irish, bethel in Hebrew) at Tara, a mound such as those used for worship in David's day. Irish legend states that the "wonderful seer," Jeremiah, is buried near the ruins of Devenish Abbey on the Isle of Devenish in Lower Lough Erne, near Innishkillen, County Fermanagh.

If the secular history be true, then the Davidic line propagated through Tephi was passed to Scotland at a later time by the marriage of an Irish princess, and finally passed to England in the same way, thus fulfilling the prophecy, "I will overturn, overturn, overturn" the throne of David three times (see Ezek 21:27). (Some translations may not permit this interpretation.) The names, dates, and places of these events are all recorded and well known. Indeed a number of Scots trace their genelogies back to David, and even before the birth of Christ, Ireland had several kings named Solomon or David. In reference to the intermediate stay of the throne of Scotland, it is relevant that Herodotus stated that the nation of the Scots was a thousand years old when he wrote, which places its beginning at around 1500 B.C., when Israel was being held captive in Egypt.

The fate of Jeremiah and the line of David related here are consistent with both history and Scripture. They are, at the same time, indefinite in places and in need of positive proof. At any rate, there is no Biblical or secular record that Jeremiah ever returned to Judea or that he died in Egypt. Moreover, it was not intended that the whereabouts of Judah, Israel, and the throne of David should be known until "in the latter days ye shall consider it" (Jer 30:24). "In the last days you will clearly understand it" (Jer 23:20 NAS).

If the saga is essentially true as it stands, then Jeremiah did indeed accomplish the task for which he was born, to pluck up and replant Judah into certain islands where he would be sent (Jer 31:9–10). "I will establish his [David's] line forever" (Psa 89:29 NIV) *(em add)*. "I will set his hand [or, sceptre] also in the sea" (Psa 89:25) *(em add)*.

The return of the remnant of Judah from Babylon occurred

roughly five hundred years before the birth of Christ. Four hundred years before His birth, Brennus led British warriors in the sacking of Rome. Nations warred, and rose, and fell. Israel and most of Judah were dispersed and churned through the tumults that beset warring man. Exiled Israel and Judah, with few exceptions, lost their identity as Israel, but were known by different names. There were Jews, in the religious sense now, in Jerusalem who were remote descendants of those whom the Assyrians and Babylonians had taken away. Some other descendents from all the tribes had made their ways back to Samaria and had interbred to a great extent with the non-Israelites there. The Jews considered the Samaritans to be mongrels. The Samaritans were not racially pure, it is true, but neither were the Jews. In addition, the Samaritans differed from the Jews in religious matters, as they accepted only the first five books of the Old Testament and none of the others. The time was almost right for the face-to-face meeting with the Messiah. A fragment of Israel was in the Holy land. "And I shall bring you out from the peoples and gather you from the lands where you are scattered . . . and I shall bring you into the wilderness of the peoples, and there I shall enter into judgment with you face to face" (Ezek 20:34–35 NAS). Before His incarnation could occur, the Romans had to be moved into position in the spiritual war.

The Roman empire had swallowed most of the Mediterranean area and interconnected it with a system of roads. At the eastern end of their empire, the Romans had conquered Judea without undue difficulty, but found the conquered Jews difficult to control. At the western ends of the Earth, Rome had little success against the Britons. From Caesar's *De Bello Gallico* we learn that Britain was far from primitive. Julius Caesar commanded the Roman invasion fleet himself in August of 55 B.C., when they crossed the English Channel at Calais. His forces were met by the Briton Casibellanus with some four thousand chariots of war. Caesar commented that "the legionary soldiers were not a fit match for such an enemy," and that "the enemy's horse and war chariots . . . inspired terror into the cavalry." Caesar tried again the next spring with more than a thousand ships carrying his armies. They established a foothold, but were no match for the British warriors, who fearlessly charged at them with the ancient war cry, "Foro!" (Pharaoh). By September of that year, the Romans had withdrawn, leaving no outpost behind in Britain.

The valor of the British in battle was understood by the Romans in religious terms. The British were not afraid to die because they believed in the immortality of the soul. The Druid-Hebrew influence was the Briton's secret weapon. The British earned the grudging respect of the Romans, a respect based largely on their valor in battle. The Rome-Britain struggle was, among other things, a religious fight, with Rome trying to stamp out Druidism, which to them was a capital offense. Caesar wrote that "the Druids make the immortality of the soul the basis of all their teaching, holding it the principal incentive and reason for a virtuous life." The Druids in Britain were also awaiting a coming Messiah, a "Curer of all ills."

The forces for the cosmic struggle for the fallen spirits were by then in place for the most important battle of the spiritual war. The appropriate time was at hand for the advent of the Savior of Israel. All Judea was expecting the Christ to come at any time. The Old Testament tells us much, albeit sometimes in veiled terms, about the where, when, and how, of the mission the Messiah would accomplish. But it does not explain why His life will set the spirit captives of Satan free. How could Satan be forced to free those whom he had trapped by his deceits? Who could force him to do so?

> Who, indeed, could force Satan to waive his rights over those, at least, who longed to return contritely to God? It is true, God Himself could have done so, but from a sense of fairness He had conceded that right to Lucifer, and for the same reason He was now unwilling to withdraw it.
>
> Only a spirit willing to enter the realm of the Prince of Darkness and to expose itself to the rigors of his tyrannous rule would have the right to do battle with him. The same situation holds good in your international law, when a nation which is oppressed and harassed by its rulers, rises against its tormentors in an effort to shake off their yoke.
>
> But it must be a spirit which would not, by deserting God, become subject to Lucifer, and thus fall irretrievably into his clutches.
>
> It must be a celestial spirit which, after assuming human shape, would invade Satan's dominion in body only, for every incarnated

being is exposed to the influence of the Powers of Evil. Hence Evil has so great a hold over all earthly creatures, even over those which are not evilly minded. The most righteous of men daily experience the influence of Evil over them, and often stumble under its impulse.

Thus the undertaking would be a great act of daring on the part of the celestial spirit which would venture upon it. Born, as it was to be, in human form, it would necessarily, as a mortal, remember nothing of its previous existence in Heaven. It would therefore be ignorant of its own identity as well as of the mission for the performance of which it had been incarnated, and would be tempted by the Evil One to sin. Moreover, God would not give it any greater spritual aid then He gave to others, for this would have offended His sense of Justice. It would have to earn whatever special Divine aid might be needed for solving its task, by repelling all advances of evil, and hence would receive such assistance only in the measure in which it withstood such attacks. That is true of all men. On the other hand, as the measure of Divine aid increased, the assaults by the Powers of Evil would grow in violence . . .

By the same token, the celestial spirit that was to assume human form would not be exposed in childhood to the evil influences with which it was to be brought into contact at maturity. Only after it should have discovered its identity and the purpose to be served by its incarnation was Hell to be permitted to unleash its full strength. Then the life and death struggle was to begin, a war to be waged by that spirit as a mortal *defensively,* against the attempts on the part of Evil to induce it to abandon God. It must be a war ending in the bodily martyrdom of the incarnated celestial spirit, provided it remained steadfast unto death, since it is the recognized procedure of the Forces of Evil, when their light and intermediate artillery fails to reduce a fortress, to bring up their heaviest batteries in the shape of physical torture, and thus to compel surrender. For this purpose they never lack human instruments and helpers.

If, in the face of the greatest torments of mind and body which the spirit could suffer as a mortal at the hands of the Powers of Hell and their human agents, it remained faithful and true to the last breath, then indeed it would have earned the final measure of Divine aid and strength which can be granted to any spirit. Armed with this Divine power it could, after its earthly death, enter upon a *war of offense* against the Powers of Hell, which as a mortal it had been able to meet in defensive combat only. Its victory over Lucifer was then assured, since the warring hosts of Heaven would be at its disposal.

Then indeed there would be war like that which had raged in Heaven when Michael and his legions overthrew Lucifer with his satellites.

This time, however, the war was to be fought in Hell, which the celestial redeeming spirit would invade, in order to overcome Lucifer on his own ground . . . By the victory of the celestial spirit, Satan was to be forced to release the *penitent* spirits from his despotism, retaining the right, however, to employ every means of corruption, as before, in order to bring about another change of heart in them and to bind them to himself anew. But no longer might he keep them under his scepter *by force* as he had done in the past. He was to be compelled, as it were, to retire his frontier guards from the bridge to be built by the Redeemer, so that no spirit desiring to return to its homeland would be forcibly prevented from so doing. (from Greber, p. 294–296.)

REFERENCES CITED

Barthel, Manfred, *What The Bible Really Says*
Breasted, James, *Development of Religion and Thought in Ancient Egypt*
Capt, E. Raymond, *King Solomon's Temple*
Capt, E. Raymond, *Stonehenge and Druidism*
Capt, E. Raymond, *The Traditions of Glastonbury*
Greber, Johannes, *Communication with the Spirit World of God: Its Laws and Purpose*
Haberman, Frederick, *Destinies of Israel and Judah*
Langdon, Stephen H., *Semitic Mythology*
Luckenbill, D. D., *Ancient Records of Assyria and Babylon*
Mackenzie, D. A., *Ancient Man in Britain*
Rawlinson, George, *Story of Phoenicia*
Roberts, L. G. A., Druidism in Britain
Waddell, L. A., *The Phoenician Origin of Britons, Scots, and Anglo-Saxons*

◇

CHAPTER 11

The Messiah Comes

C HRIST'S work of redemption began immediately after the defection of the spirit hosts of Heaven. It was He, armed with the power of God, Who worked with the loyal Holy spirits to form the dimensions of existence, of which the physical universe is but one. These dimensions constitute the ladder of ascent by which the fallen spirits of the abyss could climb back to the heights of Heaven. The climb halted, however, at the physical dimension in which we find ourselves: the highest dimension of the hells. Further ascent was not possible beyond this frontier of Lucifer's sovereignty. After fallen spirits rose to the level of human existence on Earth, Christ led them and strove to turn their thoughts Godward. Opposing Him were the ruling powers of Hell, doing their utmost to maintain their dominion over all men. This conflict forms the main theme of the Old Testament.

In order to accomplish His ends, Christ strove, long before His incarnation, to win over at least a small fraction of mankind to the service of God. That fraction was Israel. The people of Israel were to be bearers of the faith and His witnesses to the world, for their own salvation and for the salvation of later generations. In these efforts, Christ employed the good spirit-world under His command, many of them incarnating as mortals whereby they might preach the truth and set examples of righteous living. Once the Holy nation, His chosen ones, had attained a certain degree of

growth, the fullness of time would have arrived for the Redeemer
to descend to Earth as a man to complete the next phase of the plan
of salvation.

In the spiritual warfare for the souls of man, the lower forces
made cunning use of every enticement in order to lure mankind
away from God and further bind them to Satan. Many of the
people, who were ensnared by Satan, sank so low in their evil-
mindedness that their influence on those drawn to God could no
longer be tolerated. If Israel, the firstborn of the true faith, were to
fall victim to Hell, a long time would have to elapse before another
nation fit to play Israel's role could arise. The idolatrous influences
of those bound to Satan had to be removed from the physical
plane.

> The command to exterminate these peoples had led many of you to
> look upon the God of the Old Testament as a cruel Deity and to
> maintain that the writers of those portions of the Scriptures were
> incapable of conceiving of a Christ-like Divinity, since otherwise they
> would never have attributed such cruelty to the will of God. In this
> they are mistaken. One and the same Christ preached the conception
> of God which you find in the New Testament, and commanded the
> destruction of the peoples which I have mentioned. In one case as in
> the other, Christ appears as the Savior. By consenting to the exter-
> mination of those peoples, He preserved them from sinking still
> further into idolatry and depravity, and indeed gave them the opportu-
> nity of working their way, in a new existence, out of the depths to
> which they had fallen. The underlying motive was the same as that for
> which, in earlier times, the human race was destroyed by the Deluge
> and for which the cities of Sodom and Gomorrha were laid waste
> (Greber, p. 309).

The time came at last when a great part of humanity showed
their desire for God. Their minds had been prepared by numerous
men and women, prophets of God, who for the most part are not
mentioned in the Scriptures. The evil forces also knew the prophecies, and had been busily at work centuries in advance in their
efforts to thwart Christ's upcoming mission of redemption.
Countless human souls stood ready and eager to cross the bridge
which the Rescuer would build across the great gulf which divided
His kingdom from that of Lucifer.

Which celestial spirit would incarnate and attempt this dangerous mission? The highest Spirit, the King over the spirit-world, undertook the task. It was against His rule that the spirit revolt had come about and that the gulf between the two kingdoms had been established. He was the One Who would risk Himself in endeavoring to bring the fallen spirits back. The plan was kept secret from the Powers of Darkness so that they might have the least possible chance of defeating it. Even the angels, God's Holy spirits, were not privy to all of the plan of salvation (see I Pet 1:12).

Had the forces of evil known the true purpose of the human birth of Jesus, had they known that His desperate struggle against the assaults of evil and His agonizing death were prerequisite to His victory as a Spirit over Lucifer, they would never have tempted Him, but would have done their utmost to prevent His death upon the cross. Only after Christ had died a redeemer's death would the time be ripe to reveal more of God's plan of salvation, for then its revelation could no longer do harm, but only good. The consequences of a victory by Christ, as a human, would be disastrous to Lucifer and his kingdom, for by it, he would lose his subjects one by one. In the end, he would be in the position of a captain whose entire forces have deserted to the enemy and who, when at last reduced to utter helplessness, has nothing left but to admit defeat, and surrender. For this reason, Lucifer, after having been abandoned by all, would ultimately recognize his impotence before the patient love of God and be forced to tender his submission. "The last enemy that will be abolished is death [i.e., Death, or Lucifer]" (I Cor 15:26 NAS) *(em add)*.

Then would be the day on which there would be no more separation from God. On that day, all limbs broken from the tree of life would be regrafted to it, misery and anguish would be no more, and all the tears shed in such numbers by His erring children on the long road of their wanderings would be dried. That was to be the day on which the kingdom of God would once again shine in the full glory which it had before the fall of the spirits, and on which all of his children who had returned home would resume the places which once had been theirs in the Father's house.

Such was the plan of salvation conceived by God after Lucifer and his angels had fallen, but it was revealed by Him only to His first-created Son and to a few of the Holy spirits of Heaven, one of which was to declare itself ready to undertake the dangerous mission of being born of a woman, and as a human being, vanquish the Prince of Darkness. All of the spirits knew what it meant to assume human shape. All spirits knew that, as humans, they would risk being overpowered themselves by the very foe they had set out to conquer, in which event the coveted salvation would not be accomplished. Nevertheless, the King of God's spirit-world volunteered.

Two major doctrines of most Christian churches must be clarified before we can understand the life and works of Christ: first, the Diety of Christ; second, the Trinity. A misunderstanding of either of these leads to grave distortions in our concept of Christ and prohibits our understanding of His life.

First let us consider the Diety of Christ. Who was Jesus? What did He profess to be? His testimony was that He was the Christ, the Son of the living God. This was confirmed by the words of God: "This is my beloved Son, in whom I am well pleased" (Matt 17:5). Upon Him the Father has conferred the government of Creation, and, foremost of all, the task of redemption. Everything was conferred upon Him by the Father. Christ is called God's "only begotten Son" (John 3:16) and the "first-born of all creation" (Col 1:15 NAS). He is therefore God's first creation. Christ is also called the *alpha* and *omega* (see Rev 22:13), these being the first and last letters of the Greek alphabet. Christ is therefore not only the first, but also the last, direct creation of God. All other things owe their existence to Christ: "all things were made by him" (John 1:3, 1:10). The Old Testament writers add to the confusion between the Father and the Son. The writers were, in most cases, unable to distinguish between the spirits who communicated with the prophets, whether the Father, the Son, of one of the Holy spirits in Their service.

Jesus was called, among other titles, "a Son of God." By the time of His incarnation, much of the force of this title had been lost. Abraham and Moses had been called sons of God, as had other prophets and Holy men. Moses had been referred to as a god (see Ex 4:16 NEB), as had many others (see I Cor 8:5). Even evil spirits had been called sons of God (see Job 1:6, 2:1). Roman Caesars had appropriated this same title, calling themselves variously, "lord," "son of God," "God," "Savior of the world," and "high priest." It is little wonder that when Jesus made similar claims He was not widely believed. The words had lost much of their impact.

Jesus also claimed to be a savior. When the believers referred to Him as their Savior, this title was already familiar. At least eight of the Roman emperors assumed the title "Savior of the World." This must have been confusing to early Christians. To the non-Christians, it made Jesus' claims the butt of ridicule.

The titles used to describe a Caesar are frequently echoed in the New Testament. The Roman address to Caesar, "My lord and my god," is echoed by the Christian manuscripts when they sometimes address Jesus as "My Lord and my God." They were not thereby identifying the Son with the Father, though these words unfortunately contribute to that idea. On the contrary, this expression was used by some early Christians to distinguish between their allegiance to Jesus and the Roman's allegiance to Caesar. The expression emphasized that they had chosen to pay homage to Jesus rather than Caesar. They were saying, in effect, that Caesar could be a Roman's lord and god, but so far as the Christians were concerned, the only such person was Christ. Such a sentiment was a capital offense, since the religion of emperor worship held that the emperor was himself God. Hence, those persons who refused to view Caesar as God were disbelievers. The Romans called them atheists. Early Christians were martyred by the thousands to the cry of "Away with the Atheists!"

Christ's contention concerning His person, concerning the source of His doctrine and the power which He possessed, was that He had received each and every thing from the Father (see John 8:26–27, 8:42, 12:49–50, 14:24). Furthermore, all predictions Christ made of the future had been learned from the messengers sent to Him by His Father. Christ never once said, "I am God." Is it reasonable to suppose that He never once revealed the truth, despite the fact that on numerous occasions He spoke of His special relationship with the Father? No, the conclusion that Christ was God Himself is manmade, being the result of much controversy and some violence among the Christians of the first few centuries of this era. It is because we have raised Christ to the rank of God that we find insurmountable difficulties in understanding His personality, His life, His sufferings, and His death. The Father alone, and none besides Him, is God. The Father can delegate power to any spirit through which He wishes to perform His works.

> That power which [God] conferred upon Christ, could have been conferred by the Father upon any created spirit other than His First-born Son, and the great miracles worked by Christ could have been performed by any other man had God given him the necessary power. Christ Himself says frankly that the things He had done could be done by any who believed in Him. 'He who believes in me, shall have the power to do the same deeds that I do, and even greater deeds' (John 14:12). Belief in Christ is belief in God; not, however, because Christ Himself is God, but because He is the promulgator of God's teaching. 'The doctrine that I have taught is not my own; it was my Father, who sent me, that directed me what I should teach and in which words I should present my doctrine' (John 12:49) (Greber, p. 333).

That being the case, "He who believes in Me does not believe in Me, but in Him who sent Me" (John 12:44 NAS).

> Paul's salutation always runs: "Grace to you and peace from God our Father and the Lord Jesus Christ." He never says "God the Son." If therefore there is any part of your present Bible which can be construed into something else than the truth that only the Father is God, then the fault lies either in the translation, or in a falsification of the Greek text from which that translation was made, and in some cases in a combination of both. Of this last you will find an instance in Paul's letter to the Philippians (Phil 2:5–6) in the passage which reads according to your version: "Have this in mind in you, which was also in Christ Jesus: who, existing in the form of God, counted not the being on an equality with God a thing to be grasped, but emptied himself, taking the form of a servant." The unaltered text read: "Have this in mind in you, which was also in Christ Jesus; who, although in form like unto a God, counted it not a thing to be grasped to humble himself before God, but emptied himself, taking the form of a bond servant" (Greber, p. 367).
>
> Never does He weary of repeating explicitly that He can do nothing by His own power, that His words are not His own, that His miracles owe nothing to Him. It is the Father Who has sent Him; from Whom He has derived His teachings; from Whom He has received the power

to heal the sick and to raise the dead. Whatever He does is as the Father wills, and at the hour appointed by the Father (Greber, p. 331).

If Christ were Himself God, where would be the need for Him to pray to God? Should He pray to Himself, then? He would have no need of further aid or enlightenment. Yet the incarnate Christ did not know everything. There were things which God withheld, even from Christ, and which He reserved to Himself. Recall Christ's answer to the mother of the son of Zebedee: "but to sit on my right hand, and on my left, is not mine to give, but it shall be given to them for whom it is prepared of my Father" (Matt 20:23). Again, the Son did not know the day of judgment, the knowledge of which is the Father's alone. "But of that day and hour knoweth no man, no, not the angels of heaven, but my Father only" (Matt 24:36). Nor was Christ allowed by God to evade the agony of death upon the cross. Hence, His prayer in the garden of Gethsemane that the cup be permitted to pass, was not granted. As these examples show, Christ was therefore neither omnipotent nor omniscient. Only God has those attributes.

Christ's miracles are often regarded as being evidences of His Divine nature. This conclusion is illogical. Every miracle performed through Christ had been performed in the same or in a similar manner by other mortals who were envoys of God. We misunderstand God's purpose in these attesting signs. God establishes His human instruments as such by their performance of the unusual, so that humanity will recognize them as Divinely appointed. Accordingly, the miracles done through Christ were the testimony of God that Jesus was His envoy. Each miracle was familiar to the Jews as having been done by one of their prophets of earlier times. By the power of God, through His spirit agents, Jesus walked on water and Moses parted the waters. Jesus changed water into wine; Moses turned it into blood. Jesus calmed the storm; Moses called it up, the strong East wind which parted the sea. Elijah raised a widow's son from death and Jesus did the same. Elisha healed the leper. So, too, did Jesus. Food was marvelously produced at Elijah's request; Jesus fed the thousands. If we ascribe Godhood to Jesus due to His miracles, then are we not constrained by the same reasoning to view Moses, Elijah, and Elisha as likewise Divine? But it is not so. The miracles of Christ were done by "the finger of God" (Luke 11:20), the same power the Egyptians recognized as "the finger of God" when exercised by Moses (Ex 8:19).

The Son is sometimes thought to be the Father due to Jesus' statement, "I and my Father are one" (John 10:30). The statement simply means that there is a perfect unity of love and will between the Father and the Son. That same oneness is promised to all who believe, and who seek God. Christ prays for that same unity on behalf of the Apostles and all who believe in Him, "that all of them may be one, Father, just as you are in me and I am in you; . . . that they may be one as we are one . . . brought to complete unity" (from John 17:21–23 NIV). In the same vein, Christ's statements: "from now on you know Him, and have seen Him [God]" (John 14:7 NAS) *(em add),* and "he who has seen Me has seen the Father" (John 14:9 NAS), are often taken as testimony that Jesus was God, despite Christ's clarification immediately following those statements (see John 14:10–21). If Jesus' audience were, in fact, looking at the Father, this would constitute a contradiction to the words, "Not that any man has seen the Father, except the One who is from God" (John 6:46 NAS). The statements Jesus made here about God simply correspond to the modern figure of speech, "like Father, like Son."

Christ taught of one God, the Creator of Heaven and Earth. Only the Father is God. None other is His equal, neither the Son, nor what we call "the" Holy Spirit. After His resurrection, Christ said: "I ascend to My Father and your Father, and My God and your God" (John 20:17 NAS). "My Father, which gave them me, is greater than all" (John 10:29). According to those words, the Father is above all. If this is true, there is nothing equal to Him, and He is greater than the Son, a truth which Christ confirms with the words, "my Father is greater than I" (John 14:28). Furthermore, Paul calls the Father the "God of Jesus Christ" and "the God of our Lord Jesus Christ." These statements totally contradict the usual translations of the first verse of John's gospel. The apparent contradiction is removed upon accurate translation, as in: "In the beginning was the Word, and the Word was with God; and the Word was a god" (John 1:1 GNT).

The entire Bible, both Old and New Testaments, recognizes only one God in one person. The Father is God, and He only. Not one of His Sons, neither the firstborn nor any of the others, is God.

Christ is not, therefore, God Himself, but the Son, God's Highest created being. During Christ's incarnation as Jesus of Nazareth, He was as human as the rest of us, although, being the only pure and flawless Spirit ever incarnated, He naturally carried the highest spiritual gifts man might carry. Nevertheless, He had no other advantages over other men. It is precisely this that constitutes Christ's wonderful merit, that, although He was the Son of God, He was compelled to battle with human frailties and shortcomings which He shared with other men, and in spite of which He held out against the infernal powers. He was called upon to sustain their most savage attacks, directed against Him as a vulnerable antagonist who, terrified at the threat of defeat, cried out to God in prayer. He therefore knows from experience how helpless mortals feel. "For in him we have, not a high priest who has no sympathy with our weaknesses, but one whose experience in the temptations that beset him was similar to ours in every respect. Only he did not commit the sin of apostasy" (Hebrews 4:15 GNT).

With the identity of Christ clearly in mind, let us turn to the doctrine of the Holy Trinity. The Christian concept of the Holy Trinity states that the Father, Son, and Holy Spirit are coequal and coeternal, different creeds supplying their own additions and variations to these two attributes. The Trinity is said to be an "unfathomable mystery of the faith," and so it is. The most difficult thing to fathom is how the idea can be believed at all, defying as it does both Scripture and rationality. If it is possible for Christians to believe that Jesus had both human and Divine natures at the same time, if it is possible to believe the He was both the Son and the Father at that same moment, and if we can believe He was two-in-one, then it is only a little more difficult to believe God is three-in-one, both ideas being equally impossible.

The Father, the Son, and the Holy Spirit form the Trinity. The Father, only, is the one God. The first Commandment is monotheism (see Ex 20:3, Deut 6:4), one God, the God endorsed by Christ (see Mark 12:29). The "Holy Spirit," as we have seen in earlier chapters, is a term standing for any of the Holy spirit agents, the spirits of God (see I John 4:1–2). The three are by no means equal. The usual listing gives them in descending order of supremacy. They are not coequal. Instead, the three agencies are bound by bonds of love, of will, of unity of purpose, and hence have the oneness spoken of by Christ. All three are eternal, but not in precisely the same sense. The Father is eternal: without beginning and without end. The Son and all of His spirits are also eternal, for, although each of them had a beginning, each will exist forever. There are different ways of being eternal.

There is essentially no evidence in the Scriptures to back up any other concept of the Trinity. The word "Trinity" is nowhere to be found in the Scriptures. The Trinity is projected into the Old Testament by inventive minds who find the plural *Elohim,* "Gods," to be a reference to the Trinity. The New Testament is equally empty of corroboration, one of the few workable verses being I John 5:8. As is well-known, this passage is spurious and does not occur in any of the early manuscripts. It is, however, a useful, albeit vague, passage which can be interpreted as supporting the Trinity concept. It has been retained for that purpose, having been officially accorded the status of Holy Writ less than a century ago. The Father, Son, and Holy spirits are therefore distinct agencies, all with minds of their own, but joined by allegiance to the Father. Their distinctness is apparent in the words of Jesus when He says, "And I will ask the Father [not Myself], and He will give you another Helper, that He [by His agents] may be with you forever; that is the Spirit of truth" (John 14:16–17 NAS) *(em add).* The Helper, or Spirit of truth, is then identified as the "Holy Spirit" (John 14:26 NAS), or as the "holy spirit-world" (John 14:26 GNT).

With the Diety of Jesus and the Holy Trinity no longer serving as stumbling blocks, we are now in position to understand more of the life and ministry of Jesus.

A spirit of God, Gabriel in this case, told Mary of her favored status. If she were to consent to bear a child, He would be a very special child to God. She consented. Mary related to Joseph the things that had happened. It was a hard test to which he now found himself subjected. Was he to believe what his betrothed had told him? Like all other men, he was but human. Evil thoughts assailed him fiercely. The powers of Hell had but one end in view: to incite Joseph to doubt Mary and to cast her off, for, under the Jewish law, a virgin betrothed who was found to have relations with another man was stoned to death. There was nothing in the ways of distrust, jealousy, and bitterness, that the evil powers neglected to instill into Joseph. It seemed as though the burden was more than he could bear. At times he was minded to put his betrothed away "privily." Secretly it must be, for Joseph was unwilling to denounce Mary for an offense which called for the death penalty. On the other hand, he was not willing to make her his wife as long as any doubts persisted. Mary's sole defense was that God would reveal the truth to him in one way or another, for she, also, suffered terribly under his suspicions. Then an angel of the Lord appeared to Joseph, bidding him not to fear. This ended the conflict within him.

Had Joseph not passed his test of faith, Mary would have been put to death and Jesus would not have been born to her. Had Mary not passed her test of faith and consented to bear this Child, though unmarried at the time, Jesus could not have been born to her at all. In either case, Jesus would not have been born at all to Mary and Joseph. In the end, Joseph resolved to wed Mary, but she nevertheless left town for three months to stay with her relative Elizabeth, the expectant mother-to-be of John the Baptist (see Luke 1:39–56).

The human birth of Jesus was marked by angels, Holy spirits who announced Him as a Son of God. The angel told Mary, "A holy spirit will come upon you, and the power of one who is very high will overshadow you. Therefore the child, divinely con- secrated, will be called a 'son of God'" (Luke 1:35–36 GNT). Some Bibles have "a" son of God, others have "the." The transla- tion "the" greatly detracts from the heroism of Christ by implying that the secret of His identity was known. Neither Mary nor Joseph knew which son of God was being born to them, only that He was a son of God and was destined to be the true Messiah (see Luke 1:26–33). After Jesus had finished His earthly mission, it became widely known which Son of God He was: The Highest One.

It had been prophesied that Jesus would be born of a virgin. The *Good News Bible* uses "young woman" in Isaiah's Messianic prophecy (Isa 7:14) and adds the following footnote, "The Hebrew word here translated 'young woman' is not the particular term for 'virgin,' but refers to any young woman of marriageable age. The use of 'virgin' in Matt 1:23 reflects a Greek translation of the Old Testament, made some 500 years after Isaiah." Although this word could therefore mean "morally upright young woman," whether sexually a virgin or not, let us work with the usual meaning. The impact of His birth was greatly diminished by the evil inspiration that many men had been so born. A number of "holy men" and religious leaders during the prior two thousand years had claimed virgin births. Even certain of the Caesars made this claim. As a result, when the claim was made for Jesus, it carried little weight with the masses. Jesus was Mary's firstborn Son. She was thereafter as little a virgin as is any woman who has conceived and given birth to a child. She later bore four other sons and at least two daughters (see Matt 13:55–56), which in no way whatever detracts from Mary or Joseph, or from Jesus and His mission as the Messiah of Israel.

After the Babe had emerged from the years of infancy, His childhood was like that of other children. He learned to walk and to speak, and in time began to play like the rest. On occasion He misbehaved, as all children will. With the passing of His boyhood His understanding developed. Inasmuch as He was the incarnation of the highest of created spirits, He was also endowed with intelligence of a high order. Nevertheless, He had to learn things from the beginning, as does even the most brilliant child. As a child, He came to know of God exactly as we do, namely, by learning from His parents and teachers.

Jesus learned well as a child, encountering at age twelve the priests in the temple, "putting questions to them and replying to theirs out of His own wisdom" (Luke 2:41–52). He was in this respect a child prodigy, such as we find in other branches of knowledge. This Boy was a child marvel in His knowledge of God's ways of salvation. But He was human, like all other children, and the priests made no mention of having realized His true identity. Indeed, at that time even He did not yet know who He was, nor what mission He was destined to perform as a mortal. Neither did His family know, for when they found Him debating with the priests, they did not understand His comment of being "about my Father's business," which they could have understood had they known He was THE son of God (Luke 2:41–52).

As a boy, He was assailed by those temptations which come to all children and which are of a strength in keeping with a youth's powers of resistance, temptations which He overcame in measure as His knowledge of good and evil increased with His advancing years. With every victory over temptation the Boy received from God greater inner strength and knowledge of the spirit, but as His power of resistance grew, the forces of evil were permitted to increase the violence of their assaults upon Him. It is so with every mortal, and no exception was made in favor of the Boy Jesus, for it applies to all men alike that they gain in ability to resist sin with every victory over temptation.

As the Boy grew in years, the numerous errors of the Jewish faith professed by His parents caused Him many an inward struggle. These errors had been introduced in the course of time in the form of manmade doctrines and alleged amendments to the Divine commandments. When He reached the point of being able to read and understand the original texts of the Old Testament, He began to question the interpretations given to Him by His Jewish instructors, but whenever, in His youthful enthusiasm, He expressed these views to His elders, He was rebuked.

As Jesus passed from boyhood, through adolescence, to manhood, His wisdom increased, not only in the ways with all people as they mature, but chiefly by reason of the teaching which He received from the Divine spirits. Hand in hand with this went the growth of His goodness, or, as our Bibles express it, "Jesus increased in wisdom and stature, and in favour with God and man" (Luke 2:52). It was real progress and not merely a gradual disclosure of Himself. As a boy, He had to learn to choose good and refuse evil (see Isa 7:15–16). Even a spirit which enters, pure and flawless, into the garment of flesh, must fight its way step by step toward perfection against the influence of evil. To appreciate Christ, we must realize that He had "emptied Himself" to become man (Phil 2:7 NAS), and was at all times in danger of possibly failing and becoming one of Satan's victims. He, like us, had to endure to the end on faith in God, without fully knowing how God would accomplish His means. There were many difficult times, when, "In the days of his stay upon earth, Christ, amid loud lamentations and many tears sent up fervent prayers to Him, Who could save him from the spiritual death of apostasy, and was heard . . . although he was a Son of God he also had to learn through the sufferings that lay before him, and only after he had attained perfection did he become the author of salvation" (Heb 5:7–9) (Greber, p. 321).

Soon after He had reached the years of discretion, He began to exhibit great powers, enabling Him to communicate with the Holy spirits, to see the spirits, and to hear the words spoken by them. This gift with which the adolescent Jesus was endowed was nothing new. It had been possessed by prophets and many others before Him. In His case, however, the gift was developed to the highest degree attainable by man. Moreover, the manner in which the Divine revelations reached Christ were nothing unheard of or new. We have only to recall the ways in which God had communicated with His instruments in the past, how He communicated with Abraham, Isaac, Jacob, Moses, and Joshua, and with Zacharias, Mary, and Joseph. In precisely the same ways He now communicated with Jesus. God used the spirit-world to enter into communication with Jesus as with all His forerunners, and through it He revealed all things required of Christ for the fulfillment of the task before Him. Through communication with the Divine spirits He was taught everything He needed for the execution of His task, for in these matters He, as a mortal, was as ignorant as all the rest. He had no recollection of His previous state as the highest of God's spirits, because in every case the incarnation of a spirit into a material body shrouds all memory of the past.

Shortly before He was born upon Earth, Christ sent a herald to prepare for and proclaim His coming. This herald also was a celestial spirit, Elijah, the same spirit which had fought upon Earth on Christ's behalf when idolatry was at its worst. Now, as Christ's forerunner, he was born as a mortal for the second time and bore the title of John the Baptist. Even before John's birth the incarnation of God's Annointed One was foretold. The archangel

Gabriel had announced to Zacharias that he was to be the father of a son who would be the forerunner of the Messiah. The public appearance of John the Baptist was a pivotal event in the life of Jesus, who until then had not known that He was the promised Messiah. When John hailed Him before the people as the Lamb of God "that taketh away the sin of the world" He knew Himself, and was confirmed in His knowledge by the voice of God saying: "This is my beloved Son, in whom I am well pleased" (Matt 3:17). Later on, when John was in prison facing the prospect of death, he questioned whether Jesus was truly the Messiah, not to mention the Son of God. John sent two of his own disciples out to ask Jesus who He was (see Matt 11:2–3). This action would have been pointless if John already knew. John did not hear the Voice which spoke those words to Jesus.

Neither could the Apostles have heard the voice from Heaven at Jesus' baptism. They were not present. Jesus recruited them immediately afterwards. Nor did they know during His public ministry Who He was, for they often questioned among themselves Who He was. "What manner of man is this, that even the winds and the sea obey him!" (Matt 8:27). It was much later, shortly before His crucifixion, that the true identity of the Master as THE Son of God was revealed to the Apostles, and then only to Peter, James, and John. God spoke from a cloudlet, a partial materialization, and said approximately, "This is my beloved Son, in whom I am well pleased; hear ye him" (Matt 17:5; Luke 9:35; and II Pet 1:17 do not agree on the exact words). Yet even at that late time Jesus strictly enjoined them to "Tell the vision to no man, until the Son of man be risen again from the dead" (Matt 17:9). We would assume, then, that these three did not tell the other Apostles. About a week earlier (six days, Matt 17:1; eight days, Luke 9:18–36), Peter had received a revelation that Jesus was "God's Messiah," or "The Christ of God," or several other versions, depending on the translation (see Luke 9:19–20), which did not identify Jesus as the Son of God. Even this was occasioned because the crowds were speculating as to which prophet had been reincarnated as the man Jesus (see Luke 9:7–8). The crowds were likewise ignorant of His identity (e.g., Matt 13:53–57; Mark 6:1–5). On a still earlier occasion, Peter had attempted to walk on water with Jesus, the episode leading to the exclamation, "Truly, you are a son of God!" (Matt 14:33 GNT). The "a" later turned into "the" as manuscripts were written and rewritten.

Throughout most of His ministry, Jesus' true identity seems to have been known only to Himself, the exceptions being the evil spirits, whom He continually commanded to keep quiet about it (see Matt 8:29; Mark 1:24–25, 1:34, 3:11–12; and others). Hence, apparently nobody else on Earth knew who He was. Only Jesus was told at first, and His faith in the voice He heard was soon put to the test: would He believe it, or would He not? If He rejects it, then the plan of salvation fails to be carried out for lack of a champion to do it. The moment had now arrived for the spirit of God to reveal to Christ His mission in life.

> He was told that He was the highest of created spirits, God's First-born; that it was His mission to proclaim the Divine truth; that He must stand firm against the attacks of Satan who would do battle against Him to the utmost and bring about His death upon the Cross, as the Prophets had foretold. But only after His earthly body had died upon the Cross and His Spirit had departed from it, did Christ learn wherein the final victory over Satan lay. Hell recognized in Christ the Son and Emissary of God, Who was to lead humanity Godward by His teaching and Who was to be ready to die for the truth, but of the true connection between Christ's Crucifixion and a victory over Hell, not even Satan was aware. Had he been so, he would neither have tempted Christ, nor brought about His death. As it was, he sought only to render Christ, in Whom he saw only a herald of the truth, harmless, as speedily as possible. Should he be unable to induce Christ to forsake God, he hoped to discredit His teachings by preparing for Him a malefactor's death as the surest way of attaining that end. In this he reckoned upon the fact that men would naturally expect that a Son of God, such as Christ proclaimed Himself to be, would be endowed with Divine power sufficient to prevent so ignominious an end at the hands of His enemies. If He failed to prevent this, His teachings would be condemned. Such was the way in which Satan reasoned.
>
> Christ now knew Who He was, as well as the nature of his task, but before beginning with the execution of the same His powers of resist-ance must be tested, as had been those of all men who had previously served God as His instruments. He must prove Himself equal to His momentous, far-reaching Mission. It was to this end that the Spirit led Him into the wilderness (Greber, pp. 323–324).

There He was called upon to face a terrific onset by the powers of Hell. No helper stood beside Him. No word of human consolation from His mother, His brothers or sisters, or His friends, could reach Him, at the very time when He yearned for the sympathy and support of a friendly human heart. All this was denied Him in the wilderness. Instead, He heard the howling of wild beasts, and His clairvoyant eyes saw shapes from Hell before Him, coming and going without cease. He could hear them enticing, promising, threatening. Every form of appeal to which men are susceptible was employed against the Son of Man, for Satan has his specialists in every field of evil. Among them were spirits of despondency and timidity, and spirits of doubt, seeking to shake His belief in Himself as the Son of God, and in His Divinely assigned mission, and to drive Him to despair of Himself. It is true that, "God cannot be tempted" (Jas 1:13), but this was Jesus, the Son of God, and He was being tested severely. Could any man be expected to believe a Voice which no one else heard? Could a carpenter's son from Nazareth believe He was the Messiah of Israel? Easier, by far, for Him to dismiss the Voice as a hallucination. If He, in the body as a poor human, could be led to reject the revelation He had just received, then Satan would thwart the mission of salvation then and there. It would fail for lack of a human instrument.

Again, there appeared spirits of hatred, intent upon embittering Him against a God who would drive Him forth into the desert to suffer. There also came the spirits of a sinful life of pleasure, drawing the most enticing pictures of human ease and enjoyment in contrast to the dreary waste about Him. The parts which these various spirits had to play were skillfully assigned. The ablest of them were the spirits of doubt which appeared upon the scene again and again. How, argued they, could any God send His Son into a desert to suffer hunger and unspeakable torture of the soul? After all, was not everything that He had heard from the allegedly good spirits, was not the utterance of the Baptist, was not the voice of God speaking to Him by the Jordan, merely a part of a great delusion? Was not His Sonship of God a great hallucination, to which He had fallen a victim? This was the point upon which Hell centered its main attack, seeking to destroy within this Son of Man His conviction that He was the Son of God (Greber, pp. 324–325).

For forty days and forty nights this remorseless persecution continued against a victim who stood helpless and defenseless, trembling in every limb from emotion and from physical exhaustion, brought on by hunger and sleeplessness. The desert offered no nourishment. Christ fasted, indeed, not voluntarily, but because there was no food. At that time Jesus, the man from Nazareth, had no powers to produce food.

Nevertheless, all the specialists of Hell labored in vain to overcome this fever-racked Jesus, in spite of the fact that with fatigue, hunger, and thirst, He was at last unable to stand. Again and again, He cried out amidst tears for God's help in order that He not succumb to the mortal sin of deserting God, and that He be given the strength to hold out victoriously against the assaults of the evil powers. Finally, on the very last day, when the other infernal powers with all their arts of seduction had failed to make headway against their tormented victim, the Prince of Darkness arrived in person. The following account of the temptation of Christ in the wilderness is adapted from the account related to Pastor Greber by the Spirit (from Greber, pp. 325–328).

Satan stood before Jesus and taunted, "You call yourself a Son of God. If that is true you need not suffer hunger. Command that these stones become bread. But that is beyond your power, deluded man, and because of your obsession you must die here of starvation. You are not able to work miracles. You never were, and never will be, and you imagine yourself to be a Son of God!

"Look at me! I am a son of God, Whom I left, Who in His cruelty leaves you to suffer this way. I can work miracles, and will turn these stones into bread for you to eat. You will see that I am able to do this. Abandon God Who had abandoned you to starve. Worship me and the choicest foods on Earth will be yours!"

Jesus was cornered. He knew that He could not produce food, and He was, indeed, starving. But He resisted Satan and believed the Voice. "Go away, Satan, I do not want your bread, not would I want any if I could make it out of these stones. I await the Holy word that comes from the mouth of God. That word will come at the appointed time. By it I shall have food and live."

Satan, however, was not so easily discouraged. "So be it," he replied. "If you will work no miracles in my presence, nor eat the bread I offer you in pity, you may choose another way to find out for yourself whether you are indeed a son of God. I would gladly prove to you that you are not and free you from your delusion. Look at the pinnacle of the temple. I will take you there and you can cast yourself down, for it is written, 'He shall give His angels charge over thee and on their hands they shall bear thee up.' Make the test, then, You know I will not help you, since it is my purpose to prove to you that you are not one of the sons of God. I am certain the fall will break you into pieces.

Nevertheless, you should make the trial. Not even God may demand of you a blind belief that you are His Son. Unless you are willing to put your Sonship to at least a single trial, you must admit yourself lacking in understanding. If it happens that you survive the fall unhurt, even I will believe in you. But if you die, be thankful that death has relieved you of the lie which beguiled you, rather than that you should waste your life in such madness and die disappointed and despised by mankind."

Jesus was again cornered by this attack. He had no powers to survive such a fall, and He well knew it. He was as powerless as we. Jesus, tortured by weeks of suffering, controlled Himself with a mighty effort and replied steadily, "I will not make trial of the Lord. Not in this way will I seek to prove I am His Son. In His hands I leave the proof. He will not fail me, as you too will find out."

Satan still did not lose hope. He had yet another lure which had always given brilliant results in the past. The world was his, for everything material was under his sway. He could give the kingdom of the Earth to whomsoever he pleased; whether to Nebuchadnezzar, or to Caesar Tiberius, or to Jesus, was for him to decide. The kingdoms of the Earth, those kingdoms to which Jesus yearned to bring peace and the rule of God, passed in their splendor, as in a film, before the fevered eyes of Jesus. Satan pressed the attack. "I will give you all these things. If you want them all, they will be yours. If you want only one, you have only to choose it. But you must bow down to me as your overlord. In these kingdoms, I am, and will remain, supreme. But you shall be next in power."

Christ responded, "Go away, Satan, for it is written, 'Thou shalt worship the Lord thy God, and Him only shalt thou serve'."

Satan had lost the battle. In the previous days he had felt certain of his victim Whose prayers for help he had overheard and Whose signs of fear he had witnessed. That had been at a time when only Lucifer's subordinates had been engaged. Now he had come in person to reduce a fortress which seemed ready to yield, into which hunger and exhaustion had entered as his ally. He found that he had been mistaken: spiritual weapons and bribes had no effect upon this mortal. One implement of warfare remained, one before which all men tremble and grow pliant, namely, physical tortures. Satan resolved to use the most excruciating. To inflict these there was no lack of human agents. In the end he could not fail. He need only bide his time and await the most favorable moment. Therefore, when the Devil had finished every temptation, he departed from Jesus until a more opportune time (see Luke 4:13).

Suppose a person of today were to hear a voice that the others around him did not hear. Suppose that the voice were to say something rather amazing, rather different from what the person believed. Would not that person dismiss the whole event as a delusion or a hallucination? Would he not perhaps doubt his own sanity? Surely others would doubt it for him. The same was true at that moment with Jesus, and Satan's attack was centered on shaking the faith of the man Jesus in what He had just heard. It was also true at a later time when His own family came out to take custody of Him, saying, "He has lost His senses" (Mark 3:21 NAS).

Christ, as a man, had been compelled to earn painfully the strength which He would need for the mighty task before Him. Then the heavens opened and God's spirits flocked about Him. After the battle in the desert, "behold, angels came and ministered unto him" (Matt 4:11). They also gave Him earthly food, after his fast of forty days.

After successfully passing His tests, Jesus returned to Galilee, but now He was armed with the Holy spirits of God, and, accordingly, for the first time He was able to command miracles to be done (see Luke 4:14–44). It appears that God does not heedlessly distribute favors and success. He demands that everyone exert himself to the utmost, and this He demanded also of Christ.

> The problem given to Christ to solve on behalf of the kingdom of God, was the greatest ever assigned to a mortal, hence it was necessary that God send Him spirits in abundance, not only as regarded their numbers, but also with respect to their strength and ability. Among them went spirits of fortitude to infuse new strength into Him when His own began to fail in the battle with the evil powers. Often these spirits were accompanied by those of hope, joy, and peace of soul. Again, militant angels from Michael's Legion came to His side, when Satan marshalled his legions in full force, and when the fury of their assaults threatened to be more than human strength could bear. Spirits of truth and understanding instructed Him as to the best way of bringing the word of God before the multitudes or of answering questions concerning Himself or His teachings. Spirits of wisdom taught Him how to solve individual problems, but all this assistance came only after He had exhausted His own resources without avail (Greber, p. 337).

The first step Jesus took in His public ministry was to convince not only His disciples, but the people as well, of the Divine nature of His mission. He had to reveal Himself and His intentions, and prove His message with the aid of God, Whose emissary He proclaimed Himself to be. The miracles were the testimony, the identifying signs, offered by God on behalf of Jesus as the Messiah. Despite the miracles, people were slow to believe. Christ's own family, as well as the Apostles, at first saw in Him nothing more than a prophet. His conduct in public and the doctrines preached by Him did not meet with His mother's approval. She had known that His beliefs differed from the doctrines held by the Jewish religion, but to see Him proclaim His views openly to the multitudes distressed her sorely. She had pictured His mission on Earth in a very different light. When she heard that Jesus had preached strongly against the spiritual leaders of the Jewish people and had publicly branded as false many of the tenets of her ancient faith, she, in company with her other sons, sought to compel Him to return to His parental home, believing that in this way she could allay the ill will that His actions had aroused among the high priests, scribes, and Pharisees.

It is easy to understand why Jesus' behavior disturbed His mother and brothers. They believed the doctrines taught to them by the Jewish priests were true. Their ancestors had lived and died in that faith. For a son, and brother, to publicly preach that these doctrines were full of errors was more than these simple people could bear. In addition, they were in fear of the ban of the priesthood, and of the harsh words of their fellow men. "For not even His brothers were believing in Him" (John 7:5 NAS). Jesus' family questioned His sanity, thinking He had "lost His senses" (Mark 3:21 NAS). His mother and brothers surely could not have reacted in these ways if they had known His true identity at the time. Mother Mary had apparently kept her secret well, as suggested by Luke (Luke 2:19, 2:51).

His words impressed other hearers so deeply that they asked of one another where this man obtained all His wisdom and the power of His eloquence. Was He not the son of the carpenter? Was his mother not Mary, and His brothers named James, Joseph, Simon, and Judah? Did not His sisters also live there? How did He come by this? (see Matt 13:54–56). How did it happen that of all of the family, Jesus was the only one who was so wonderfully gifted?

A number of false messiahs had already come to Jerusalem from other places. The fake messiahs briefly had their followings, then each fell by the way. Several of them even had the name "Jesus," a common name in that time and place. Then came another Jesus claiming to be the Messiah. After having seen the deceivers, people were reluctant to follow another Messiah. His miracles, or attesting signs, were therefore of vital importance in lending authority to His words. The most awe-inspiring sign of His Sonship was the raising of the dead.

To raise the dead was something that Christ could undertake only when He had been assured by spirits (angels) from God that such was the Divine will, for all signs which bore testimony to the power of God were manifested solely when they were of special service in promoting the kingdom of God or the sanction of His emissary and His teachings. What Christ did could not have been accomplished by any human power, but only through the power of God. Divine spirits interceded, accomplishing whatever was needed to allow the return of the spirit into the body. It does not occur to people that such things are done in accordance with Divine laws, that there is no magic anywhere in all of creation. This is true not only of the raising of the dead, but of all other miracles performed by Jesus. When He turned water into wine, this task also was accomplished by the Divine spirit-world, and for this reason not even He was able to bring about the transmutation instantly, as His mother wished. His "hour was not yet come," because the spirits had not completed the necessary work. Time is required, even by spirits. It is because people do not understand these processes that they fail to grasp the meaning of certain words found in the Bibles, such as in the Scriptural account of the raising of Lazarus. At first it seems utterly incomprehensible that "he [Jesus] was deeply moved in spirit and troubled" (John 11:33 NIV) *(em add)*, and that "Jesus wept" (verse 35). "Jesus, once more deeply moved, came to the tomb" (verse 38). Why should the Master of Life and Death be troubled? Jesus had postponed arriving for three days, knowing that Lazarus' death was imminent. He further knew that Lazarus could be restored in an instant.

The problem here is in the rendering by translators unfamiliar with spirit influences and their physical symptoms. Most simply put, it was the presence of the spirits of God, whose task it was to restore Lazarus upon Christ's command, which Jesus felt. The strong presence of spirits often produces a shivering, or shaking (as in Job 4:14–15), and may result in involuntary tears. The sensation is an uplifting and agreeable one in the presence of Holy spirits, and unpleasant when due to the evil ones, but the physical symptoms are the same in either case. It was this sensation, produced by the nearness of God's spirits, which passed through Christ on this occasion. A clearer translation reads that Jesus, "was so affected by the power of a spirit of God that he trembled" (John 11:33 GNT). And then Jesus wept.

At first Jesus taught and healed, and the crowds praised Him (see Luke 4:14–15). At that time, He was referring to Himself only as the Son of Man, but even that was too strong a claim for most of the people. The crowds followed Him, to be sure, but it was to be healed of diseases and miraculously fed (see Luke 6:19), not out of allegiance to His teaching. On the contrary, His teachings went against their religion. Christ broke their religious law by associating with unclean people (see Luke 7:34) and violating the Sabbath, saying it was "made for man, and not man for the Sabbath" (Mark 2:27). He altered the Law of Moses concerning divorce (see Matt 5:31–32). He forbade taking of oaths (see Matt 5:34–37), whereas oaths were allowed by Moses (see Num 30). He spoke with authority in doing all these things.

In spite of this, He gathered a certain number of disciples, but when Jesus revealed a bit more, and began to speak of His special relationship with the Father, many of them deserted and "walked no more with him" (John 6:66). What men do not understand, they regard as foolishness and dismiss from their minds. This was true also in the days of Christ. Whatever lay outside of the people's daily experience, or conflicted with the creed inherited from their ancestors, could not be brought home to them any easier than it can be today. For this reason Christ did not devote Himself to expounding truths at length, but confined His teachings to proclaiming the truth concerning God, the fulfillment of the Divine will, and His own mission on behalf of the Father. Everything else He left to the truth-bearing spirits which He intended to send to mankind.

The priests warned the people against Jesus and His teaching.

They slandered Him as a false prophet, a man possessed by a demon, a winebibber, and a man who kept company with wayward women and broke bread with publicans and sinners. The priesthood could not bear for the people to accept as truth His teachings, doctrines that differed from what they taught and which, in some places, frankly contradicted them. The priests were in danger of losing their followers. What they did not believe, the people must not believe. "No one of the rulers or Pharisees has believed in Him, has he? But this multitude which does not know the Law [the Books of Moses] is accursed" (John 7:48–49 NAS) *(em add)*.

Jesus did not go to the religious authorities to make His claim of Messiahship. He announced Himself to them (see Luke 4:16–21), and occasionally denounced them, but His message was delivered to the common people. The common people understood little of the Scriptures, in contrast to the scribes and priests. Their minds were therefore less encumbered by manmade dogma, false theological deductions, and misinterpreted prophecies. They were more able, therefore, to accept Him first and verify Him by the Scriptures later.

It is no easy task, even today, to start from the Old Testament descriptions of the Messiah and then to conclude that Jesus of Nazareth was He. It is easier to first believe, then to gloss over the troublesome prophecies and regard only the applicable ones, for Jesus did not fulfill most of the prophecies concerning the Messiah. Of those He did satisfy, some seemed wrenched out of context. A case in point is the explanation given in Matthew of Jesus' return from early childhood in Egypt. That event is said to fulfill the prophetic words, "Out of Egypt have I called my Son" (Matt 2:15). These words seem, to the mortal reader, to refer to Israel. "Israel is My son, My first-born" (Ex 4:22 NAS), of whom it is written, "When Israel was a youth I loved him, and out of Egypt I called My son" (Hosea 11:1 NAS). If the writer of Matthew has interpreted Hosea correctly, then he appears to have had spiritual help, as Christians believe. It is little wonder that the religious authorities of Jesus' day could not conclude He was the Christ. It is easy to see how a sincere, intelligent thinking Jew of those days could reject Christ's claim that He was the Messiah.

After all, He clearly, to them, did not fulfill the Scriptures as they had come to think they understood them. Can we be sure we would have recognized Jesus for who He was had we been there?

The surest and most powerful testimony of His identity consists of the miracles He commanded, attesting signs sent by God. Jesus told the people that even if they could not bring themselves to believe His words, they surely must be able to believe Him because of the works He did. He emphasized that the signs and miracles done through Him were God's witness to the multitudes that this Jesus was indeed the Christ. "But the witness which I have is greater than that of John [the Baptist]; for the works which the Father has given Me to accomplish, the very works that I do, bear witness of Me, that the Father has sent Me" (John 5:36 NAS) *(em add)*. "Jesus answered them, 'I told you, and you do not believe; the works that I do in My Father's name, these bear witness of Me' " (John 10:25 NAS). With Jesus having the Father's stamp of authenticity upon Him, we need not be concerned about problems of prophetic interpretations regarding the Messiah.

The Messiah chose His Apostles from among the common people. We revere the Apostles greatly today, but we do not always distinguish between the Apostles after Pentecost, when they had received the Holy spirits, and the Apostles before then. The faith, courage, and heroic exploits of these men after Christ left are well known. Let us look at what they were like before then, when they walked with Him.

Jesus' years of public ministry were years of constant activity and harassment, with crowds clinging at His garments, very little time to eat a meal in peace (see Mark 6:31–32), sometime anger and sadness at the obstinacy of the religious leaders (see Mark 3:5–6), tears shed over the fate in store for Jerusalem (see Luke 19:41), and sorely tried patience, leading to words such as "O unbelieving generation, how long shall I be with you? How long shall I put up with you?" (Mark 9:19–21 NAS).

Even the Apostles on occasion felt doubts as to their Master, for they had formed a different concept of the Messiah. Not until the day when Simon Peter uttered his conviction, "Thou art the Christ, the Son of the living God" (Matt 16:16), did His Apostles know that in Jesus of Nazareth the Son of God had come upon

Earth. Even at that, Peter had not reached this conviction due to Christ's words or acts, but by a revelation from God (see Matt 16:17).

There must have been a number of times during these years when His own Apostles were a particular burden to Him, yet He patiently taught them and nurtured their spiritual growth. The Apostles had to learn, just as we must. Their spiritual growth, just as ours, required time and effort. These men did not understand a great deal of what Jesus was preaching. Part of the reason was that He preached only in parables (see Mark 4:33–34). They frequently mumbled among themselves as to what the teachings meant (see Matt 16:5–12; Luke 9:43–45; John 6:61), although Jesus would take them aside and explain to them the parables and various other things He did not tell the public (see Matt 13:10–12, 13:36–52; Mark 4:9–12). Jesus' frustration with His helpers is apparent in His rhetorical question, "Are you as dull as the rest?" (Mark 7:17–18 NEB).

The Apostles did not know what to make of the prophecy that Elijah had to come again before the Messiah (see Mark 9:11–13). They puzzled among themselves as to who this Jesus was (see Mark 4:40–41). They apparently had more awe of Jesus than love, for they were sometimes afraid to approach Him to ask questions (see Mark 6:49–52, 9:30–32; Luke 9:43–45). Jesus gave the Apostles power to heal and to cast out evil spirits, but, due to their lack of faith, they could not always do it (see Matt 10:1; Mark 3:13–16, 6:7–9, 9:16–19, 16:14–18).

The Apostles seem to have let their miracles and the thought of being friends with a future earthly king carry them away a bit. They were at times prideful and jealous as to which of them was the greatest. At the last supper, "a jealous dispute broke out: who among them should rank highest?" (Luke 22:24 NEB). It was not the first time they had argued that point (see Mark 9:33 et seq.). James and John had made a special request of Jesus, perhaps at the insistence of their mother, that they be seated at His right and His left when He became King over Israel (see Matt 20:20–24, Mark 10:35–37). Upon hearing this request, the other apostles became indignant with the two brothers (verse 24). The Apostles were indignant at Christ's being annointed with oil in the house of

Simon the leper (see Matt 26:6–9). They tried to keep the children from approaching Jesus, for which He rebuked His Apostles (see Mark 10:13–14).

As the end drew near, the Apostles were still falling short. Jesus referred to Peter as a "stumbling block to Me" (Matt 16:23 NAS). In the Garden of Gethsemane, these men were unable to sacrifice a few hours of sleep to pray with Jesus as he had asked them (see Mark 14:32–42). Although the Apostles had recently sworn they would never desert Jesus, they scattered in all directions when He was arrested (see Mark 14:50). One of the twelve, Judas Iscariot, had betrayed Him, and another, Peter, would repeatedly deny he had ever known Him. Nor did they know what Jesus meant by His talk of rising from the dead (see Mark 9:9–11). The Master was also moved to scold them, "Do you still not understand? Are your minds closed? You have eyes: can you not see? You have ears: can you not hear? Have you forgotten?" (Mark 8:17–21 NEB). Immediately after the resurrection, the situation with the Apostles had not improved a great deal. "Afterwards while the Eleven were at table he appeared to them and reproached them for their incredulity and dullness" (Mark 16:14–15 NEB). Thomas had to touch His body before he would believe. It was during the next forty days, when these men were taught by the Lord, and during which they had each received a spirit from God, that they became the Apostles whom we revere today (see Acts 1:3, 2:1–4).

In the last day Jesus was alone. The Apostles had fled and the crowd, which had escorted Him into Jerusalem to be their king against the hated Romans, were now an angry mob demanding His blood. He had been told what He had to do to secure deliverance for His people. And He knew the prophecies full well. His heart quailed at the thought of the last hours, being "grieved and distressed" (Matt 26:36–46 NAS). In Gethsemane, He was depressed and heartsick to the point of death (verse 38), and that at a time when the tortures had not yet begun. He would soon be subjected to a test worse than that in the wilderness, the test of going to the death without turning from God, nor sinning against His fellow man.

On the evening before His death, Jesus was in the guest-chamber of a house, in the company of His disciples. The feast of the

Passover, which He was observing with them, was also His farewell feast. Who among us can measure the anguish in His soul? He knew that all preparations for His arrest and speedy execution had already been made. He knew that one of His disciples had had dealings with the high priests, and had declared himself ready to deliver his Master to them. At that very moment, the traitor was eating with Him. Judas, who dared not meet his Master's eye, was anxiously awaiting the moment when he could leave the chamber without attracting attention. The Master's heart bled on seeing before Him His traitor in this youth, whose terrible end He foresaw.

As He looked upon him, Christ's eyes filled with tears, for His heart was filled with love for even this lost brother. In His mind arose a picture of what within a very few hours was to be reality; Judas, despair in his soul, standing, rope in hand before the tree on which he was to end his own life, and beside him Lucifer, ready to take the spirit of him whom he had led astray, into the Pit (Greber, p. 343).

After Judas had left the guest-chamber, and even as Jesus gave to His Apostles the wine and the bread symbolical of His approaching death, His heart was bleeding from a thousand wounds. He was human, as you are, and had no advantage over other mortals during this hour and those which were to follow. On the contrary, He lacked even those things which are most men's, to fortify and console them in the hour of suffering (Greber, p. 345).

As for the other Apostles, would they stand by Him and console Him in the hour of His martyrdom? The events that the next twelve hours were to bring forth passed before His mind's eye. He could see them all fleeing in terror for their own lives, and Peter, shaking with dread before a maid, denying all knowledge of his master with oaths and curses. He saw the devils crowding about the door of the guest-chamber, ready to seize upon His disciples as they went out, and in this very night fill their minds with doubt of their Master, in order that they might offer no support or help to One Who was doomed to die. "Satan hath asked to have you, that he might sift you as wheat." Why had Satan desired this? Only now it had been divinely revealed to him what he had at stake in this war. God's sense of justice did not permit Him to conceal any longer from Lucifer the fact that the battle which was now to open between him and Christ was to decide the sovereignty of Hell over the fallen spirits. God had revealed to Lucifer that Christ, should He remain steadfast throughout the death-agony which was at hand, would thereafter as a spirit advance to an attack upon Hell at the head of the celestial legions; that he, the Prince of Hell would be overcome and would be deprived of an essential part of his sovereignty. At this news, Satan trembled; then, appealing to that sense of the Divine justice which on one occasion had given him absolute sovereignty over the fallen spirits, he demanded that God observe strict neutrality in the decisive battle which was impending. What Satan asked was, that God withdraw His hand entirely from Jesus, leaving Him not even any human support, while allowing Hell to have a free hand. Should God accede to these demands, Lucifer hoped that by doing his utmost, he would succeed in breaking the spirit of this Jesus of Nazareth at the last moment, and in driving Him to despair of His cause (Greber, pp. 343–344).

God granted the terms asked by Satan with the sole exception of reserving to Himself the right to strengthen Christ's purely physical vitality. Had He not done so, Christ would have died in the garden of Gethsemane. The weaknesses of every human body react upon the spirit which it houses. The incarnated spirit, however perfect, must constantly wrestle with the weaknesses of the physical body in which it resides and can never quite free itself from them during its earthly existence. This is a part of human nature from which not even Christ was exempt. To His last breath He was compelled to fight against these weaknesses. In the garden of Gethsemane even this mighty conqueror turned faint, praying that the Father might let the cup pass away from Him, yet adding, "nevertheless, not as I will, but as thou wilt." He knew that it was the Father's will that He must suffer, and His outcry reveals the mortal whose nature quails and rebels at the thought of an agonizing death. Saint Paul has recorded this truth in his Epistle to the Hebrews, in words which may offend those who deny the possibility on His part of sin or of rebellion against God:

> In the days of his stay upon earth, Christ, amid loud lamentations and many tears sent up fervent prayers to Him, Who could save him from the spiritual death of apostasy, and was heard because of his piety. But although he was a Son of God he also had to learn through the sufferings that lay before Him, and only after He had attained perfection did he become the author of the salvation (Heb 5:7–9) (Greber, p. 321).

Even the highest of created spirits is exposed by incarnation to the danger of being overcome by evil and to being persuaded to desert God. This danger threatened Christ Himself, Who was fully aware of it.

At Lucifer's desire, all the mental and physical anguish on earth, crowded into a few short hours, was to be concentrated upon his antagonist, coincidently with an attack to be launched upon Him and His followers by the entire infernal hosts. For Jesus, alone, betrayed by one of His disciples, deserted by the others, denied any Divine aid against the forces of Hell, Lucifer hoped to prepare an end worthy of a Judas (Greber, p. 344).

Picture Him now, going out into the dark of the night to the garden of Gethsemane, overwhelmed with sorrow. His disciples, on whom the evil spirit forces are already at work, walk silently beside Him, in dread of what is to come. Under the burden of His mental torments, He too is silent. Lucifer is in wait with his ablest assistants. This is the very opportunity which the Prince of Darkness had awaited (see Luke 4:13). Human words would fail to portray the terrors of the visions held up by Hell to its victim in this brief hour. Lucifer exhibited to Christ all that is fearful and detestable in mankind, causing to pass before His eyes pictures of blaspheming, sinful humanity in its full viciousness and corruption, in a steady succession of hideous pictures. Next he showed to Jesus the supposed fruits of His years of endeavor among the Jews as God's people, pointing mockingly to His disciples, one of them actually approaching at the head of a mob, the others fast asleep nearby with no words of comfort for their Master. Before the clairvoyant eyes of this trembling Victim there now passed the scenes of the suffering in store for Him: His capture, the flight of His disciples, Peter's denial, the roar of the multitude which but a few days earlier had hailed His entry into Jerusalem, and which now thirsted for His blood, the death sentence, the flagellation, His captors' brutality, the crown of thorns, Calvary, the Crucifixion, everything painted in its most terrifying aspect, in order that He might give way to despair and abandon His resistance. All the while, the spirits of hopelessness and desperation were driving the maddest of thoughts into the mind of their Victim Whom all had forsaken. His pulse throbbed, His whole body was shaken with fever, His heart threatened to burst. Through it all, His disciples were sleeping peacefully.

The meager outlines preserved by our Bibles fail utterly to convey to our minds the anguish of soul and body suffered by our

Redeemer. Many of the worst tortures are not even mentioned. Nothing whatever is said of the frightful hours He was compelled to spend in the underground dungeons of the courthouse, fetid and swarming with vermin, into which the soldiers had thrust Jesus after they had scourged and mocked Him and crowned Him with thorns, and after they had rubbed salt into the gashes left by the lash upon His body and had bound His hands, lest by removing the salt He might find some relief from his torments.

> Never did man endure such torture as did this Son of God incarnated. Through its human tools, Hell did its worst, for in Him it recognized its greatest foe who could ever appear on earth. But not even the physical sufferings which it prepared for Him could equal those which His soul had to endure; moreover, both forms of torment, mental and bodily, were applied to Him simultaneously. Add to this that to the last He was without any human consolation, and, what was still harder, without any Divine aid. God had withdrawn His protecting hand and had left Him helpless to the devices of Hell . . . Satan should never be able to allege the excuse that his failure to reduce this mortal to submission was due to the help received by his victim from external sources. He should be forced to confess that he had met his match in an unaided human being, who, in spite of the most excruciating torments of mind and body, could not be driven to desert His God (Greber, p. 346).

How desperate, then, were the efforts on the part of evil to break the power of the greatest Truth bearer Who ever came upon Earth. The bodily tortures which Jesus had to undergo and the mental suffering He had to endure, until His last breath, were so great that His predecessors, the prophets, could not have withstood them victoriously.

It is true that the sufferings of Christ had a higher significance than did those of the Divine Prophets. For them, death spelled the fulfillment of their tasks, if they had remained true to God. For Christ, however, the end of His earthly life marked the fulfillment of only a portion of His mission, the more important part of which was still to be completed by gaining a victory over the Prince of Darkness.

> His crucifixion was a condition precedent to that victory, not indeed, crucifixion in itself, but His ability to endure it without faltering in His loyalty to His Master. He might, indeed, while yet alive upon

the Cross, have lost faith in God at the last moment, and gone over to the Enemy. Had He done so, He would have died upon the Cross nevertheless, but defeated and apostate. Until that moment, He had stood upon the defensive against the terrific hail of missiles that Hell poured upon Him; had He yielded, all would have been lost. The effort at redemption would have failed and Christ would have been a prisoner of the Prince of Darkness (Greber, p. 342).

Although Jesus could have quit His mission at any time by calling down "legions of angels" to His rescue, He elected to take on the last torments at great personal risk. From noon until His physical death at midafternoon, Jesus was without the help of God or angels, and all human support had long since vanished. Jesus had seen the angels leave, but did not understand why they departed, as registered by the anguish in His cry, "My God, my God, why hast thou forsaken me?" (Matt 27:46). Jesus, the man, had to hold out on His own, by faith.

When He saw the angels returning in triumphant joy at His achievement, Jesus uttered a loud cry and sighed, "It is finished!" (John 19:30 NAS). Then He, the angels, and one of the thieves crucified with Him, ascended in spirit into Paradise, leaving their physical bodies behind. Christ was once again in His position as King of Creation, once again in possession of His full mental faculties and powers.

Christ had held His ground against the anguish of body and soul inflicted upon Him by the hellish powers. The moment of His physical death marked the beginning of the second part of the war of redemption. He, Who as a mortal, had stood on the defensive against the powers of Hell, would now, as a Spirit, advance to attack them on their own ground to render His victory complete. To force the decision, He would descend into Hell. As a man, He had repelled all the attacks of His mighty opponent. He had done all that men can do. Now, however, He could, as a Spirit, advance upon His enemy and descend into Hell, relying upon the all-conquering Divine power which He, as a mortal, had earned by His loyalty to God. He descended with the Heavenly Legions of Michael as His army. Now began a struggle like that which had occured when Lucifer with his adherents had battled with the Heavenly Legions in the days of the great revolt of God's spirit kingdom. This mighty conflict raged until it had invaded the lowest depths of Hell, into which Lucifer and his followers were forced to retreat. When Lucifer saw that all was lost, he begged for mercy. He, who in the desert had tried to tempt the Son of God, now stood quaking before Him Whose faith in His Sonship he had sought to undermine. Christ disclosed to him that he was not to be deprived at that moment of all of his power, but that it was to be restricted to those of his subjects who were whole-heartedly devoted to him. Any who desired to leave his kingdom and to return to God must be released unconditionally. Satan might, if he wished, attempt to bind these spirits to himself by artifice and guile, but not by force, as previously. And so it remains today. The time approaches, however, when Satan and his henchmen will be removed from this sphere altogether.

Thus was concluded the mighty task of redemption. In all of its critical aspects, God's Plan of Salvation had been accomplished. The gulf that yawns between the Realm of Darkness and the Kingdom of God had been spanned by a bridge which could be crossed freely by all who desired to leave Satan's domains and to return to their old home in the land of God. No sentinel in the service of Hell could prevent them from passing the frontier. This great victory in the lower spirit-world was, of course, unknown to Christ's followers on Earth. To them, it appeared that His mission had failed. Joseph of Arimathea had hastily entombed the body of Jesus in his own tomb. There it remained while the real Jesus, in His real Spirit-body, ascended into Paradise and then descended into Hell. As we have seen in earlier chapters, the flesh body was of no further use. The physical body does not leave the physical universe. It is the spirit in its spiritual body which ascends into Heaven or descends into Hell.

Not even of Christ was the physical body rejuvenated, being unneeded in the spirit-world. It was not intended, however, that the corpse of Christ become an object of worship, nor to undergo decay. "Neither wilt Thou allow Thy Holy One to undergo decay" (Psa 16:10 NAS). The body vanished from the tomb before the stone sealing the entrance was rolled away. It was God's spirits who performed this task, the process being the same as that by which the body of Gabriel was dematerialized after he finished speaking with Daniel, and by which Raphael vanished after walking with Tobit (see Apocryphal book, *Tobit*). Similarly, the bodies of Enoch and Elijah had been dematerialized when those spirits returned to Heaven without physical death.

Christ was raised from the dead, it is true, but it was from among the dead in the kingdom of the Dead, Christ being the first Spirit ever to ascend from there to Heaven after the fall. In this He was "the first-born of the dead" (Rev 1:5 NAS), a description which cannot allude to physical revival, since many people, such as Lazarus, had had that experience before Him. It is now obvious, in view of previous chapters in this book, that Christ's amazing comings and goings during the next forty days followed precisely the same principles as did the appearances and disappearances of any of the other high spirits. His materialization before the Apostles in the upper room was precisely the same phenomenon as that by which the angels materialized and ate with Abraham. No magic was involved in either case. To the Christians of today the resurrection of the dead means the revival of the physical body, and Christ's resurrection on Easter Sunday is regarded as the reunion of His spirit with His body which had lain in its grave for three days. "These are wholly mistaken ideas, for, to repeat it once more, Christ's resurrection from the dead merely signifies His return from the realm of the spiritually dead, His return from Hell, into which His Spirit had descended" (Greber, p. 386). The dematerialization of the physical body of Jesus, and the removal of the stone after three days to display the empty tomb, constitute the final and ultimate sign that He was the Messiah of Israel (see Matt 12:39–40).

Christ appeared to two of His disciples on the road to Emmaus (see Luke 24:13–35) and explained the Scriptures concerning Himself, beginning with Moses. The last Redeemer of Israel had accomplished a mission whose counterpart was the mission of Israel's first liberator, Moses, through whom it had been given, "The Lord your God will raise up for you a prophet like me from among you" (Deut 18:15 NAS). There are many similarities between Christ and Moses, the servant of Christ. All the male children under two years of age were slain by Herod's men, but Jesus escaped. Moses likewise escaped when the Hebrew infants were slain. Christ delivered from bondage all those captive spirits who may choose to follow him. Moses led the Israelites out of Israel.

Christ's mission was accredited by signs and miracles, as was that of His predecessor Moses. The things that Christ taught were taught to Him by the spirits at God's behest, just as Moses was taught from Above by inquiring of God in the tent of testimony. In both cases, the bodies of Jesus and Moses were not to remain on Earth to become objects of veneration (see Jude 9).

With Moses as with Christ, the mission involved two clearly defined steps. As regarded Moses, it was necessary above all that he remain firm before Pharoah, and not allow himself to be diverted from his God-given mission either by threats or by enticements, lest God's plan amount to nothing by reason of Moses' lack of resolve. The people of Israel, on their part, had to do their share by declaring themselves willing to leave when the time came. It then rested with God to grant them a decisive victory over Pharoah and to make possible their deliverance. The manner in which this was to be achieved was not the concern of either Moses or the people: that was for God alone to decide.

> So too it was with Christ. He had nothing to gain by telling the people how the redemption was to be accomplished. It was His duty only to proclaim to them that the hour of their deliverance was near; that they must strive to make themselves worthy of the gift, and that it was He Whom God had sent as their Savior. On His own part, He must beware of succumbing to the Princes of Darkness who left no stone unturned to induce Him to forsake His God and to abandon His Divine mission. Like Moses, Christ must guard against being vanquished by the foe whom He had come to conquer. If He could hold out in His entrenchments against the assaults of Evil, it was for God to determine how the defense could be turned into a successful attack, for obviously, as a mortal, Christ could not wage an offensive campaign against spirits (Greber, p. 329).

Christ could advance for an attack upon Satan only as a Spirit, and only after His earthly death.

Moses had led the chosen Israelites, the nation of witnesses for God, to freedom from their bondage. Christ led His followers to freedom from this entire dimension of creation, and sent forth witnesses to declare His message to all the world. "Go into all the world and preach the gospel to all creation" (Mark 16:15 NAS).

REFERENCE CITED

In addition to the passages quoted, much of the other material in this chapter is adapted from the information the Spirit related to Pastor Johannes Greber. The complete story is found in the section entitled "Teachings Concerning Christ—His Life and His Work" of his book:

Communication with the Spirit World of God. Johannes Greber Memorial Foundation, 139 Hillside Avenue, Teaneck, NJ 07666

———————————◇———————————

CHAPTER 12

The Word Goes Forth

CHRIST materialized before those who had been closest to Him on Earth, assigning them the mission of preaching the gospel to all the world (see Mark 16:15). The gospel, or "good tidings," proclaimed Christ's long awaited redemption of the fallen spirits, freely offered to all spirits who chose to accept it.

The world into which His witnesses ventured was dominated by the Roman empire. Cities such as Rome, Corinth, and Ephesus come to mind when we think of the evangelizing efforts of Christ's disciples. However, these disciples spent most of their efforts in places not even mentioned in the New Testament. The lack of mention of these other cities and countries results in a distorted picture of the spread of Christianity. To rectify this omission, this chapter will focus on the unpublicized labors of these early bearers of the light to the dispersed Israelites in Europe.

We have already related how Israel and Judah fled from their respective captivities and dispersed into all the world, while only a few Jews returned to Jerusalem to rebuild the temple. Scholars have traced the descendants of these tribes, who carried the name of King Omri, to the Kimmerii-Cymry-Celtoi-Celts. Those bearing the name of Isaac became the Scythians and Saxons. Herodotus tells us that the Scythians never used pigs for sacrifice and would not even breed them anywhere in the country. The Israelites taken from Galilee were called Galutha by the Persians, the name meaning "prisoners," or "captives." As the Galileans fled through Europe, the name evolved into Galutha-Galatians-Gauls, from which our word gaol, or jail, is thought to have originated. Certain Judahites became known as Jutes, while certain of the tribe of Dan became the Danes. Other of the Israelites migrated slowly across Europe, carrying before them a replica of the Ark of the Covenant, and carrying in their hearts the memory of a covenant with the one God. Some became known as Angles, or "God-men", due to their mode of worship. Others received the name Gaels, Ga-el meaning "God's men," although this name may possibly be still another derivative of "Gauls."

These people drifted westward for several centuries, many of them eventually arriving at the western-most edge of Europe, the British Isles. Winchester and York were hundreds of years old by the time of the Apostles. London predated King David. Marseilles had been a major seaport for the Phoenicians, and then the Greeks, for over five hundred years. The ancient trade route between Phoenicia and Britain passed through the seaport of Marseilles and overland along the Rhone River valley, finally crossing the English Channel from Brittany in France. The ancient traders arriving in the British Isles found the old world's primary source of lead and tin, along with considerable amounts of gold, silver, copper, and iron. Lead samples, mined in Britain, have been found dating to the first century A.D., one bearing the inscription: "British lead, the property of the Emperor Nero." Ruins of Hebrew mining sites dating from that time are still visible.

The coast of Britain had numerous ports and harbors which served shipping fleets. Inland were the lands under cultivation, and the sheep and cattle herds. A definite British coinage had been in existence for some two hundred years before the birth of Jesus. Less than a decade after Him, a British coin minted under Caradoc bore an eagle with spread wings, almost identical to the one on the United States quarter that preceded the version in current use.

The art of enameling was identified with Britain, whose artisans taught it to the Romans. Julius Caesar wrote with admiration of the British culture, character, and ingenuity in commerce and craftsmanship. He referred to their populous cities and numerous universities, their architecture, and their Druidic religion with its teaching of a coming Messiah and the immortality of the soul.

Neither was Gaul so primitive as we may have believed. Strabo, who wrote about Marseilles and its neighboring cities, wrote: "All who profess to be men of taste turn to the study of elocution and philosophy. The city [Marseilles] for some time back has become quite a school for the barbarians [non-Romans] and has committed to the Galatae [Gauls and Galatians] such a taste for Greek literature that they even draw contracts on the Greek model. Further, at the present day it so entices the noblest of the Romans that those desirous of studying resort thither in preference to Athens." Strabo adds that they employed professors of the arts, sciences, and medicine not only for private tutelage, but also by towns for public instruction. This land was prosperous and cultured, with a strong Phoenician, Greek, and Hebrew heritage, including the propensity for planting olive orchards and vineyards as in Judea. It was through the cosmopolitan port of Marseilles that Paul would likely travel to Iberia, stopping, if possible, along the way with friends and relatives in Rome (see Rom 15:24, 15:28). Iberia, translated "Spain" in most Bibles, included at that time not only modern Spain, but also southwestern France.

The Israelite tribes lost their identities and languages, for the most part, during their migrations. Although they frequently maintained some version of the patriarchical Hebrew religion, they were by no means faithful to the pure faith. On the contrary, they frequently succumbed to the worship of Bel, or Baal, Diana, Astarte, the Mother of Heaven, and others. The sins which caused their exile from the promised land traveled with them.

The religious climate in the world during the lifetime of Jesus was varied. Hinduism was then very old in India. China had had Confucianism for several centuries. Taoism had spread throughout the Far East. Judea had a form of Judaism, though contaminated by ideas brought back from Babylon. The Roman empire was more pagan than all of these, worshipping a large assortment of major and minor dieties, as, for that matter, did many of the Judeans and Samaritans. In the western confines of Gaul and Britain, the Druids maintained an impure faith, but one which still bore a strong resemblance to the faith of Moses, as well it should, since the Isles had been settled and developed by branches of the enterprising Hebrews since the time of Abraham.

It has been claimed that Druidism was nationally organized among the British clans around 1800 B.C., approximately contemporary with Abraham. The Celts, by commandment and custom, did not commit their Druidic religious teachings to writing. No man could enter the Druidic order who could not prove his descent from nine generations of free forebears. In this, the Druids showed a reverence for genealogies reminiscent of the Old Testament Hebrews. The Druidic priesthood were not permitted to bear arms or to serve in war, much like the Levites among the Hebrews. The priests wore white linen robes, with no other metal but gold worn on any part of their garment. A Druidic cross was wrought in gold down the back of the priestly garment. The Druids avoided using iron tools in building their stone altars, a custom long followed by the Hebrews (see Deut 27:5; Josh 8:31). Diodorus relates that some of the Druids sang to the music of harps.

Druidism is said to have been founded in Asia by Seth of the Mosaic genealogy, in the year when the equinox occurred in the first point of Taurus, the bull. This puts the date at 3,900 B.C., or about fifty years after Seth was born. The bull became the symbol of Druidism, in time being corrupted into an object of idol worship in the religions of Baal, of Brahma in India, of Apis in Egypt, and of the so-called "golden calves" in Israel. While the ensign of the lion was assigned to the tribe of Judah, the bull was the sign of the ten Israelite tribes under Ephraim. They were sometimes known historically as the "bull tribe," and sometimes as the Taureans. Today, both these signs are combined on the royal standard of the British monarchs.

Gildas, the ancient British historian, reported that the Druidic universities at that time were the largest in the world, with over sixty such universities in existence, and with an average attendence of over sixty thousand students. His statement is confirmed by Greek and Roman testimony, stating that the nobility of Rome and other nations sent their children to study law, science, and religion in Britain. The Druids were renowned for their study of astronomy, to which the remains of Stonehenge bear silent witness today. It required twenty years to master the circle of Druidic knowledge.

The Druidic beliefs included the belief in an infinite universe created by the God in Whom there is no darkness, a familiar Christian concept. The Supreme Being was also referred to as "Governor," "The Wonderful," and "The Ancient of Days," all familiar Old Testament terms. They believed in a type of Druidic Trinity: the creator in the past, the savior in the present, the renovator in the future. The three aspects were known as Beli, Taran, and Esu (or Yesu). In these beliefs, nature was held to be the action of God through the medium of matter, so that the laws of nature were, in the strictest sense, the laws of God. God's creatures were in a lower state of existence due to the consequences of their errors. The sufferings they endured were held to be indispensable in rehabilitating the fallen beings. Every man had been in the angelic state in Heaven and would reenter there if his soul willingly chose the good and abided by its choice. If his soul preferred evil, it relapsed back into the cycle of purification by suffering. The soul would repeat the cycle, countless times, until it learned by experience. A soul which had finally achieved the heavenly happiness after death could, however, return to human life for the good of mankind. Such a reincarnation was considered a great blessing. Julius Caesar observed that: "The Druids teach that by no other way than the ransoming of man's life by the life of man, is reconciliation with the divine justice of the immortal gods possible."

Although the Jews never knew the name of their Messiah to come, it was a name familiar to the Druids. A translation of one of the Celtic triads reads:

> The Lord our God is One.
> Lift up your heads, O ye gates and be
> ye lift up, ye everlasting doors, and the
> King of Glory shall come in.
> Who is the King of Glory? The Lord Yesu;
> He is the King of Glory

This triad reveals a Hebrew connection by its close resemblance to one of the Psalms of David:

> Lift up your heads, O gates,

And lift them up, O ancient doors,
That the King of glory may come in!
Who is this King of Glory?
The Lord of hosts,
He is the King of glory (Psa 24:9–10 NAS).

The arch-Druid, Taliesen, long ago stated that: "Christ, the Word from the beginning, was from the beginning our teacher, and we never lost His teaching. Christianity was a new thing in Asia, but there was never a time when the Druids of Britain held not its doctrines." Britain, the only free country in the Roman world, was prepared to accept the new Christian faith when it arrived from Jerusalem. The pagan Caesars, therefore, met unprecedented resistance in their attempts to subdue Britain, resistance which had religion at its core. The Romans, before Christianity, regarded Druidism as their greatest religious opponent because of its direct opposition to Roman and Greek mythology. Druids could not bow to the Romans and at the same time live up to Druidic teachings such as: "Three duties of every man: worship God, be just to all men, die for your country." Orders were issued from Rome to exterminate, at any cost, the chief seat of Druidism among the Cimry, or Western Britons, in the region of Glastonbury.

At the time, Tiberius was emperor and Pilate was still the governor of Judea. According to Paulus Orosius, Pilate told Tiberius about the resurrection of Jesus and the miracles wrought by Him and His disciples. The story had already reached Rome by way of the Romans present at Pentecost, and earlier. A growing multitude believed that the Nazarene was a god. Simon Magus (see Acts 8:9–24) had already been deified by the Roman Senate and his statue erected in the harbor for all to see. Why Simon Magus and not Jesus the Nazarene? Paulus Orosius tells of the attempt: "Tiberius, with an approval of great popularity, proposed to the senate that Christ be given the status of a god. The senate, roused with indignation because the matter had not, according to custom, been first referred to them, in order that they might be the first to decide upon the acceptance of the cult, refused to deify Christ, and by an edict decided that Christians were to be banished from the city." Tiberius countered with an edict threatening the accusers of the Christians with death.

In Jerusalem, the Jews could not tolerate the growing Christian movement. Saul, later to be called Paul, had persecuted followers of Christ and had agreed with the stoning of Stephen (see Acts 8:1–3). Soon afterward, the disciples of Christ fled Jerusalem, carrying the Gospel with them (see Acts 8:1–4), while the Apostles lingered in Judea. The words, and even the names, of many of these disciples are all but forgotten. The New Testament makes no mention, even, of Lazarus, Mary Magdalene, or Mary, the Mother of Jesus, after their flight from Jerusalem.

Joseph of Arimathea is one of the greatest of those forgotten disciples. Joseph had a home in Arimathea, identified by modern Bible authorities as the village of Ramah, birthplace of the prophet Samuel. Joseph was a member of the Sanhedrin, but was also a secret disciple of Jesus (see John 19:38). As such, he could not have agreed to the priests' plots to kill either Jesus (see Luke 23:51) or Lazarus (see John 12:10). After Christ's death, Joseph and another secret disciple, Nicodemus, buried the body of Jesus. Joseph had boldly requested Pontius Pilate's permission to claim the body. This raises the questions of why Joseph could obtain an immediate audience with Pilate, and why Pilate would grant his request for the body of Jesus.

The ease with which Joseph gained access to Pilate, the top Roman official in Judea, was likely due to his influential position in the Sanhedrin, to his wealth, and to the implied connections he had with Roman power. The latter point is suggested by Joseph's title of "Decurio" in the Latin *Vulgate* (see Mark 15:43; Luke 23:50 of the *Vulgate*). This Roman title designated an official in charge of metal mines, and the associated farms and fortifications. Joseph is called *"nobilis decurio"* by Gildas Badonicus (516–570 A.D.), the British historian. Joseph's political influence with the Romans is evident from Cicero's remark that it was easier to become a senator of Rome that a decurio in Pompeii. Joseph's authority over mines naturally connects him with the shipping fleets, the port of Marseilles, and the Jewish mining industry in the Glastonbury area of western Britain.

Regarding the ease with which Joseph obtained Jesus' body, the probable answer, as several writers have pointed out, is that both Hebrew and Roman law required the male next of kin, the legal guardian of the family, to make such a claim. Joseph's apparently valid claim for the body suggests that he and Jesus were close relatives. Old traditions do, in fact, claim such a relationship. The Jewish Talmud asserts that Joseph was the uncle of Mother Mary, and therefore the great-uncle of Jesus. If so, then the act of Joseph is immediately understandable. He alone, and none of the women, disciples, or Apostles, would have had both the right and the responsibility to claim the earthly remains of Christ.

But in the eyes of the Jews, the Arimathean and his friend Nicodemus were marked men. So, too, was Lazarus, whom the Jews had already considered putting to death a second time (see John 12:10–11). The closest friends and relatives of Jesus fled to Caesarea, a major port for Roman ships and the ships of Tarshish. In Caesarea were gathered Peter, Lazarus, Barnabas, Clement, Joseph of Arimathea, and certain of the women. The Jews at that time still had no authority to impose the death penalty, Rome having retained that authority to itself a few years before the Crucifixion. Some church writers state that the Jews put Joseph, Lazarus, Mary, Martha, Marcella their maid, and perhaps others, including Mary, the Mother of Jesus, into a boat without sails or oars and abandoned them in the Mediterranean where they later drifted ashore near Marseilles.

Numerous local traditions and data trace these disciples up the Rhone valley and, from there, into western Britain. In the following, we will look at a condensation of this information, referring the reader to other sources for details and corroboration. We will also bear in mind that centuries of persecutions and wars have destroyed most evidence of events in the first few centuries. Accordingly, some of the details given by different early writers are inconsistent. In spite of this, the broad outline of the story appears reliable.

The best listing of the members of Joseph's party is, possibly, that given by Cardinal Baronius. According to him, the group consisted of Joseph, Sidonius (or, Restitutus, the man born blind), Trophimus, Martial, Maximin (thought to be the rich young ruler of Luke 18:18–23), Mary Magdalene, Martha, Marcella, Lazarus, Mary (wife of Cleopas), Eutropius, Salome, Cleon, and Saturnias. Many other writers insist that Mary, Jesus' mother, was among this party, since Joseph, her uncle, had been appointed her guardian by John.

The company proceeded to Avalon, later named Glastonbury, in the domain of Arviragus in Britain. There they were free from both Jewish and Roman persecutions, as no Roman army ever entered this region. The troops of Arviragus carried the banner of the cross on their shields through the bitter battles against the Roman legions. In later days, the lion, emblem of Judah, was superimposed on the cross. In using the cross as an ensign, Arviragus pre-empted, by some two hundred and fifty years, Constantine, who is usually credited with first using the emblem of the cross in battle. The Roman writer, Juvenal, indicated how greatly the Romans feared Arviragus, stating that his name trembled on the lips of every Roman, and that no better news could be received at Rome than the fall of this royal Christian leader. Juvenal writes: "Hath our great enemy Arviragus, the car-borne British King, dropped from his battle throne?" Arviragus, in 36 A.D., presented to Joseph as a perpetual gift twelve parcels of land, each parcel containing 160 acres. This was the first land dedicated in the name of Jesus Christ.

Additional evidence that disciples reached Britain is given by Eusebius (260–340 A.D.), who wrote: "The apostles passed beyond the ocean to the Isles called the Brittanic Isles." St. Hilary of Poitiers (300–367 A.D.) writes: "Afterwards the apostles built several tabernacles, and through all the parts of the earth wherever it was possible to go, even in the Isles of the Ocean they built several habitations for God." The testimony of the erudite Bishop Ussher is: "The British National Church was founded in A.D. 36, 160 years before heathen Rome confessed Christianity." As the message of Christ spread through the Isles, an Irish king sent his priests to Avalon to commit the Christian law and its teachings to writing, naming them "The Celestial Judgments." Clement of Rome (30–100 A.D.), a traveling companion and coworker of Paul, refers to the disciples in Britain in his *Epistle to the Corinthians,* Polydore Vergil concludes that "Britain, partly through Joseph of Arimathea . . . was of all kingdoms the first that received the gospel." Further testimony is added by Sir Henry Spellman in his *Concilia,* in which he writes, "We have abundant evidence that this Britain of ours received the Faith, and that from the disciples of Christ Himself, soon after the Crucifixion of Christ." Spellman concludes that, "For anyone to longer doubt the historic authenticity of Glastonbury, and the Mission of Joseph, is ridiculous."

Gildas Albanicus (425–512 A.D.) says, "Christ, the True Sun, afforded His light, the knowledge of His precepts, to our island in the last year, as we know, of Tiberius Caesar." This puts the date at 36 or 37 A.D., consistent with the time of the persecution of the Christians by Saul. Gildas also wrote that, "Joseph introduced Christianity into Britain in the last year of the reign of Tiberius." Joseph and his company settled in Avalon and built their wattle church. It was sixty feet in length and twenty six feet wide, following the pattern of the Tabernacle of Moses. The task was completed between 38 and 39 A.D. The wattle church was encased in boards and covered with lead by Paulinus (625–644 A.D.), the Archbishop of York, to protect it from the elements. A stone church was later erected over the "Ealde Churche," or "Church of the Refugees," the first Christian Church above ground, which perished in a fire in 1184.

The antiquity of the British Church was officially reaffirmed by four Church Councils, those of Pisa (1409), Constance (1417), Sienna (1424), and Basle (1434), which held that, "The Churches of France and Spain must yield in point of antiquity and precedence to that of Britain, as the latter Church was founded by Joseph of Arimathea immediately after the Passion of Christ."

Not all of the group that arrived in Avalon with Joseph stayed there. Some of them went back to Gaul and assisted Phillip in founding churches there. Traces of these disciples abound in southern France, particularly among the old metal trading route up the Rhone valley. There is abundant evidence that the disciples of Christ brought His message to the lost sheep of Israel in the West. We will list the barest of details about a few of those messengers. Scientific precision is not possible at this late date, forcing us to rely on early church records and traditions. As a result, there are occasional differences in dates, names, and locations as cited in different sources. With this caveat once stated, we will mention a few of the earliest evangelizers according to the best evidence of them. Further information is available in the references at the end of this chapter.

Trophimus came with Joseph's band to Marseilles. He was

mentioned by Paul as one of his helpers (see Acts 20:4; II Tim 4:20), and was commissioned by Peter. Trophimus founded the church at nearby Arles, where we find numerous traces of his visit. He is generally believed to have died at Arles on November 28, 94 A.D., although Hippolytus (born c. 160 A.D.) says he was martyred in Rome along with Paul.

Aristobulus was one of the seventy whom Christ had sent out (see Luke 10:1–17). He was chosen by Paul to be a missionary to Britain. In Britain he built churches and ordained priests for the island. Dorotheus (303 A.D.) and Hippolytus call him the "Bishop of Britain." He either died at Glastonbury in 99 A.D., or he was martyred under Nero, about 38 A.D. He is buried in Britain.

Maximin, the rich young ruler who encountered Jesus, labored near Marseilles, where now is found the village of St. Maximin, commemorating his name. He was said to have been one of the seventy disciples, also. Rabanus reports that "Maximinia" was the chief of the Christians next to the Apostles.

Barnabas, another companion of Paul, was stoned to death in Cyprus. He was buried by Mark outside the city. The grave of Barnabas was opened during the reign of Justinian. His body was found with a copy of the Gospel of St. Matthew lying on his chest.

Simon the Zealot first came to Britain in 44 A.D., the year when Claudius exiled several thousand Jews from Rome to Sardinia. Simon had already preached in northern Africa before arriving in Britain. Nicephorus (758–829 A.D.) says, "and the same doctrine he taught to the Occidental Sea, and the Isles called Britanniae." Simon the zealot was crucified by the Romans in Lincolnshire, in Britain, on May 10, 61 A.D.

Martial is supposed to have been the apostle of Limoges. He is believed to have arrived there in the first century along with his parents, Joseph of Arimathea, and Zaccheus, the publican of the Gospels. Joseph moved on, while local traditions have Martial remaining at Limoges, and Zaccheus residing at Rocamadour.

Zaccheus was called Amadour by his early converts in Gaul. His traditional dwelling place is Rocamadour, where he is said to have died and been interred. The burial chamber was later rifled and his body burned. Visits to Rocamadour are among the oldest of French pilgrimages.

Restitutus is best remembered from the Gospel as the man born blind. His evangelizing work was mostly in southern France, where the village of St. Restitut bears his name. Restitutus was buried there. His body was burned and the ashes scattered during the religious wars in the Middle Ages.

Luke is best known as the helper of Paul and the writer of *Luke* and *The Acts of the Apostles*. However, Luke also taught in Greece, Italy, and, principally, in Gaul. From Gaul he made frequent trips to Britain, visiting Joseph's enclave at Avalon.

Mary Salome (or, Salome) and Mary Cleopas spent most of the remainder of their lives in southern France. A church erected there in the eighth or ninth century enshrines their reputed relics. Annual pilgrimages are made there in honor of the two Marys and their handmaiden, Sara.

James, the brother of John, can be traced to Sardinia and Spain immediately after Christ. Old and definite traditions have him being martyred upon his return to Jerusalem. Cressy relates that, "In the one and fortieth year of Christ [41 A.D.] St. James, returning out of Spain, visited Gaul and Britain." James was executed in 44 A.D. by Herod (see Acts 12:1–2). His body was brought from Palestine to Spain and buried there.

Philip headed north from Judea on his missionary journey, traveling over part of Scythia (house of Isaac). He preached with Bartholomew for some time. Philip spent a great deal of time in Gaul, where the early church there referred to him as the Apostle of Gaul. He was crucified by the Romans at Hieropolis in Phrygia and buried there with his four daughters. His daughters had all been revered as prophetesses.

Crescens, another companion of Paul, also went to Gaul, or Galatia (see II Tim. 4:10). The churches of Vienne and Mayence, both in southern France, claim him as their founder.

Beatus learned Christianity at Joseph's settlement in Avalon. Beatus worked in Wales and introduced Christianity into Switzerland, where he and his converts built hospitals and churches. Though he died in 96 A.D., his humble dwelling is still being preserved today.

Mansuetus was another British missionary out of Avalon. Originally from Ireland, he was converted and baptized by Joseph, whereupon he set out to work in Europe. Mansuetus was called the friend and student of all the disciples. He was martyred at Illyria in 110 A.D.

Andrew, the brother of Peter, has always been associated with Scotland, although it seems that he never visited there. It appears, rather, that he visited the Scythians, predecessors of the Scots. The Scottish Declaration of Independence at Arbroath, April 6, 1320, derives the Scots from Greater Scythia, roughly tracing them to Scotland "twelve hundred years after the people of Israel crossed the Red Sea, to their home in the west where they still live today." It adds that Christ called them "almost the first to His most holy faith" and "confirmed them in that faith by . . . the most gentle Andrew." Eusebius tells us that Andrew headed north of the Black Sea to Scythia upon the dispersal from Judea. Other records say he taught chiefly in Greece, where he was martyred at Patras in 69 A.D. Andrew was crucified on a cross in the shape of an X. Such a cross is known to this day as "St. Andrew's Cross." His bones were reportedly taken to Scotland in the fourth or fifth century and buried at a place called St. Andrewa. Today they are in a cathedral at Patras built to house his relics. Due to his work among the Scythians, Andrew is the Patron Saint of Scotland. St. Andrews's cross became the national emblem of Scotland, and was later superimposed upon St. George's cross to form the Union Jack, the flag of Great Britain.

Martha, Mary, and Lazarus, the family from Bethany, also came west as teachers for the Lord. Martha is traditionally associated with the southern French towns of Avignon and Tarascon, near Marseilles. Martha died a natural death at Tarascon with her handmaiden Marcella at her side. The church of St. Martha at Tarascon is reputed to house her body and certain relics.

Mary, the sister of Martha and Lazarus, better known as Mary Magdalene, is associated with the French village of St. Baume, where she stayed. Her body is said to have been originally at the church of St. Maximin there. A skull and an arm bone attributed to Mary Magdalene are still in the possession of that church. The belief that Mary lived and was buried at St. Baume was so strongly held in the earlier centuries that many thousands of pilgrims, including Popes and kings, made pilgrimages to St. Baume.

Lazarus left Britain and returned to work in Gaul. Church records at Lyons reveal that he brought Martha and Mary back with him. He left behind in Britain his guidelines for living the Christian life. *The Triads of Lazarus* are still in the ancient Celtic records of Britain. One of them reads: "Believe in God who made thee; Love God who saved thee; Fear God who will judge thee." Lazarus was the first Bishop of Marseilles, serving until his death seven years later. His body was, perhaps, transferred to Glaston-bury some time later. To many minds, Lazarus was the Apostle of Gaul, despite the work there of Philip and others.

Peter preached in many places. Eusebius Pamphilis (c. 306 A.D.) puts Peter in Britain as well as Rome, Gaul, and Babylon. It is likely that Peter first visited Rome in 44 A.D., staying at the home of Rufus the senator, whose son, Rufus Pudens, later married Claudia. This family is the one saluted by Paul in his letters (see Rom 16:13; II Tim 4:21). In that year, Claudius banished the Jews from Rome, with Peter going to Britain. Evidence has been advanced that Peter visited both Gaul and Britain several times. An old British tradition holds that Peter founded the church which later became Westminster Abbey. At the same time, he is also the Patron Saint of Chartres, perhaps the oldest Druidic site in Gaul. Clement, in his first *Epistle to the Corinthians,* said that Peter preached both in the East and the West, including "the extreme limit of the West." Peter reportedly had just come from a visit in Britain at the end of his life when he was imprisoned in Rome. He was manacled to a post for nine months in fetid darkness, during which time he converted his jailers and several dozen others. In the end, Peter was crucified upside down in 67 A.D., judging himself unworthy to be crucified in the same manner as his Savior.

Mary, the Mother of Jesus, is another of the illustrious persons who disappear from the New Testament after the resurrection. None of the New Testament writers mentions her death or the location of her tomb. Their absence of comment on this point is conspicuous in view of the importance of Mary, and in view of the Old Testament penchant for naming the burial places of important servants of God.

Three hundred years after Christ, the mother of Constantine spent much time, effort, and money in locating and preserving

Holy sites and relics from Judea. She did not find the graves of Mother Mary or Joseph of Arimathea. Less than a century after that, the learned St. Jerome, by special commission of the church at Rome, recorded sacred places in the Near East. Jerome made no mention of the burial places of either this Mary or this Joseph. The most obvious explanation is that their burial sites were not in Judea or Rome. Nevertheless, there is a site near Jerusalem, the Chapel of the Dormiton, where tourists are told Mary is interred. It is of doubtful authenticity, however, because this location was unknown to the expert searchers of the first few centuries. Many other sites have been proposed as her authentic tomb. The Roman Catholic Church eventually formed the doctrine that Mary ascended physically into Heaven, thus supplying an explanation for the apparent absence of her body. An alternate possibility is simply that she was not buried in the realm of the Roman empire.

Jesus had entrusted the care of His mother to the Apostle John. The New Testament record states that, "From that hour the disciple took her into his own household" (John 19:27 NAS), or "home" (NEB, NIV). At this point, readers usually assume that John took care of Mary for the rest of her life. It is generally ignored that John left Jerusalem after a few years and served as an Apostle in Ephesus. It is unlikely that he carried Mary with him on this dangerous mission, particularly as he makes no mention of it in his Gospel. It is more likely that John continued to care for her as he would have cared for his own mother, as Christ instructed him to do, and that, upon his departure from Jerusalem, he entrusted her to the care of her powerful and rich uncle, Joseph of Arimathea.

Several manuscripts substantiate this. For example, the *Magna Glastoniensis Tabula* affirms, "St. John, while evangelizing Ephesus, made Joseph *paranymphos* [guardian]." In the Biblical record, Mary is last seen "dwelling among the disciples" in Jerusalem, those very people whom the Jews soon dispersed. The obvious likelihood is that Mary went with them wherever they fled from Jerusalem. Family ties and human nature suggest she would have gone with her uncle, Joseph, and her sister Mary Cleopas (see John 19:25), both of whom sailed to Marseilles and journeyed from there to Britain. If we can believe this tradition, Mary came to Avalon. A clue supporting this tradition comes from St. Augustine (c. 600 A.D.) in his letter to Pope Gregory, where he mentioned the island (Avalon) and the crude church built there by "the first neophytes," adding that God "continues to watch over it as sacred to Himself, and to Mary." Another clue is supplied by William of Malmsbury in his *Acts of Kings of the English,* in which he wrote of the sacredness of the old church wherein so many saints were buried under the protection of Mary. This church, St. Mary's of Glastonbury, was held in the deepest veneration, so much so that men swore oaths by it in the way that we swear legal oaths on the Bible. Over the ages, the Roman Catholic Church has referred to the Old Church as "Our Lady's Dowry." Other than this church at Avalon, churches were not dedicated to Mary until the twelfth century. The Old Church also carried the names "Secretum Domini" (The Secret of our Lord), and "Domus Dei" (The House, or Home, of God). A special significance is apparent.

So strong was the belief in the first centuries that the mother of Jesus was buried in Glastonbury, that St. David (c. 546 A.D.) erected a stone addition to the old church over what he believed to be the grave of Mary. A pillar with a brass plaque bore record to the holiness of that place. The plaque reads: "The first ground of God, the first ground of the saints in Britain, the rise and foundation of all religion in Britain, and the burial place of the Saints." Copies of the Arimathean story from old documents tell that Joseph came to Britain and cared for Mary fifteen years until her death in approximately 48 A.D. at Avalon. A native of Avalon known as Maelgwyn, Latinized to Melchinus (c. 500 A.D.), writes: "Ye ealde chyrche was built over the grave of the Blessed Mary." A worn and weathered stone on the ruins of a wall of the chapel bears two simple words: "Jesus-Maria." Its date and meaning are unknown.

Upon the death of Mary, Joseph's role as guardian ended. He is later found in Gaul, where Philip and others had by then established churches.

The numerous missionary churches in Gaul sprang from notable disciples of the Lord. In addition to those disciples, Paul, Peter, Andrew, Luke and Philip taught widely in Gaul. In view of that fact, it would be remarkable if Paul wrote no letters to those churches. Did he write to Corinth, Ephesus, and others, but inexplicably ignore the churches he visited along the Rhone valley? A good case can be made that he did write to them.

The New Testament letters of Paul were addressed to the church at Corinth, the church at Ephesus, and the ones at Rome, Philippi, Colossae, and Thessalonica. In contrast, he wrote a letter to the group of churches in Galatia (see Gal 1:2). Certain ancient writers claim that the *Epistle to the Galatians* was written to the inhabitants of Gaul, not the small colony of Gauls in Asia Minor, the traditional location of Galatia. Baronius said that the phrase, "to the Galatians," must be corrected to read, "to the Gauls." Theodoret, in reading "Galatia," also understood it to refer to Gaul, because the Greeks had given that name to Gaul, "and the Galatians had been thus named because they were a colony of the Gauls."

Other sources tell us that Paul sent Crescens to Gaul, where the churches of Vienne and Mayence claim Crescens as their founder. Paul wrote that Crescens was gone to "Galatia," so translated, although some ancient manuscripts read "Gaul" (see II Tim 4:10 footnote, NAS), or "Gallia" (see II Tim 4:10 footnote, NEB). Epiphanius (315–407 A.D.) wrote: "The ministry of the divine word to St. Luke, he exercised it by passing into Dalmatia, into Gaul, into Italy, into Macedonia, but principally into Gaul, so that St. Paul assures him in his epistles about some of his disciples— 'Crescens,' said he, 'is in Gaul.' In it must not be read in Galatia, as some have falsely thought, but in Gaul." All of the above strongly suggests that *Galatians* was, in fact, written to the churches in what we call Gaul. One of the oldest and most reliable manuscripts, the *Codex Sinaiticus,* specifically says Galia in Galatians 1:2.

Various references exist which place Joseph among the Gauls, or Galatians, if so they are, from the time of Mary's death (c. 48 A.D.) until his return to Britain with another group of disciples (c. 62 A.D.). He was believed to have died at Avalon on July 27, 82 A.D. Maelgwyn described the Isle of Avalon, "greedy of burials," which received thousands of sleepers, among whom Joseph of Arimathea entered his perpetual sleep." Maelgwyn also wrote that "Joseph of Arimathea, the noble decurion, received his everlasting rest with his eleven associates in the Isle of Avalon."

For over a thousand years annual pilgrimages were made to the tomb of Joseph by Christians from all parts of the old world. The stone lid of his sarcophagus was said to have borne the words: "*Ad Brittanos veni post Christum Sepelvi. Docui. Quievi* [To the Britons I came after I buried the Christ. I taught. I have entered my rest]." The body of Joseph remained there until 1345 A.D., when Edward III gave permission to dig for it. A monk wrote in 1367 A.D. that "the bodies of Joseph of Arimathea and his companions were found at Glastonbury." Joseph's bones were placed in a silver reliquary. His stone tomb was still reported seen as late as June 2, 1662. John Ray, fearing another wave of Puritanical desecration of churches and relics, had the altar tomb secretly removed and buried in the churchyard. Its location remained unknown until 1928. In that year, an empty sarcophagus matching the old descriptions of Joseph of Arimathea's tomb, and bearing the inscription "J.A.," was accidentally discovered in the cemetery adjoining St. Mary's chapel. Many believe that the tomb of Joseph had been found.

The foregoing pages recount the barest outlines of the coming of Christianity to the west of Europe immediately after Christ. This account has been drawn from secondary sources. The original sources themselves are often meager and sometimes disagree in minor ways, making it impossible to establish every point with certainty. What the sources do provide, however, is a remarkable agreement among early writers and traditions that certain disciples did labor in Gaul and Britain. The agreement comes both from old British writings and from sources antagonist to Britain and the British Church during those times. It requires extreme skepticism to assert that the stories so recounted are purely fictional. Much more likely, they are fundamentally true.

Recent excavations in the ruins of a church built by Constantine (c. 326 A.D.) over the reputed tomb of Jesus have uncovered a polished stone slab on which is boldly pictured a small Roman ship. The ship is shown with the sails furled and the mast either broken, or lowered. The Latin caption beneath it reads: "*Domine Ivimus* [Lord, we went]," which forms a speculative link with, "Go therefore and make disciples of all the nations" (Matt 28:19 NAS). Its true significance is unknown.

Paul, the Apostle to the Gentiles, traveled to a number of cities in the countries bordering the Mediterranean. Bibles frequently contain maps showing the supposed routes of Paul's missionary journeys, as deduced from the New Testament. Consequently, the travels and activities of Paul which are not mentioned in the Bibles are, necessarily, not shown on the maps. Moreover, the years between Paul's liberation from his first imprisonment and his martyrdom in Rome are absent from the New Testament. The lines of evidence locate Paul in Gaul and Britain during those years.

Paul wrote to the Roman Christians that he would try to visit them on his way to Iberia (roughly, Spain). As already noted, Iberia included the territory up to the Rhone valley in present day France. This implies that Paul would necessarily visit the Christians at Marseilles, and the other new churches in Gaul, for they lay directly along his proposed route. We have no record that Paul ever joined James in evangelizing Spain. There is, however, evidence that he followed the route of the Jerusalem refugees up the Rhone River to Britain. Among the earliest writings to this effect is the *Epistle to the Corinthians* by Clement, a traveling companion and coworker with Paul (see Phil 4:3). Clement (30–100 A.D.), who became the third bishop of Rome, wrote that Paul was the herald of the Gospel to the West, having been "to the extremity of the West" just before his martyrdom. The extreme limits of the West were the British Isles.

Bishop Theodoret, some three hundred years after Clement, wrote that Paul and others went also to the Scythians (roughly, Germany), the Britons, and the Cimmerians. Theodoret specifically states that Paul "brought salvation to the Islands of the sea." Several other authors from the first millenium concur that Paul reached Britain perhaps twenty years after Joseph of Arimathea. Venantius Fortunatus, Bishop of Poitiers, writing in the sixth century, relates that Paul crossed the ocean and visited "Britain and the extreme West." It therefore appears that Paul followed after two of his helpers: Aristobulus, whom he had sent to Britain, and Crescens, whom he had sent to Vienne in Gaul. If the inveterate apostle Paul neglected to visit the Gentiles in Gaul and Britain, then this negligence would be difficult to explain.

When Paul was traveling the West, the Roman population of London was perhaps 80,000. It was as easy for Paul to find London as it was for the thousands of Romans. At the present day, Paul is the Patron Saint of London. His emblem, the sword of his martyrdom, is incorporated into the coat of arms of London. Old traditions are strong that he preached there, at the location where St. Paul's Cathedral now stands. Another ancient tradition assigns to this Apostle the founding of Bangor Abbey, whose rule was known as the Rule of Paul, and whose abbots claimed to be his successors. Over every gate of the Abbey was Paul's saying: "If any will not work, neither shall he eat" (from II Thess 3:10). Capellus, in his *History of the Apostles,* writes: "I know scarcely of one author from the time of the Fathers downward who does not maintain that St. Paul, after his liberation, preached in every country of the West, in Europe, Britain included." In concluding the case for Paul's travels to Britain, we note that Bishop Burgess concluded: "Of Paul's journey to Britain we have as satisfactory a proof as any historical question can demand." We have ample reason for believing that Christ's disciples, lesser known ones and the more famous Peter, Paul, Joseph of Arimathea, Philip, and James, carried the Gospel to the lost sheep of Israel, the Gentiles of the extreme west in Gaul, Iberia, and Britain.

According to martyrologies, Paul was interred at the estate of Pudens on the Via Ostiensa at Rome. Constantine excavated Paul's grave, had his remains placed in a stone coffin, and caused a church to be constructed over the tomb, located outside of Rome. A stone marker at the church, later rebuilt, bears the name "Pauli." No stone casket is seen. Similarly, the remains of Peter do not seem to be in his traditional burial place at Rome. It may well be that neither of these Apostles to the West remained where they were first interred. Bede (673–735 A.D.) recorded that the British King, Oswy, brought the remains of many disciples of Christ to Britain. This king requested the bodies of Peter and Paul and four other saints to be moved from Rome and interred at Canterbury. A letter (c. 656 A.D.) from Pope Vitalian to King Oswy permitted the transfer of their bodies. The Pope's remarkable agreement to yield such Holy relics to another state implies that the connection between Peter, Paul, the early apostles, and Britain, was strong, clear, and beyond controversy in those days.

The introduction of Christianity into Britain immediately after Christ, coupled with the Britons' monotheistic Druidic faith and their stubborn resistance to Roman arms, spurred Claudius to invade the Islands which supplied his tin and lead. He also issued an edict in 42 A.D. making the acceptance of the Druidic or the Christian faith a crime punishable by death. Claudius assembled a mighty army to invade Britain, a challenge which yielded Julius Caesar only limited success a century earlier.

Parenthetically, we recall that history has perpetuated Julius Caesar's famous words, "*Veni, Vidi, Vici* [I came, I saw, I conquered]," although the British warriors routed his armies and forced them to withdraw from Britain after only two weeks. In the ten years of conflict which followed, the Roman armies never penetrated inland more than a few miles. Upon Julius Caesar's first return from Britain, he was openly satirized by the pens of Roman writers, who changed "*Veni, Vidi, Vici*" into "I came, I saw, but I failed to stay."

The military efforts of Claudius against the British were little more successful than those of Julius. Roman arms encountered fierce resistance directed by able leaders, among whom Caradoc is of special interest to us. Caradoc, called Caractacus, or Caratacus, by the Romans, was captured along with his wife (or sister), his daughters, Euergen and Gladys, and his son, Linus. (Tacitus says the captives were Caractacus, his wife and daughter, and his brothers.) A sister of Caradoc had earlier married Plautius, one of the Roman generals. Gladys married Aulus Rufus Pudens Pudentinus, a young Roman senator, while the captured British royal family was held in Rome. Euergen became the first female British saint. Linus became the first bishop of the church at Rome. Gladys came to be known as Claudia, or as Claudia Rufina, in reference to Emperor Claudius. Claudia wrote several books of odes and hymns. She was highly praised by Roman writers for her beauty, charm, and intelligence. The Roman poet, Martial, mused: "Since Claudia wife of Rufus comes from the blue-set Britons, how is it that she has so won the hearts of the Latin people?"

The royal family was detained in comfort, quite in contrast to the Roman custom of executing captured leaders. Their spacious estate became known as the Palatium Britannicum, and the Hospitium Apostolorum. Known in earlier days as the Titulus, it is more commonly known today as St. Pudentiana. As the names suggest, the palace of the British was the haven for Apostles who passed through Rome. The building and grounds were bequeathed to the Christian church at Rome, constituting that church's only real estate until the time of Constantine.

The British royalty had dwelt in the very area of Britain where Joseph of Arimathea and his band had settled only a few years earlier. As we see from the writings of Paul, they were already Christian before he met them. Paul sent greetings to "Rufus, a choice man in the Lord, also his mother and mine" (Rom 16:13 NAS), to his kinsmen Andronicus and Junias, "who are outstanding among the apostles" (verse 7), and to his relative Herodion (see verse 11). Quite obviously, Paul had relatives in Rome who were well known to Rufus Pudens. When Paul was in Rome and wrote to Timothy, he sent greetings to him from Pudens, Linus, Claudia, and others (see II Tim 4:21). Paul wrote to the Philippians: "All the saints greet you, especially those of Caesar's household" (Phil 4:22 NAS). At least two of these friends of Paul were British royalty. Several authors from the first centuries identify Claudia as the first harborer of both Peter and Paul when they came to Rome. There is little doubt that both Peter and Paul knew the British royal family in Rome, that they, and others, lodged at the Hospitium Apostolorum at times, and that they knew the way to Britain.

The influence of the efforts of Joseph the Arimathean and his British converts bore fruit in Rome. Linus, the first bishop of Rome, was the son of a British king. Clement, who succeeded Linus, is, likewise, traceable to Britain. Mansuetus, the third bishop of Rome, was born in Ireland, and converted and taught in Britain. Some writers insert Cletus into this trio of early bishops. Whether or not Cletus belongs in the list, the British hand in establishing the church at Rome is evident. Those of the lost sheep who had wandered to the Islands were beginning to recognize the voice of the Shepherd.

The Messiah had won liberation for His errant spirits on Earth. His story had gone forth, borne in the hearts of those who loved Him, to be told to His unfaithful bride, Israel. She, having been driven into the wilderness several hundred years earlier, received from Him the invitation to return to God, to receive healing of spirit, and to become the light-bearing nation by which His kingdom would be established on Earth. The lower spirits spared no efforts in attempting to remove from this dimension as much of the Truth of God as He had given us. To that end, human instruments were ever ready, driven by greed, pride, and intolerance. They continued to persecute Jews, and added Christians and Druids to their list of victims, encompassing all those humans who had caught a glimpse of the Light. The acts of the pagan Roman Empire against Christians will not be detailed here. It suffices to recognize that over six million Christians were slaughtered and entombed within the catacombs under Rome during the first two hundred years of Christianity. That city had the curious distinction of having more Christians beneath it than in it. It is notable that nearly all of the martyred Christians, who came from throughout the entire Roman Empire, were converts of evangelists from Jerusalem and Britain, rather than Rome.

During the time when the empire of the Caesars was Satan's tool for decimating Christian communities, Britain was becoming a Christian nation. Arviragus, the compatriot of Caradoc, had fought against Rome under the sign of the cross, probably the Celtic cross, while Paul was evangelizing to the west of Judea. A mere hundred years later, King Lucius (or, Lleurwg) of Britain was baptized at Glastonbury by Timotheus, grandson of Claudia. Lucius proclaimed Christianity the national religion of Britain, making Britain the first officially Christian nation. Ephesus was then the central church, rather than Rome, and Greek, not Latin, was the language of the church. According to Sabellious, "Christianity was privately confessed elsewhere, but the first nation that proclaimed it as their religion, and called itself Christian after the name of Christ, was Britain." Bede declares that "the Britons preserved the faith which they had received under King Lucius uncorrupted and entire, in peace and tranquility, until the time of Emperor Diocletian."

In the spiritual struggle against the Gospel, the lower spirit forces made full use of the human penchant for violence. The pagan empire of Rome was the major weapon by which Christians were murdered, thereby removing those combatants from this dimension of the spiritual war. By the end of the third century, the Diocletian persecution raged across Europe. When it reached Britain, however, the tide of battle shifted visibly in favor of the higher spirits. A series of events began which culminated in Christianity being declared the state religion of the Roman Empire. While this fact is common knowledge, certain relevant circumstances surrounding it are not. Knowledge of these facts, which are presented in the following, places that period of history in a clearer perspective in regard to the Redemption of the fallen spirits and the role of lost Israel.

The Diocletian persecution lasted about eighteen years on the continent, but upon reaching Britain it encountered massive resistance. In Britain, Constantius Chlorus ruled as emperor from York. The name Chlorus means "pale," intimating that Constantius may have been of British rather than Roman stock. His wife was Helen, the British granddaughter of King Lucius. Melancthon noted that: "Helen was unquestionably a British princess." Under the leadership of Constantius, and amidst great bloodshed, the British warriors stopped the persecution of Christians in Britain within a year. Constantius Chlorus was buried in the ancient city of York, where several other Roman emperors had ruled and were also buried. Constantine, the son of Constantius, assumed the emperorship immediately upon the death of his father. He attempted to repair the damage resulting from Diocletian's edict to exterminate the Christians, their churches, writings, and possessions. Constantine amassed a powerful army, said to have been composed almost exlusively of British warriors, and sailed with it to Germany. There they routed the Roman legions and ended the persecutions. Next, Constantine and his Celtic-Saxon army of Israelite descendants marched on Rome, where he received a jubilant welcome. He ascended to the imperial throne amidst great rejoicing, being acclaimed emperor by the senate and the populace of Rome.

The silence of our culture regarding these matters misleads us into thinking of them as internal affairs of the Roman empire, instigated by one of the Romans. We note, however, that Constantine's mother was a British princess. His father might have been British. His army was British. He ruled from York, not from

Rome. And his religion, Christianity, had long since been the state religion of his native Britain. The genealogy of Constantine, as recited by his descendant, Constantius Palaeologus in *The Panegyrics of the Emperors,* demonstrates that Constantine was a Briton descended from Caradoc. According to Polydore Vergil, "Constantine, born in Britain of a British mother, proclaimed Emperor in Britain beyond doubt, made his natal soil a participator in his glory." And so wrote the eminent Cardinal Baronius: "The man must be mad who, in the face of universal antiquity, refuses to believe that Constantine and his mother were Britons, born in Britain."

Rome, which Claudius mobilized to conquer Britain and annihilate Christianity nearly three centuries earlier, was now conquered by its intended victim. The first Christian church had been founded at Rome by the British royal family, and before Paul came there. That same family, under Arviragus, had used the sign of the cross as their fighting emblem. Their descendents, under Lucius, had nationalized the faith in Britain, where Joseph the Arimathean and other illustrious disciples had planted it. Lucius had placed the sign of the cross for the first time on coins. His granddaughter, Princess Helen of Colchester, and her husband, Constantius, smashed the Diocletian persecution. Their son, Constantine, backed by a British army, nationalized the Christian faith in Rome. The end result found a Briton reigning over the Roman Empire from York, with British warriors fighting for him under the sign of the cross of Christ.

Constantine's objectives are spelled out in one of his edicts, where he says: "We call God to witness, the Saviour of all men, that in assuming the government we are influenced solely by these two considerations: the uniting of the empire in one faith, and the restoration of peace to a world rent to pieces by the insanity of religious persecution." Constantine's first act as Emperor of Rome was to declare the empire Christian, ending forever the persecution of Christians by the empire. He made land gifts to the church at Rome, whose only previous gift was the Palace of the British and its estate, bequeathed by the Claudia-Pudens royal family. Baronius observed that, until the reign of Constantine, the Roman Christians had no other church in which to worship.

Two years after he was proclaimed emperor in Rome, Constantine convened a church council at Arles, the first council since the one in Jerusalem recorded in the *Acts of the Apostles*. A decade later, he called another church council at Nicaea. These meetings took place in the area of Gaul where Christianity was first brought to the continent. Both councils seated British bishops in positions of seniority. At Nicaea, scarcely ten of the three hundred and eighteen bishops present were from churches which spoke Latin, most of them being from Africa, Spain, Gaul, Britain, and other countries. At these councils, and at a third one held in Constantinople, the doctrines of Christianity hardened, amidst much disagreement, into creeds which would be recited by millions of Christians over the next two thousand years.

Constantine and his mother set up his government at Constantinople. It has been stated that during his long reign, Constantine made only two short visits to Rome, ruling instead from York, Colchester, and Constantinople. For nearly fourteen hundred years the sword of Constantine was a treasured relic of the British coronation regalia. It was always handed to a new king when he was crowned, as a symbol of his heritage as defender of the Christian faith. The sword was stolen during Puritan desecrations and was never recovered.

Constantine's mother, Helen, spent the latter years of her life working for the faith at Constantinople. Helen diligently collected and preserved relics of the early Apostles found in and around Jerusalem, and restored churches and sacred sites in Palestine. This former British princess came to be known as "Helen of the Cross" due to the claim that she found the cross of Christ buried near Jerusalem.

In declaring Christianity the national religion of the Roman Empire, Constantine did for Rome what King Lucius had done for Britain a century and a half before. The state could no longer martyr the Christians, but the spirit attack on the Truth continued and now assumed a more subtle form. In this new phase of the struggle for the fallen spirits, the Scriptures would be declared closed, thwarting Christ's promise of further revelation (see John 16:12–15). The choice of those writings which constituted Scripture became irrevocably established. Creeds, believed to embody the basic truths of Christianity, were formulated, and, thereby, virtually denied the believer his right and responsibility to discern the truth for himself. The church soon became the major instrument for force-feeding a mixture of truth and error to God's Truth-starved children.

At that time the Scriptures were not accessible to ordinary people. Toward the end of the century which began with Constantine, St. Jerome did translate the Scriptures into the everyday language of Latin. The difficulties he faced in that task have already been mentioned in an earlier Chapter. Still, the church held itself to be the sole interpreter and dispenser of the truth, even after the Scriptures were available in the language of the common man. While attempting to serve Christ, the churches unwittingly aided Satan by persecuting those Christians who did not accept the church-held beliefs. This practice continued for a thousand years, reaching its climax during the Inquisitions, during which the church slaughtered hundreds of thousands of Christ's adherents who dared to differ with it. In the name of God, untold numbers of human souls endured torture or death, from duly authorized clergy, for having differed in some way from the authorized creed. At times it was a criminal offense to own, or even read, a Bible.

One wonders why the evil forces would go to such great lengths to enforce orthodoxy. It could only be that it was to their advantage.

Against this background, each grain of the Truth glistens as a pearl of great price.

Much of what we think true is only partly true: incomplete at best, misleading at times, contaminated always. Everyone celebrates St. Patrick's work in Ireland, but few in America know that he was a Briton who spent many years at Glastonbury and is buried there. Every child learns that St. Augustine brought Christianity to the British Isles around 596–597 A.D., but few are taught that he found a flourishing British church already in existence, a church which gave him a cool reception. Popular myths often blur our vision. The reader is left to discern the truth, with the help of the spirit of truth, which Christ has sent him.

Historical truth is sometimes difficult to ascertain, particularly when the bulk of the records have been destroyed. In the case of

Britain, almost nothing written by Britons during the first five centuries has survived. Such recollections that exist are largely of Roman origin, written by men with an adversary view of Britain. In that case, perhaps the maxim of Napoleon applies: "What is history, but lies agreed upon?" With the burning of the great library at Glastonbury in 1184 A.D., Satan effectively destroyed the preeminent source of information about the first thousand years of non-Roman Christianity in the West.

As civilization emerged from the dark ages, the light of understanding and religious freedom dawned across Europe. The last few centuries have left us better, and more plentiful, historical records. Many of the relevant historical events are common knowledge and need not be discussed in detail here. Each Christian knows of the reformation of the church of Rome, of the rise of Protestantism, and of the strong pull of religious freedom which helped lure pilgrims to the new lands in North America. In the present context, we merely note the remarkable fact that, after nearly two thousand years of struggles, a nation arose in North America whose very foundation included the right of religious freedom.

Nearly a million days have elapsed since the tribes of Israel were driven into the wilderness as punishment for deserting God. Yet the pledges God made to the Israelites are still valid and show many signs of imminent fulfillment. Christians look for the regathering of scattered Israel, followed by their finally fulfilling God's assignment to be witnesses for Him among the nations of the world. Upon the establishment of the tribes of Israel in the land promised to them, the End of the Age will be fast approaching, to culminate in the rule of Christ on Earth. Then will the plan of salvation of the fallen spirits enter its most important phase since Christ's first advent on Earth.

REFERENCES CITED

Capt, E. Raymond, *The Traditions of Glastonbury*
Jowett, George F., *The Drama of the Lost Disciples*
Lewis, Lionel Smithett, *St. Joseph of Arimathea at Glastonbury*
Morgan, Rev. W., *St. Paul in Britain*
Stoker, Robert B., *The Legacy of Arthur's Chester*
Taylor, John W., *The Coming of the Saints*

❖

CHAPTER 13

Thy Kingdom Come

THE regathering of Israel into the land God promised them has been the subject of countless books, articles, and sermons. Accordingly, detailed expositions of differing views on this subject are readily available to anyone wishing to read them. The following synopsis of that information will quote only a few of over a thousand Scripture verses regarding Israel, thereby outlining the usual explanations given by most denominations.

The story of the covenant people begins with the man with whom the covenant was first made, Abram. "Now the Lord had said until Abram, Get thee out of thy country . . . unto a land that I will shew thee: And I will make of thee a great nation . . . and in thee shall all families of the earth be blessed" (Gen 12:1–3). Abram, certain of his kin, and others (Gen 11:31, 12:5), then left the land of the Chaldeans and travelled to Canaan, approximately the Palestine area of today, but much larger. In Canaan, Abram received this word from God: "Unto thy seed will I give this land" (Gen 12:7). Somewhat later, the promise was repeated to Abram with additional details: "all the land which thou seest, to thee will I give it, and to thy seed for ever. And I will make thy seed as the dust of the earth . . . Arise, walk through the land . . . for I will give it unto thee" (Gen 13:15–17). Abram learned that his descendants would be an enormous multitude who would someday possess the land in perpetuity.

God changed Abram's name to "Abraham," said to mean "father

of multitudes," "father of nations," or "father of a ruling nation," depending upon the choice of translators. Sarai's name was changed to Sarah (princess).

The covenant is repeated with still further clarification in Genesis 17, where it is revealed that from Abraham's exceedingly great number of descendants shall come forth kings (see verses 6 and 16), and that "all the land of Canaan" (verse 8) shall be their everlasting possession, "and I will be their God" (verse 8).

The covenant passed to Abraham's son, Isaac (see Gen 17:21), and then to Isaac's son, Jacob: "the land whereon thou liest, to thee will I give it, and to thy seed; and thy seed shall be as the dust of the earth . . . in thy seed shall all the families of the earth be blessed . . . I . . . will bring thee again into this land" (Gen 28:13–15).

Jacob had twelve sons and one daughter, Dinah, but only two of the sons, Joseph and Benjamin, were sons of Jacob's chosen wife Rachel. Jacob was the inheritor of the covenant promises (Gen 32:12). God changed Jacob's name to Isreal (Gen 32:28, 35:10), and his descendants were called by various titles, such as "the house of Israel," "the children of Israel," simply "Israel," and others. The covenant was confirmed to Jacob, renamed Israel: "a nation and a company of nations shall be of thee, and kings . . . the land which I gave Abraham and Isaac, to thee I will give it, and to thy seed after thee" (Gen 35:11–12).

Jacob-Israel and his clan were brought to Egypt (Gen 46:1–7) where Joseph, his first-born son from Rachel, had authority over Egypt under the Pharaoh. At the end of his life, Israel blessed Ephraim and Manasseh, the two sons of Joseph born in Egypt, with: "let my name be named on them, and the name of my fathers Abraham and Isaac; and let them grow into a multitude in the midst of the earth" (Gen 48:16). Manasseh was to produce a great nation, with Ephraim's descendants becoming a "multitude [or family, aggregation, union] of nations" (verse 19) *(em add)*. The transfer of Joseph's birthright to Ephraim and Manasseh has the effect of producing thirteen Israelite clans, rather than the original twelve tribes. Ephraim is to receive the various great material blessings passed to the first-born son: "for I am a father to Israel, and Ephraim is my firstborn" (Jer 31:9).

The saga is well-known of the stay of the Israelites in the land of Egypt, of their exodus from that land, and of their return to the promised land. Moses led the Israelites to the land which God had sworn to their fathers to give them (see Deut 31:20). Moses had transgressed, however, and was forbidden to enter the promised land (see Deut 32:50–52). Joshua received the Divine commission to succeed Moses: "Be strong and of a good courage: for thou shalt bring the children of Israel into the land which I sware unto them: and I will be with thee: (Deut 31:23).

The promises of God were thus fulfilled. The covenant people were settled in their promised land according to the pledges God made to them: "So the Lord gave Israel all the land which He had sworn to give to their fathers, and they possessed it and lived in it. And the Lord gave them rest on every side, according to all that He had sworn to their fathers, and no one of all their enemies stood before them; the Lord gave all their enemies into their hand. Not one of the good promises which the Lord had made to the house of Israel failed; all came to pass" (Josh 21:43–45 NAS). An important phase of history had been concluded. Israel was living safely in a land of their own under Divinely appointed rule, having no earthly king. Their destiny had been clearly explained to them: they were to be witnesses and servants of God, a nation of priests who would be God's instruments for establishing His rule on this sphere. As it happened, the generations who followed drifted away into idolatry and left their first God. They craved a king and God gave them Saul, then David, then Solomon. Under human leadership, although it was Divinely appointed, the tribes could not maintain their union. Most of the tribes, including the tribe of Joseph (in the form of Ephraim and Manasseh), and including many from Judah and Benjamin who were among them, seceded from the union. These northern tribes formed a kingdom carrying the Biblical name of Israel and retaining the pledges made to Israel. Only portions of the tribes of Judah and Benjamin remained in the southern kingdom, where they were collectively known as Judah in the Scriptures. These descendants of Jacob (Israel) in the two kingdoms fell further and further into idolatry and evil ways. After roughly three centuries, the Lord allowed the Assyrians to be the "rod of mine anger" by carrying away almost everyone except part of Judah. Over a century later, the Babylonians were used to carry Judah into captivity, thereby finishing the dispersal of all the children of Israel. Nevertheless, the Abrahamic covenant still was in effect. A time would come when they were to be in permanent possession of that same land. "And they shall live on the land that I gave to Jacob (Israel) My servant, in which your fathers lived; and they will live on it, they, and their sons, and their sons' sons, forever; and David My servant shall be their prince forever" (Ezek 37:25 NAS) *(em add)*.

Although a small remnant of Judah, the Jews, returned from Babylon and rebuilt Jerusalem and the Temple, that was not the promised regathering when all the prophecies were to be fulfilled. Indeed, Jerusalem was conquered several times in the next few centuries. In 70 A.D., Titus destroyed Jerusalem and the temple, with a quarter of a million Jews perishing. The remaining Jews continued to revolt until Caesar ordered the desolation of Judea in 135 A.D. About a thousand towns and villages were left in ashes, fifty fortresses were razed, and the survivors were scattered in all directions. Nothing seemed to remain of the Israelite people or of their nation. Yet the promises of God still stood.

A new covenant had been prophesied for Israel (Jer 31:31–32) to replace the Mosaic covenant. God promised repeatedly through His prophets that, although Israel had been cast off, it would not be abandoned. Instead, the children of Israel would be chastened, cleansed, cured of their idolatry, and recalled to the land of their own (for example, see Isa 61:8–9; Jer 32:37–40; Ezek 37:21–28). The Scripture passages elaborating upon these events are too numerous to list here. At some time after their dispersion, Israel was to be replanted and rebuilt (see Jer 31:28), at which time there would be worldwide knowledge of the Lord (see Isa 11:9; Jer 31:34). "For the Lord will have mercy on Jacob, and will yet choose Israel, and set them in their own land" (Isa 14:1).

The children of Israel were to be recalled from among the nations where they were dispersed and brought into their own land (see Ezek 37:21–22), the land "wherein your fathers have dwelt" (verse 25). This regathering was to happen only after the coming of the Messiah, the period of history referred to as "the latter days" (Hosea 3:5). Thus, the Israelites have waited for centuries for God to "perform the truth to Jacob, and the mercy to

Abraham, which thou hast sworn unto our fathers from the days of old" (Micah 7:20).

Let us now go forward in time to the year 1897. In that year, Theodor Herzl announced that the purpose of the Zionist movement was to "create for the Jewish people a home in Palestine secured by public law." The Turks were then in control of Palestine, having held it since 1517. In 1917, it was taken by the British under General Allenby upon Turkey's defeat in World War I. By this act, the land promised to Israel was liberated by an army and a general who were of Israelite ancestry. On November 2, 1917, British Foreign Secretary Arthur J. Balfour made the famous "Balfour Declaration": "His majesty's government views with favor the establishing in Palestine of a national home for the Jewish people." The Arab nations quite understandably opposed the idea of losing some of the land in their possession, and little came of the idea over the next generation. However, after World War II, the British turned the fate of Palestine over to the United Nations, who divided it into a Jewish and an Arab state. Israel was able, finally, to proclaim itself an independent state on May 14, 1948. Although they were attacked by Egypt, Jordan, Iraq, Syria, Lebanon, and Saudi Arabia, on that same day, they prevailed and are still firmly established on the ground where Jacob had his dream. The regathering of Israel sets the stage for the fulfillment of the end time prophecies in Ezekiel, Daniel, Revelation, and other books, and for "the time of Jacob's trouble [Israel's trouble]," which closely precedes the return of Christ to earth. A clear understanding of the fate of Israel is most important in deciphering those prophecies. We must necessarily go back a step, then, and consider the larger body of prophecies about Israel, and search for their meanings.

We immediately find that a considerable number of prophecies have not been fulfilled by the gathering of Jews in Palestine. Many are yet to be fulfilled. And there are some contradictions. As Bible scholars have realized, a great many prophetic passages are either confusing or completely baffling, and there are frequent obscure allusions which have not been deciphered. It is, therefore, difficult to discuss the tribes of Israel and arrive at many incontestable conclusions.

The difficulty is multiplied by the fact that over two thousand

Bible verses refer to either Israel or Judah, and many other verses which mention Judah or Israel use symbolic names. For example, some of the other names for Israel and/or Judah are: house of Israel or Judah, nation of Israel or Judah, Samaria (Isa 10:11; Jer 31:5; Hosea 7:1), Ephraim (Isa 7:2; Jer 31:6; Hosea 12:1), Jacob (very many references), holy mountain (Isa 2:2; Joel 3:17), Joseph, Isaac, Rachel, Zion, daughter of Zion, city, Jerusalem, and others. Were this profusion of literal and symbolic names not enough, there are also other symbolic usages such as cedar (a nation), highest branch (king), tender young twig (daughter), high mountain (great nation), shoots and boughs (children), as used by Ezekiel (Ezek 17).

There are further problems in understanding the prophecies. Symbolic prophecies must be interpreted. Daniel was wonderfully inspired to interpret accurately. The same cannot be verified for modern interpreters. Moreover, prophecies are not necessarily given in chronological order. That is, the order of events is not necessarily the same as that in which the prophecies occur in the Bibles. In addition, prophecies are sometimes taken out of context. This can happen naturally and honestly if the context itself is subject to interpretation. Furthermore, the prophetic statement may in actuality be given somewhat out of context in the Bible, as though it were inserted in passing.

Finally, we must not assume that the children of Israel were to realize that they were fulfilling prophecy during their dispersal and regathering. As a parallel, there were very few people in Jerusalem at the time of Christ who understood what was happening to them. When the time came that people had to make a choice and take sides, almost all of them deserted Christ and "walked with Him no more." They knew the Scriptures well enough, but they could not recognize that prophecies were being fulfilled before their eyes.

The congregating of Israel in Palestine marks the end of a long phase in the history of the descendants of Abraham and prepares for the fulfillment of end time prophecies. The time of the restoration of Israel is of importance in verifying that events have truly happened in the way they were predicted in the Old Testament, for "He has weighed the world in the balance, and has measured the times with a measure, and carefully counted the hours, and He will not move or disturb them until the prescribed measure is reached" (II Esdras 4:36–37, Goodspeed translation). The Lord threatened Israel with severe punishment and correction if they failed to live according to the Divine laws given them: "If . . . you do not obey Me, then I will punish you seven times more for your sins" (Lev 26:18 NAS, repeated in verses 21, 24, and 28). The sevenfold punishment could imply seven times as intense, as in the story of the "fiery furnace," seven times as long, or seven prophetic *times:* that is, seven prophetic years. A year in prophecy is twelve months of 30 days each, or 360 days, as we see from the parallel prophecies in Daniel and Revelation (see Dan 12:7; Rev 12:6, 13:5). When Moses was leading the exodus from Egypt, the people were punished by forty years of wandering in return for a forty-day transgression, the principle being a year for a day (see Num 14:34). A similar correspondence was applied to a task assigned to Ezekiel (see Ezek 4:5–6). Therefore, we will work from this premise, from which we see that seven prophetic times, or seven prophetic years, would equal seven times 360, or 2,520 calendar years.

Let us add this time interval to the beginning of the period usually given for the Babylonian conquest of Judah, from 604 to 585 B.C. If we add the punishment time (2,520 years) to the beginning of the conquest (604 B.C.), then we arrive at the year 1917. In that year, the British did issue the Balfour Declaration in favor of establishing a national home in Palestine for the Jews, and led the liberation of Palestine during the following year. Certainly 1917/1918 can be accorded significance in that regard.

The last part of the book of Daniel contains several puzzling prophecies which are not to be understood until "the time of the end" (Dan 12:4, 12:9). A curious figure of 1,260 days, expressed as "time, times, and half a time" (Dan 12:7 NAS), was to elapse before certain unspecified events were to take place. Another time period of 1,290 years is given (see Dan 12:11), which is to be measured from the end of the daily sacrifice and the "abomination of desolation" set up in the Holy place (see also Matt 24:15). In Old Testament usage, "abomination" usually refers to an idol or false religious symbol. The Dome of the Rock built on the site of the old Holy Temple, therefore, qualifies according to the meaning. The Dome of the Rock, a mosque of architectural splendor built by Caliph Abd al-Malik to replace the primitive Mosque of Omar, was built atop the ruins of the Temple of Solomon. This Islamic edifice, for the worship of Allah, now encloses the rock once consecrated by the children of the Exodus as the site where Abraham had offered to sacrifice his son, Isaac. When this rock was first exposed, as Caliph Omar and his soldiers cleared the debris on Mount Moriah, he exclaimed: "This is the place described to us by the Apostle of Allah. Let us make this place for a mosque." Sophronius, the Patriarch of Jerusalem, who had been forced to accompany the caliph, is said to have uttered in horror: "Verily, this is the abomination of desolation spoken of by Daniel the Prophet, and it now stands in the Holy Place" (Landay, p. 18). Whether or not these utterances have been preserved with total accuracy, the Dome of the Rock, which rises on the location of the Holy of Holies, stands as a Biblical "abomination."

Unfortunately, for students of Biblical prophecy, it is not clear when to begin counting the years, as the construction of the Mosque of Omar was begun in 637 A.D., and the Dome of the Rock was not dedicated until 691 A.D. If the counting were to begin with 657 A.D., then the passage of 1,260 years would bring us to the year 1917/1918. Similarly, the 1,290 year period would bring us to 1947/1948, the time Israel was established as a nation in Palestine. In the event that these times are correctly interpreted, some special event should be in store after the 1,335 days (Dan 12:12). That is, in 1992.

Several other lines of reasoning have been proposed for other prophecies which project dates toward the end of this century as being significant times of prophetic fulfillment. However, the various arguments do not result in the same dates. In addition, it is often unclear, as in the previous examples, when the counting should begin. Dates for ancient events, especially in the era before Christ, are, by no means, as certain as they sometimes appear. In fact, even our present calendar may be in error by a decade, or more, according to some estimates. If Jesus were born as early as 6 or 7 B.C., as many Bible historians conclude, then the current year is incorrectly dated for that reason, alone. In summary, the dates arrived at by scholars interested in end-time events seem significant enough to warrant close attention, but not convincing enough to accept as necessarily true.

The Old Testament contains other verses leading to the conclusion that the present-day State of Israel is the regathering promised long ago, and so the world believes. Yet there are quite a few prophecies which are in strong disagreement with this conclusion. The following list contains some of the prophetic requirements which modern Palestinian Israel does not meet.

"And I will walk among you, and will be your God, and ye shall be my people" (Lev 26:12) (See also Jer 31:3). The Son, Jesus, did indeed walk among some of the descendants of Israel two thousand years ago, but He is not accepted by the Jews, and they are not called His people.

Judah was to retain the sceptre (the kingship): "The Sceptre shall not depart from Judah, nor a lawgiver from between his feet, until Shiloh come; and unto him shall the gathering of the people be" (Gen 49:10). Modern Israel has no king, and no royal bloodline tracing its nonexistent monarch to David. On the other hand, Jeremiah apparently transplanted the royal line to the British Isles, where a monarchy still exists.

Israel, in particular through Joseph's sons, Ephraim and Manasseh, was to become a "nation and a company of nations" (Gen 35:11) (See also Gen 17:1–6, 48:19). They were to become a plurality of nations, and kings were to be numbered among Abraham's progeny (Gen 17:6, 17:16). Ephraim would become greater than Manasseh, and his descendants would become "a multitude of nations" (Gen 48:19). Palestinian Israel is only one nation, however. In contrast, the British Commonwealth is such a company of nations. The phrase "multitude of nations" could equally well have been translated as "congregation of states," so that the company of fifty states called the United States also qualifies.

"Behold, I will allure her, and bring her into the wilderness, and speak comfortably unto her" (Hosea 2:14). The exodus of the Jews from Europe into Palestine in the 1940's might conceivably be viewed as an alluring of them, but it seems more accurate to view them as being driven by the Nazi plague. Furthermore, Palestine was not a wilderness or an uninhabited area, at that time, as any Arab will testify.

God will "make thee high above all nations which he hath made, in praise, and in name, and in honour" (Deut 26:19). Palestinian Israel cannot claim to be the chief nation in the world. The richest and most powerful nation is easily the United States.

"The abundance of the sea will be turned to you. The wealth of the nations will come to you" (Isa 60:5 NAS). Yet the Palestinian Israelites are not a great seafaring people, nor are they the world's economic leaders.

Biblical Israel (Joseph) is to be blessed with great natural resources, including minerals, things from the ground (petroleum?), abundant harvests and cattle, and other material blessings (see Gen. 39:2, 39:23, 49:25–26; Deut 33:13–17). These promises are not fulfilled in Israel to any greater degree than any of many other countries.

The chosen people are to bring the light of salvation to the ends of the earth, and be witnesses for the Lord (Isa 43:10–12). Yet, the earth is not covered by Jewish missionaries from Jerusalem preaching Christ. The earth is covered, however, by missionaries from the English-speaking nations.

"Thy seed shall possess the gate of his enemies" (Gen 22:17, 24:60). The "gates," or national entrances and passageways, of the enemies of modern Jerusalem are not under control of the Jews. There was a time, however, when most of the world's entrances were controlled by the two-nation complex of Britain-USA, but never by the Jews. At one time, Britain-USA controlled the Suez Canal, the Cape of Good Hope, the Panama Canal, Singapore, Hong Kong, the Straits of Gibraltar, and others.

"And thou shalt lend unto many nations, but thou shalt not borrow; and thou shalt reign over many nations, but they shall not reign over thee" (Deut 15:6). This clearly has not happened to the Jewish people. The only nation which lends to everyone but does not borrow from them, or necessarily even receive repayment of its loans, is the United States.

"For with stammering lips and another tongue [language] will he speak to his people" (Isa 28:11) *(em add)*. Therefore, wherever Biblical Israel is, they must be speaking languages other than Hebrew. The national language of modern Israel is still Hebrew.

"I would make the remembrance of them to cease from among

men" (Deut 32:26). The Jews have never been forgotten or mis-
placed at any time during history. Just the opposite, they have been
known, identified, pursued, and persecuted for over two thousand
years. It was not the Jews, but the Israelites, who seemed to vanish
from history.

"And thou shalt be called by a new name, which the mouth of
the Lord shall name" (Isa 62:2). He will "call his servants by
another name" (Isa 65:15). The names Jew and Israel do not satisfy
this requirement. A clue to what the name is can be found in the
next verses. "And they shall put my name upon the children of
Israel" (Num 6:27). The Lord's name is not upon Palestinian Israel.
Neither "Israel" nor "Jew" is the Lord's name. Speaking to Israel,
the Lord said: "I have redeemed thee, I have called thee by thy
name" (Isa 43:1). "I will bring thy seed from the east, . . . west
. . . north . . . south . . . my sons from far, and my daughters
from the ends of the earth; even every one that is called by my
name" (from verses 5–7). The only one of the world's nations or
population groups which is named after the Savior of Israel is the
group of people named after Christ: the Christians.

The preceding quotations show that the true Biblical nation of
Israel shall not know who it is, shall not be recognized or recognize itself as being Israel, shall occupy a land populated by immigrants mostly from Europe where the Israelite tribes were driven,
shall have a land blessed with enormous wealth and natural resources, shall speak a language other than Hebrew, shall be called
after the Redeemer, and shall have other identifying characteristics. The English-speaking Christians satisfy all of these criteria, to the extent of having a monarch in Britain whose
genealogical line can be traced to King David. There are a sizable
number of other verses which could be quoted here in support of
the Christian-Israel connection, but most of them are subject to
interpretation. In contrast, the verses quoted above are unambiguous. The principle of using the parts of the Scriptures which
are clear as a guide for understanding the parts which are obscure
now applies, resulting in a much longer list of supporting verses.
That, however, is beyond the scope of this brief discussion.

On the face of it, the Christian nations would not appear to be
Biblical Israel because they have not regathered in the promised

land of Canaan, roughly Palestine. However, Abraham's heirs were to become many rulers and nations, not just one.

And Canaan was not the only promised land.

The Bibles mention other lands promised in addition to Canaan, but are mostly silent on their exact locations. The Lord spoke through the prophet Nathan to King David and told of a place for Israel which had not yet been assigned (see I Chron 17:7–15). An almost identical statement is repeated in another place: "I will appoint a place for my people Israel, and will plant them, that they may dwell in a place of their own, and move no more; neither shall the children of wickedness afflict them any more, as beforetime" (II Sam 7:10). The task of transplanting the root of the nation was assigned to Jeremiah (Jer 1:10). As we have previously seen, Jeremiah probably transplanted the throne to Ireland upon the fall of Jerusalem.

If the people were already in the promised land, where the Israelites were at that time, why were they promised a promised land to be appointed later? The verse is in the future tense, so that the land had not already been appointed. The only possible conclusion is that there must be another place in addition to Canaan into which descendants of Israel were to be gathered.

The promises made to Abraham and his descendants are in no way violated if God gives Palestine to some of the descendants of Jacob-Israel and, at the same time, places the main body of the descendants in an entirely different place. This is apparently what He has done. The Jews who have gathered in Palestine are indeed children of Jacob-Israel; thus, the promise that Canaan would again belong to Jacob has been fulfilled at the time predicted. The particular descendants of Jacob who now occupy that land are derived mainly from the fraction of the Judahites who returned from Babylon, those original captives being themselves only a portion of Judah. These Jews have mistakenly believed that they are all of Biblical Israel. Modern political and geographical Israel is more accurately pseudo-Israel, those descendants of Israel who did not recognize Israel's Messiah. Pseudo-Israel, the Jews, are those of Abraham's lineage, and their converts to Judaism, to whom it was said: "And you will leave your name for a curse to My chosen ones, and the Lord God will slay you. But My servants will be called by another name" (Isa 65:15 NAS). These Jews are specifically mentioned by Jeremiah as the "remnant of Jerusalem" (Jer 24:8 NAS). "And I will make them . . . as a reproach and a proverb, a taunt and a curse in all places where I shall scatter them" (Jer 24:9 NAS). What we seek is the large majority of Israelites, that vast multitude identified as Biblical Israel. Where is the place appointed for the main body of Israel, the portion carrying the birthright blessings through Joseph and his sons, Ephraim and Manasseh?

Archaeological evidence has traced the bulk of them to Europe and to the British Isles. The westward push did not end there, however. The opening up of the North American continent allured many of these people into the great American wilderness, where no cities had ever been built. A new nation called the United States of America was formed, with the love of religious freedom and of Christ in its heart, and with rebellion against unwarranted taxation as the precipitating factor. Curiously, it was also heavy taxation which originally caused Israel to split from Judah. The population grew by the millions during the next century, so that the USA was indeed formed by immigrants allured from those very places where the tribes of Israel had been driven. It is an interesting fact that the 1980 census shows that there are about as many Americans having English ancestors as there are Englishmen having English ancestors. There are more Americans having German ancestors than the present population of Germany. And the United States has over six times as many people of Irish descent as Ireland has.

God placed on His people a most conspicuous mark for the very purpose of labeling them. The mark, or "sign," is the Sabbath. It had been said that the children of Israel would always have a Holy seventh day as an identifying mark: "Wherefore the children of Israel [all the tribes] shall keep the sabbath, to observe the sabbath throughout their generations, for a perpetual covenant. It is a sign between me and the children of Israel for ever" (Ex 31:16–17) *(em add)*. According to these words, the sign of the Sabbath will be always and unconditionally on the Israelites. A sign is an identifying mark, in the same way a sign in front of a store identifies the store. The only groups of people who carry the identifying sign of the Sabbath are the Jews and the Christians.

While both Judah and Israel of the divided kingdom carried this mark, the mark was altered soon after the death of Solomon. When the full nation of Israel divided into Judah and Israel, the Israelite king, Jeroboam, accommodated the heathens in various ways, including moving the Sabbath back one day so that it coincided with the day of the pagan sun worshippers. The Sabbath celebrated by the Israelites then fell on Sunday, the day after the Sabbath of the tribe of Judah. Today, the Christians celebrate their Holy seventh day on Sunday, the day after the Jewish Sabbath. It appears that Biblical Israel and the remnant of Judah have carried their labels, God's sign, for all to read for centuries. It further appears that the Israelites have been brought to their other promised land, where they are to dwell in safety and where they "shall no more be pulled up out of their land which I have given them" (Amos 9:14–15).

As noted earlier, the Babylonian conquest of Judah extended over the approximate period 604–585 B.C. The prophesied punishment was to last for 2,520 years, which, if added to 604 B.C. brought us up to 1917 when Britain, part of Biblical Israel, liberated Palestine and moved to establish it for their brethren, the Jews. The Assyrians had conquered Israel over a century before Babylon took Judah. The conquest of Israel, likewise, took a period of years, from about 744 B.C. to about 721 B.C. If we follow the approach that worked for Judah and add 2,520 years to the beginning of the Assyrian conquest, we find that prophetic Israel should have been established in about the year 1776, and was to result in a great and powerful nation. If this be true, we need not be puzzled by our not having realized it. The Israelites were not intended to know about the deed until after it had been accomplished.

Nebuchadnezzar was used as an object lesson to Israel. Daniel relates how Nebuchadnezzar, who can be interpreted as symbolizing Israel, deserted God and worshipped idols. He lost his mind and his understanding left him. He lived as an ox, or bull, eating grass for seven human years, which is 2,520 human days, or 2,520 years in prophetic equivalent. "Israel is stubborn like a stubborn heifer" (Hosea 4:16 NAS). "I have surely heard Ephraim's moaning: 'You disciplined me like an unruly calf" (Jer 31:18 NIV). At the end of that time the king's symbolic spiritual blindness was removed and his mind restored. "Who is blind, but my servant" (Isa 42:19). "Blindness in part is happened to Israel" (Rom 11:25). Nebuchadnezzar immediately recognized the might and majesty and mercy of God and was cured of his apostasy. He vowed never again to desert God. Israel was, and largely still is, in just such an unaware state as was the Babylonian king. "For the Lord hath poured upon you the spirit of deep sleep, and hath closed your eyes: the prophets and your rulers, the seers hath he covered" (Isa 29:10). "And the vision of all is become unto you as the words of a book that is sealed" (verse 11), which no one can read and understand until the appointed time.

Daniel wrote that the prophecies will be understood at the time of the end of the age by certain people, but not by everyone. The angel speaking to Daniel elaborated on the duration of the exile of God's people as "time, times, and half a time," meaning prophetic "years" (see Dan 12:7 NAS, marginal note), when Daniel asked about the outcome of those events. The angel's response was: "Go your way, Daniel, for these words are concealed and sealed up until the end time" (Dan 12:9 NAS), and "none of the wicked will understand, but those who have insight will understand" (Dan 12:10 NAS), or, "but the wise shall understand" (Dan 12:10). The word "wise," of course, does not refer to high intelligence, nor to great amounts of education, nor even to the wisdom of scholars and theologians, but to the spiritual insight of those people who revere God, to whom His spirits reveal the truth. The love of God is the beginning of wisdom.

"The fierce anger of the Lord will not turn back, until He has performed, and until He has accomplished the intent of His heart; In the latter days you will understand this" (Jer 30:24 NAS). The next verse reads: "At that time . . . I will be the God of all the families of Israel, and they shall be My people" (Jer 31:1 NAS). In other words, near the time of the end, God's children shall have their understanding of these matters awakened, but the followers of the Adversary will not understand.

The conclusion which best matches the prophetic Scriptures is that the modern nation called Israel is in reality pseudo-Israel, Jews from the remnant of Judah, while the people called Christians are true Biblical Israel, with Britain and the United States playing the leading roles. In retrospect, this conclusion is not surprising. Numerous Biblical references allude to the islands, or "coastlands," to the west. Isaiah, in particular, makes frequent mention of those islands. "Surely the islands look to me; in the lead are the ships of Tarshish, bringing your sons from afar, with their silver and gold, to the honor of the Lord your God, the Holy One of Israel" (Isa 60:9 NIV). An old map in the British museum specifically calls the British islands Tarshish. The Bible is equally as specific: "Keep silence before me, O islands . . . thou, Israel, art my servant, Jacob whom I have chosen, the seed of Abraham my friend" (Isa 41:1, 41:8). The identification of the British Isles as the home of much of Israel is a thread which runs through their history. In the fifth century, Saint Patrick wrote: "We turned away from God and did not keep His Commandments, and did not obey our priests who used to remind us of our salvation. And the Lord brought over us the wrath of His anger and scattered us among many nations, even unto the uttermost parts of the earth." Gildas, in the sixth century, referred to the people of Britain as "God's Israelites, whether they loved Him or not." In the ninth century, Alfred the Great told his people: "Be ye kind to the stranger within thy gates, for ye were strangers in the land of the Egyptians."

Although many years passed during which the promises given through the prophets were not all understood, they were, nevertheless, in force. In fact, Christ came "to confirm the promises made unto the fathers" (Rom 15:8). The dispersed tribes of Israel had been lost sheep scattered throughout the earth, and their Shepherd came for them. "Behold, I Myself will search for My sheep and seek them out" (Ezek 34:11 NAS). "For the Son of man is come to seek and to save that which was lost" (Luke 19:10). "I am not sent but unto the lost sheep of the house of Israel" (Matt 15:24). The Shepherd then sent His Apostles to those same sheep: "go . . . to the lost sheep of the house of Israel" (Matt 10:6). His sheep have recognized their Shepherd and are called by His name: Christians.

In this same vein, Isaiah was told that God would call His Israelites from the mostly European lands where He had driven them: "Behold, I am going to send for many fishermen, . . . and they will fish for them" (Jer 16:16 NAS). When Christ called the

Galilean fishermen to be His Apostles, He said: "Follow Me, and I will make you fishers of men" (Matt 4:19). His Apostles and disciples fished among the scattered Israelite tribes as He had instructed them. Their catch: Christians. James wrote his epistle to the dispersed tribes of Israel (Jas 1:1). They are reading his letter today in churches throughout Christendom.

It is certain that, among the Christian people counted as Israel, there are many whose bloodlines did not originate with Jacob (Isa 56:6–8). It is also true that Israelite genes somewhere among a man's forebears do not qualify him as a member of Biblical Israel: "For they are not all Israel who are descended from Israel; neither are they all children because they are Abraham's descendants" (Rom 9:6–7 NAS). What criterion does God apply to reckon Israelites? Who are the recipients of His promises? "It is not the children of the flesh who are children of God, but the children of the promise are regarded as descendants" (Rom 9:8 NAS). "Therefore, be sure that it is those who are of faith who are sons of Abraham" (Gal 3:7 NAS). "And if ye be Christ's, then are ye Abraham's seed, and heirs according to the promise" (Gal 3:29). People who belong to Christ are known as Christians.

The outcasts have been largely regathered, both the fragment of Judah, the Jews, into Palestine, and the full body of Israel, the Christians, into the western nations. "And he . . . shall assemble the outcasts of Israel, and gather together the dispersed of Judah from the four corners of the earth" (Isa 11:12). Many verses distinguish between Judah and Israel, and, like this one, may be read as two separate regatherings.

Even if the explanations suggested here are correct, many prophecies are still unexplained. Perhaps they are yet to be fulfilled, perhaps simply misunderstood. Nevertheless, it is conspicuous that the English-speaking Christians of today are the greatest believers in, and distributors of, the Holy Books of the ancient Israelites. Of all nations, we are the chief worshippers of Israel's God and Israel's Messiah. Further, we are fulfilling the task God assigned to His chosen servants: that of serving as witnesses to the world. This country, above all other nations, has sent out missionaries by the thousands, Bibles by the millions, and countless evangelistic messages worldwide on radio and television.

Certain writers have sought the markings of Israel on Britain and the United States. Their speculations point out that the United States has the official motto: "In God We Trust" (Joint Congressional Resolution, July 30, 1965), and has proclaimed the Bible as "the Word of God" (Joint Congressional Resolution, October 4, 1982). The United States is a gathering, if not a regathering, of people primarily from the Israelite descendants of Europe. As our currency says, we are gathered out of many into one *(E Pluribus Unum)*. God has truly prospered our beginnings *(Annuit Coeptis)*, and the formation of this country may well have marked the beginning of a new order of the ages *(Novus Ordo Seclorum)*. The Great Seal of the United States, as shown on a dollar bill, has thirteen stars arranged in a star of David formation, surrounded by clouds of glory. On the reverse side of the Great Seal, also shown on the dollar, is an ancient Egyptian monument, a curious unfinished pyramid of thirteen levels. Hovering above it is the all-seeing eye of Providence, as the structure waits for the coming of its capstone, Christ (see Zech 4:7; I Pet 2:6). Although these, and other, speculations may be valid interpretations, they will not be pursued here.

The reader of this book now knows of his origin in the spirit-world of God, of his fall from heaven due to his part in the rebellion against Christ, and of the cause and ultimate purpose of his human existence. In addition, the Christian reader knows that he is an Israelite, and heir to the promises made to Abraham and his progeny, and a chosen member of the bride of Christ—His people, His saints, His church. Armed with this knowledge of identity, and of the workings of the spirit-world, the Christian reader is in position to discern the signs of the end times.

There is a profusion of books now available devoted to end time prophecies and the return of Christ. Unfortunately, they do not agree in all details, nor do they agree with the Scriptures as considered here. Consequently, the Christian who has only traditional knowledge may easily misunderstand events when they happen.

Consider, as one example, the 144,000 mentioned in Revelation (Rev 7:3–8, 14:1–5). There are to be 12,000 from each of the twelve tribes, all undefiled by women (Rev 14:4). A popular teaching is that they are 144,000 Jewish bachelors. However, it is quite clear they are not Jewish, for they are Christ's (see Rev 14:4), and therefore Christians. Furthermore, they are drawn from the Christian Israelites who, as we have seen, are concentrated in the western nations, not in Pseudo-Israel. Finally, they need not be bachelors, for there is nothing inherently impure about the Divinely blessed institute of marriage. Nor could sexual activity within marriage be construed as defiling, for each nerve and organ was designed by the Creator with full knowledge of their intended use in carrying out His directive to "be fruitful and multiply." This cannot be a commandment to defile oneself, because it is God's commandment. It is even written that husband and wife are not to consider their bodies as their own exclusive property (see I Cor 7:4). Among the 144,000, therefore, may be an elderly, widowed Frenchman, a teenage Scot with no wife, a married Messianic Jew cab driver from Brooklyn, and a rural farmer with six children, all of whom would be unidentifiable according to the usual interpretations of Scripture. The reader of this book may be one of that number.

The realization of reincarnation also casts new light on the end times. God's messages were often directed to "you," not "them." "Your dead will live . . . and the earth will give birth to the departed spirits" (Isa 26:19 NAS). "I will open your graves, and cause you to come up out of your graves, and bring you into the land of Israel" (Ezek 37:12). "And there shall ye remember your ways, and all your doings, wherein ye have been defiled; and ye shall loathe yourselves in your own sight for all your evils that ye have committed" (Ezek 20:43). Evidently, those very spirits were to be purified and incarnated again. "And it shall come to pass in that day, that the great trumpet shall be blown, and they shall come which were ready to perish in the land of Assyria, and the outcasts in the land of Egypt, and shall worship the Lord in the holy mount [or, nation] at Jerusalem [or, Israel]" (Isa 27:13) *(em add)*.

It also appears that David will receive another chance to govern Israel, but this time under direct supervision of Christ. "Then I will set over them one shepherd, My servant David, and he will feed them; he will feed them himself and be their shepherd. And I, the Lord, will be their God, and My servant David will be prince among them; I, the Lord, have spoken" (Ezek 34:23–24 NAS). "But they shall serve the Lord their God, and David their king, whom I will raise up unto them" (Jer 30:9) (See also Ezek 37:24–25 and Hosea 3:5.) And what role will Daniel play? "But as for you [Daniel], go your way to the end; then you will enter your rest and rise again for your allotted portion at the end of the age" (Dan 12:13 NAS) *(em add)*.

Has God actually reassembled those very people who followed Moses and Christ, along with their offspring? Are we among those reincarnated ones, those fallen angels, who have finally learned to choose Christ over Satan? It might be that some of us were Hebrews who made bricks for Pharaoh, others were in his army which drowned. Some of today's Christians were perhaps martyred in the Roman arena, while others of us were cheering in the stands of the Coliseum. Certain ones of us could have been among the thousands who heard Christ and took miraculously provided bread and fish from the hands of the Apostles. Others may have been among the throng chanting for the release of Barabbas. It could be that many of us were there and are personally responsible for whatever karmic debt we now carry. Whatever the exact case may be for each individual, the stories of the slavery in Egypt, of the Exodus from Egypt, of Sodom and Gomorrah, of the Assyrian and Babylonian captivities, of the days of Jesus, and of the Roman persecutions of the Christians, all take on more personal and immediate meanings.

But the days of spiritual darkness, and of wanderings through the wilderness, both physical and spiritual, are rapidly coming to an end. Even the most casual student of the Scriptures can see that the "fullness of time" is upon us. The "time of Jacob's trouble" is near its catastrophic culmination. Before us lie earthquakes, wars, famine, and devastation; spirit manifestations, healings, signs, and religious turmoil. A time approaches when there will be great dismay: "Men's hearts failing them for fear, and for looking after those things which are coming on the earth; for the powers of heaven shall be shaken" (Luke 21:26); "Men swooning the panic and foreboding of what is to befall the universe" (Luke 21:26, Moffatt translation). But again, Jacob-Israel will be saved out of it (see Jer 31:3–10). "And when these things begin to come to pass, then look up, and lift up YOUR heads; for YOUR redemption draweth nigh" (Luke 21:28) *(em add)*.

The crowning event which ends these times is the return of Christ, with the establishing of His rule on Earth.

Christ is soon to claim this dimension of creation, His hard-won right, and "the Lord God shall give unto him the throne of his father David: And he shall reign over the house of Jacob for ever; and of his kingdom there shall be no end" (Luke 1:32–33). God is surely granting the prayer His Son left with His people: "Thy kingdom come, Thy will be done on earth, as it is in Heaven." And the paths of His people shall be made straight, and their progress complete.

REFERENCE CITED

Landay, Jerry M., and the Editors of the Newsweek Book Division, *Dome of the Rock*